Making Your Mark

Effective business communication in Germany

Coursebook

Marianne Howarth
Coventry Polytechnic

Michael Woodhall
Dorset Institute of Higher Education

A multi-media package from
BBC OUPC, DTI – The Department for Enterprise, London Chamber of Commerce, Open College, Open University and Pitman Publishing

Pitman

PITMAN PUBLISHING
128 Long Acre, London, WC2E 9AN

First published in Great Britain 1988

ISBN 0 273 02926 6

Phototypeset by Wyvern Typesetting Ltd, Bristol

Printed and bound in Great Britain at
the Bath Press, Avon

Further copies of this coursebook and the complete
Making Your Mark package (video, video transcript, coursebook and four audio cassettes)
are available from:
The Sales Department,
Pitman Publishing,
128 Long Acre,
London, WC2E 9AN.

Contents

Preface

Making your Mark is a new and innovative business language pack designed to help British exporters improve their ability to do business in Germany. This market offers great potential to British companies, but to succeed, the exporter needs to be properly equipped. *Making your Mark* provides both the communication skills and an understanding of the German market which will greatly assist the job of winning orders.

The pack has been designed using both open and distance learning techniques. As such it can be used successfully by those people whose heavy schedules make study on a regular basis difficult. Equally, the unique nature of the material will provide the basis for in-company training courses and will have wide application to the educational sector.

The particular distinguishing feature of *Making your Mark* is that it is based on authentic, unscripted business situations. It therefore responds to the needs of the language learner as well as the language trainer for 'real', rather than 'realistic' material. In this pack, very few words have been put into the mouths of the business people concerned, but a very great deal has been taken out, then analysed and used as the basis for practical, flexible language learning exercises.

Making your Mark represents a unique collaboration between organisations and individuals dedicated to supporting Britain's export drive. The original concept developed from early conversations between the Series Consultants, Professor David Liston and Professor Nigel Reeves and producers from the BBC Open University Production Centre at Milton Keynes. This led to the proposal for a business language course, based on the real experiences of British exporters overseas. The proposal attracted support from a number of influential bodies: the DTI –

Department for Enterprise, the London Chamber of Commerce, Open College, Open University and Pitman Publishing. The BBC Open University Production Centre undertook the management of the project.

Sincere thanks are due to the above organisations for the support given. A debt of gratitude is owed also to the authors of this book who worked to seemingly impossible schedules. Particular thanks go to the two language authors, Marianne Howarth and Michael Woodhall, for their tireless efforts, without which the project would not have been possible. They in turn wish to thank Michael Shea, M.D., of SIHI–Ryaland Pumps, Martyn Unwin, Project Manager Bayer Dyestuffs, Peter Warham, Export Operations Manager, IMI for their help in testing the materials; special thanks to John Sharp for the grammar guide and Richard Oldnall for many years of encouragement and help. The valuable support and advice provided by the series consultants, Professor David Liston and Professor Nigel Reeves have been essential to the quality of the pack. There are many others whose vision, experience and support have played a vital part in the development of *Making your Mark*.

While few people will claim that exporting is all 'fun' it is an area of endeavour which is increasingly important to the survival of the United Kingdom. The men and women who travel abroad, representing their companies, fighting for and winning orders are a special breed. They share a determination, humour and self-reliance not often found so comprehensively in other professional groups.
This pack is dedicated to you.

Viel Erfolg!

Project team

Project Managers

Roger Penfound, Angela Jamieson (BBC OUPC)

The BBC at Milton Keynes produces a wide range of educational programmes, most of which are made in partnership with the Open University. Through its involvement with the Open Business School, BBC OUPC has developed extensive experience in the production of management education programmes.

Series Consultants

Nigel Reeves OBE MA DPhil CIEx FIL, FRSA is Professor of German and Dean of the Faculty of Human Studies at the University of Surrey. He is also a member of the Southern Universities Joint Examination Board; the BOTB Study Group on Foreign Languages for Overseas Trade; Chairman of the Institute of Linguists Council; Chairman of the National Congress on Language in Education; Member of the National Council for Modern Languages in Higher and Further Education; Chairman of the Management Committee of the BOTB/LCCI/Lloyds Bank Foreign Languages at Work scheme. He has also contributed to *Languages and Export Performance* (Royal Society of Arts 1979) and *The Language Key in Export Strategy* (Birmingham Chamber of Commerce 1981); and is a member of the study group for the earlier BOTB report, *Foreign Languages for Overseas Trade*.

David J Liston OBE MA CIEx FRSA is Honorary Education Adviser to the BOTB. Following thirty years with the Metal Box Company, he became the first Assistant Director of the Manchester Business School. His other academic appointments have included Pro-Rector and Visiting Professor of the Polytechnic of Central London; Professor at the European Business School; Visiting Fellow, Henley School of Management; External Assessor for the Open University course in International Marketing. For three years he was Industrial Adviser to the Government, and has led UK teams to EEC seminars on East–West trade. He is author of the original BOTB report *Education and Training for Overseas Trade*, and co-author with Professor Nigel Reeves of the books *Business Studies, Languages and Overseas Trade* (Pitman) and *The Invisible Economy, The Changing Profile of Britain's Invisible Exports* (Pitman).

Language authors

Marianne Howarth BA MPhil
In her current capacity as Director of Language Consultancy Services at Coventry Polytechnic, Marianne Howarth is responsible for providing a comprehensive range of language training programmes and services to business and industry.

She has a special interest in the needs of the open business learner and is frequently consulted by companies on appropriate language training options in this area.

Marianne Howarth has specialised in German. She has lived and worked in the Federal Republic of Germany and has wide experience as a broadcaster, interpreter and translator. She has translated several books into English and, with Michael Woodhall, is a principal translator of the *Handbook of German Business Management*.

Michael Woodhall BA MA
Michael Woodhall, Director of the Language Centre of the Dorset Institute of Higher Education, specialises in providing language training with a management skills focus to business and industry regionally and nationally. In addition, he runs management training programmes in English for overseas companies.

In the past he has set up and run similar centres at Manchester Business School and the École Supérieure de Commerce de Lyon. Michael Woodhall is a published translator and is currently Translation Manager of the *Handbook of German Business Management*. He and Marianne Howarth have collaborated on this and a number of business language related projects since 1980.

Introduction

Making Your Mark is a multi-media package, led by a video which follows British people doing business in Germany. The pack consists of: • the video cassette • the transcript booklet • the coursebook • a language audio cassette for listening practice – the 'car cassette' • a language audio cassette for speaking practice – the 'study cassette' • business audio cassettes 1 and 2 for practical information and advice.

How to use the coursebook

The coursebook consists of seven sequences which run parallel to the video. Each sequence covers the following:
1 Preparation for the sequence
2 Practising listening and understanding
3 Consolidation of language
4 Development of language
5 Practising speaking
6 Review of sequence
7 Business guide

We recommend you, the learner, to follow the workplan outlined below when working through each sequence. We have designed it to help you to learn in the most effective way. At various points you are able to exercise your own freedom of choice, based on your existing language level, language learning needs and the time you have available.

1 Preparation for sequence

This stage will help to familiarise you with the German dialogue contained in the video sequence.

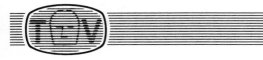

- read the preparation for the video sequence
- study the list of key words
- refer to Vocabulary Guide if necessary
- proceed to Stage 2

2 Practising your listening and understanding

This stage aims to develop your listening and understanding of the German dialogue contained in the video sequence.

- watch video and listen for key words
- study information questions (Exercise A)
- watch video again and answer questions
- compare your answers with those in coursebook
- study summary questions (Exercise B)
- watch video and answer questions
- compare your answers with those in coursebook
- read transcript and check comprehension
- decide whether to try the questions for close listening (Exercise C)

if yes: • study questions in Exercise C
       • answer questions in Exercise C
       • compare your answers with those in coursebook
       • listen to car cassette to revise sequence
       • proceed to Stage 3

if no: • listen to car cassette to revise sequence
       • proceed to Stage 3

This symbol will show you which exercises are on the car cassette:

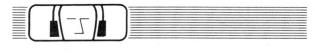

- carry out same exercises in alternative medium
- compare answers
- proceed to Stage 5

3 Consolidation of language

In this section, you will be practising various language points which occur in the video. For many of you, this will be a revision exercise. If you need help with this section refer to the grammar guide at the end of the book.

- read instructions for exercise(s)
- complete exercise(s)
- compare your answers with those in coursebook
- proceed to Stage 4

4 Development of language

This section aims to extend your range of language skills by focusing on two or three specially selected language points. Some of the exercises are included on the study cassette as well as in the book. Make your own choice about which to tackle first – but make sure you try both. This symbol will show you which exercises are on the study cassette:

- read instructions for exercise(s)
- decide whether to try book or audio exercises first
- complete exercise(s)
- compare your answers with answers given

5 Practising speaking

Dialogue chain will help you to prepare for participation in conversations or presentations in which your own products or services figure.

- listen to scripted dialogue on study cassette
- study plan of dialogue in coursebook
- listen to dialogue while following plan in book
- take role of missing person on study cassette
- prepare and practise your own role(s)
- proceed to Stage 6

6 Review of sequence

This sequence enables you to take stock of and review your progress.

- read language comment
- learn key phrases
- check progress against sequence summary
- identify areas for further practice
- practise your understanding again by listening to extra unscripted dialogue on car cassette
- proceed to Stage 7

7 Business Guide

Each business guide has been prepared by a specialist with direct experience of the topic covered. The guide is designed to give you a series of practical hints about doing business effectively in Germany, as well as an insight into the German business environment. It is intended primarily for those who are fairly new to exporting, but 'old hands' will find useful hints and reminders, as well as many references to valuable sources of advice and information. For detailed information, addresses and phone numbers of organisations mentioned in the business guide, consult the 'Where to Go' section at the end of the book.

- listen to appropriate sequence on business cassette. This symbol reminds you when to refer to the business magazine cassettes:

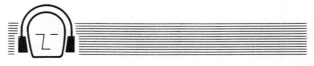

- proceed to next sequence

The business environment in Germany

Introduction

This introduction to the German market has been written by Collin Randlesome who is senior lecturer in European Management at Cranfield School of Management. He is a co-author of the Handy Report (*The Making of Managers*) and has spent seven years teaching in Germany and Switzerland.

Nature of the market

The outstanding feature of the market in the Federal Republic of Germany (FRG) is that it is one where the consumer or buyer is looking to purchase products of a high standard, and at German prices. Germans have been educated to be quality-conscious because they have been constantly told that high quality is the main selling point of the goods which they themselves produce. At the same time, the German purchaser is a very sophisticated 'value engineer', extraordinarily adept at making subconscious price/value trade-offs when buying.

The market in the FRG is open, and one in which there has not been a 'Buy German' campaign since 1945.

It is a lucrative market but one which is difficult to penetrate. Germans have no shortage of goods to choose from because domestic industry provides almost universal coverage, and foreign suppliers have not been slow to discover the rich potential of the market.

For the British exporter, the German market is especially difficult because, as recent research has revealed*, British suppliers have an unfortunate image in Western Europe, including the FRG.

Facts and figures

Land area

The sovereign territory of the Federal Republic of Germany covers 248,630 square kilometres, 54% of which is agricultural land and 29% forest. The longest north-south distance is 853 kilometres, and longest west-east 453 kilometres. A strongly fortified border strip measuring 1,381 kilometres separates the FRG from the German Democratic Republic (GDR).

Population

The population of the FRG and West Berlin was estimated in 1985 at 61,035,000 including almost five million foreigners. Since 1974, the population has been declining slowly by approximately 200,000 persons per year. With 10.1 births per 1,000 inhabitants per year, the FRG has the lowest birthrate in the world. The average number of children per woman is only 1.4 and if the decline

* 'The Image and Reputation of British Suppliers in Western Europe', P. W. Turnbull, in *European Journal of Marketing*, Volume 19, No. 6, 1985.

DENMARK

Flensburg

Schleswig

Kiel ▫

SCHLESWIG-HOLSTEIN ●Neumünster

Lübeck
Cuxhaven Pinneberg

Wilhelmshaven ●HAMBURG

●Emden

Bremerhaven
Oldenburg Lüneburg

○ BREMEN

LOWER SAXONY

●Celle

NETHERLANDS W. BERLIN ▲

●Osnabrück ▫Hannover

Braunschweig

Hildesheim

Münster Bielefeld Salzgitter GERMAN

NORTH RHINE - WESTPHALIA DEMOCRATIC

Bochum Göttingen REPUBLIC

Duisburg ●Dortmund

Krefeld Essen

Mönchengladbach ▲ Wuppertal Kassel

●Düsseldorf Solingen

●Köln HESSEN

●Aachen

FEDERAL REPUBLIC

BELGIUM **OF**

BONN

RHINELAND Koblenz Fulda

PALATINATE **GERMANY**

LUXEM- Wiesbaden▫ ▲Frankfurt Selb●

BOURG Mainz▫ Schweinfurt

●Trier Darmstadt Bayreuth CZECHO-

Würzburg Bamberg SLOVAKIA

SAAR- Kaiserslautern Mannheim

LAND Fürth

Saarbrücken▫ Pirmasens Heidelberg Nürnberg

Ludwigshafen

Heilbronn

●Karlsruhe Regensburg

Pforzheim

●Stuttgart Ingolstadt

FRANCE BADEN- Ulm BAVARIA Passau●

WÜRTTEMBERG

Augsburg

—·—· International
       Boundaries Freiburg ▲München AUSTRIA

– – – – Land Boundaries

▫ Land Capitals

○ City States

▲ British Commercial
  Representative

SWITZERLAND

Miles 0   50   100

Kms 0   50   100   150

continues at the same rate the population is expected to fall by three million by 1990.

Moreover, the population of the FRG is ageing. There are already 3.5 people over the age of 61 to every 10 of working age. By the year 2030 this ratio will be 6.5 to 10 if present trends continue.

Main cities

The major centres of population (in thousands) as at the end of September 1984 were:

West Berlin	1,852	Dortmund	585
Hamburg	1,600	Düsseldorf	571
Munich		Stuttgart	563
(*München*)	1,277	Bremen	535
Cologne (*Köln*)	932	Duisburg	528
Essen	629	Hanover	
Frankfurt/Main	605	(*Hannover*)	518

Climate

Temperate

Language

German

Weights and measures

Metric system

Holidays

The public holidays celebrated throughout the FRG do not always coincide with those in the UK. There are also a number of regional public holidays. Moreover, annual holiday entitlement for 77% of employees was in excess of five weeks even in 1981.

Summer holiday periods for schools vary from one federal state (*Bundesland*) to another in an attempt to avoid overcrowding on German motorways (*Autobahnen*). They also rotate on an annual basis so that no state can claim that it is always allocated the worst of the weather.

Germans are determined to make the maximum use of their leisure time, and this means that it is essential for the British in the German market to possess precise information about a German partner's holiday arrangements.

Currency

Deutsche Mark (DM) = 100 Pfennig

Time

One hour or two hours ahead of GMT depending on time of year. UK businesses should note that many German companies start work at 07.00 and finish at 15.30 local time. It is therefore advisable to restrict telephone calls from the UK to the FRG to mornings only.

Political environment

Federal system

The FRG consists of the ten federal states (*Bundesländer*) of Baden-Württemberg, Bavaria (*Bayern*), Bremen, Hamburg, Hesse (*Hessen*), Lower Saxony (*Niedersachsen*), North-Rhine Westphalia (*Nordrhein-Westfalen*), Rhineland-Palatinate (*Rheinland-Pfalz*), Saarland and Schleswig-Holstein. In addition, there is the city of

West Berlin which retains a special status but is fully integrated in the legal and economic system of the FRG.

The federal system is not only a reaction to past abuses of power by central government but also recognises the historical roots of Germany. Each of the federal states and West Berlin has its own constitution, parliament, government, administrative agencies and independent courts.

The different regions of the FRG are very distinctive and perhaps more individualistic in nature and taste than the various parts of the UK. Regional preferences must therefore be given serious consideration by any British company operating in the market in any part of the FRG.

Central powers

The Basic Law (*Grundgesetz*), or provisional Federal Constitution, is binding upon all the states, and the Federal Parliament (*Bundestag*) is responsible for major legislation and policy, particularly in such areas as defence, foreign affairs and finance.

Political parties

The major parties in the FRG are the Christian Democratic Union (CDU) and, in Bavaria, its sister party, the Christian Social Union (CSU), the Social Democratic Party of Germany (SPD), the Free Democratic Party (FDP), and the Greens.

Central government

A centre-right coalition between the CDU/CSU and the FDP, led by Dr. Helmut Kohl, came to power in the Federal Parliament in October 1982, after the defeat of Helmut Schmidt's Social Democrats. It should be noted that the FRG has the most successful ecology party in Europe, the Greens, who polled 8.3% of votes and obtained 44 seats in the 1987 federal elections.

Not only the Greens but the vast majority of Germans are concerned about dying forests and polluted rivers, so a British manufacturer exporting to the FRG would have to ensure that goods are what the Germans call environment-friendly (*umweltfreundlich*).

Social environment

Order and the law

Society in the FRG is ordered and orderly: it is a society in which there are rules and systems governing most aspects of life. Indeed, it may well be true that, whereas the general attitude of the British is that they are free to do whatever the law does not specifically forbid, the Germans assume that anything not specifically permitted by the law is forbidden (*verboten*). Germans appear to feel comfortable when order prevails even if this means being encompassed by rules and regulations.

The laws governing the conduct of business in the FRG are enshrined for the most part in the Commercial Code (*Handelsgesetzbuch*), and German companies employ vast numbers of law graduates to ensure that neither they nor their business partners infringe any of the laws. Indeed, a legal background is held in such high esteem by German firms that some 20% of the members of their management boards (*Vorstandsmitglieder*) trained as lawyers.

Bearing in mind the litigious tendencies of Germans in general and the legalistic attitudes displayed by some German companies, British business people would be advised to acquaint themselves with those facets of the law which affect their dealings with the FRG. It could be disastrous for them to assume that what is regarded as standard commercial practice in the UK will find legal acceptance in the German environment.

A useful source of information on such matters is the Legal Department of the German Chamber of Industry and Commerce in London.

High performance

Many Germans pride themselves on belonging to what they call a high performance or achievement society (*Leistungsgesellschaft*). This aspect of contemporary German society finds its expression in several aspects of life but it is perhaps most pronounced in education and business.

Children attending primary school (*Grundschule*) from the ages of six to ten are expected to work hard, bring home good school reports and, if possible, be selected for a place at grammar school (*Gymnasium*). Here they will eventually take six or seven subjects at 'A' level (*Abitur*) before entering university. But even the 64% of children failing to be chosen for a grammar school do not cease to compete, or begin to underachieve. They realise only too well that they have to continue to perform if they are to obtain a position as an apprentice (*Lehrstelle*) in a good company at the end of their school careers.

Equally, their parents work hard and with meticulous thoroughness in their firms. Even the best-qualified young talents entering German companies cannot hope to impress their superiors other than by their successful performance.

Not unnaturally, Germans expect from their foreign partners this same commitment to high performance through hard work and attention to detail.

Affluence

As a consequence of their achievements, most Germans enjoy the rewards of an affluent society (*Wohlstandsgesellschaft*). Although there is no absence of thrift in the FRG, with average savings per household constituting 13% of disposable income, these same households are nonetheless equipped with a dazzling array of consumer durables. In 1983, 94% of all households possessed a television set, 88% a telephone, 83% a washing machine, 65% a car, 65% a freezer and 24% a washing-up machine. It would appear that Germans are quite unabashed about showing off the spoils of their achievements.

At the same time, it should be pointed out that only 36% of German families either own or are buying their homes as compared to a figure of 63% in the UK. Indeed, residential property has recently been a very bad investment in the FRG. In 1987, there were more than one million empty houses or flats, and over the past decade property prices have stagnated or even fallen in some areas. What is more, the decline in the property market has been masked by the growth of one-person households: a third of the homes in the FRG have only one inhabitant.

Leisure

A further clearly-discernible trend in the FRG over recent years has been towards the leisure society (*Freizeitgesellschaft*). Even in 1982, actual annual hours put in by the average German industrial worker were 1,773 as compared to 1,833 in the UK and 2,101 in Japan. In 1984, the German metal workers went on strike for seven weeks for a 35-hour week, the outcome of the strike being a compromise which sees the official working week reduced to 38.5 hours. Moreover, polls carried out among young people confirm that they no longer believe that they should work long hours and produce ever more. They are increasingly unwilling to sacrifice leisure time for more money.

The older generations are appalled at what they see as a decline in the German hard-work ethic among the young.

They remember the 'rubble women' passing bricks from hand to hand to rebuild a country devastated by war; men who put in long hours in factories and produced an economic miracle (*Wirtschaftswunder*); union leaders who sat down with the bosses, not to argue over shorter working hours, but to plot strategies for greater efficiency. However, the older generation can still console itself with the thought that, despite the growth of leisure, productivity per capita in the FRG is equal to that in Japan. The good old German work ethic may not be quite what it was but the high performance society is still very much intact.

Economic environment

Macroeconomic scene

The FRG has a social market, or mixed, economy which is the third largest in the non-Communist world. In 1984, the economy began to expand again, with real growth GNP averaging approximately 3% over the next three years. The principal source of growth was domestic demand in 1986 and 1987.

The rate of inflation in the FRG was 2.4% in 1984, 2.2% in 1985, and prices actually fell by 0.3% in 1986. These impressive figures reflect not only the *Deutsche Bundesbank's* tight control of the money supply but also a widespread German fear of inflation. Having suffered the traumas of hyper-inflation twice this century, the Germans are determined to keep their domestic rate of inflation as low as possible. At the same time, they do not wish to import inflation. Therefore, any attempt by a foreign supplier to export rising domestic costs to the FRG will encounter very stiff resistance.

In 1985 and 1986, the FRG achieved record current account surpluses of DM 38.9 and DM 77.8 billion.

In common with most Western European countries, unemployment has remained for the FRG an almost intractable problem. The figures for 1984, 1985 and 1986 show some 9.0%, 9.1% and 8.7% of the workforce on the unemployment register.

Structure

Over recent years, the structure of the German economy has undergone a number of significant changes. The contribution of agriculture to GDP has fallen steadily to approximately 2%. Similarly, industry's contribution dropped from 47.7% of GDP in 1979 to 42.6% in 1985. Services other than commerce and transport have compensated for the decline in agriculture and manufacturing industry, and if government and administration are included, the FRG has become predominantly a service sector economy.

Despite the impression given by the raw GDP data that manufacturing is contributing an ever-lower percentage of total output, it nonetheless remains the backbone of the German economy. In the FRG, there is almost universal coverage of capital and consumer products. The country's bedrock industries are mechanical engineering, vehicle building, electrical engineering, precision instruments and optical goods, food, and chemicals.

In 1984, the FRG had 36,392 companies registered in the manufacturing sector. Fewer than 500 companies employed over 500 workers, and the greatest concentration of companies, particularly in engineering, was among those with between 20 and 100 workers. The ownership structure is predominantly private but government has holdings in over 900 companies, among them Volkswagen and Veba.

The main industrial area is the Ruhr, the centre of the iron, steel and coal industries. But it is here that the decline in the smokestack industries has been most heavily felt over recent years. If the demise of shipbuilding on the northern coast is also taken into account, the focal point of industrial power is seen to be shifting towards the south, especially towards Hesse and Bavaria. It is therefore not surprising that, with the majority of sunrise industries also emerging in Baden-Württemberg and Bavaria, the Germans are beginning to speak of a North-South Divide.

Foreign trade

It has already been noted that the FRG enjoyed record current account surpluses in 1985 and 1986. These were due mainly to record surpluses in the balance of visible trade, with invisibles showing a growing deficit.

In 1985, exports rose by 10% in value terms, with 5.9% of this deriving from increases in the volume of goods sold. Imports rose by 6.8%, of which 4.2% was due to increases in important volumes. The terms of trade improved slightly in 1985 as a result of the fall in the value of the dollar and a subsequent fall in raw material prices.

In 1986, the FRG's trade surplus reached a massive DM 112 billion. The surplus was due to a large degree to a sharp drop in import prices which began in the final quarter of 1985. The nominal figures reveal that the FRG exported goods worth DM 526.4 billion. Her main exports were road vehicles, chemicals, machinery, iron and steel. Imports in 1986 totalled DM 414.2 billion, the principal goods being petroleum and petroleum products, iron and steel, non-ferrous metals, electrical machinery, road vehicles, and clothing.

Detailed information on the German economy can be obtained from *Country Profile West Germany*, which appears annually, and the quarterly *Country Report West Germany*, both of which are published by the EIU (Economist Intelligence Unit).

Anglo-German trade

Although the UK balance of trade with the FRG showed a rising surplus in favour of the Germans from 1983 to 1985, the British share of the German import market actually rose over the same period from 7% to 8%. In 1986, it dropped back

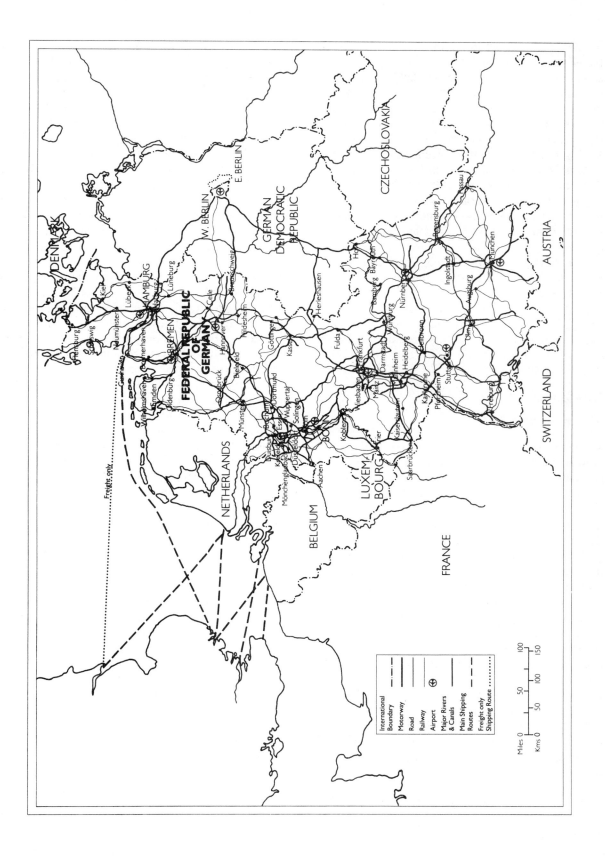

to 7.2% with the fall in the oil price being the factor responsible. In 1985, unrefined petroleum constituted 29% of total German imports from the UK as compared to only 16% in 1986. The FRG imports some 60% of its energy requirements, and the UK provided 28% of total imports in 1986, thus remaining the country's largest supplier of oil. If oil products are excluded from the calculations, UK market share increased only slightly, from 6.2% to 6.3%, during the 1985/1986 period. UK exports of computers, office machinery, aircraft, motor vehicles, electrical engineering products, and pharmaceuticals were the major items involved.

The average value of the £ against the DM fell by 15.9% from 1985 to 1986 when it was worth DM 3.184.

Further information on German imports from the UK and British goods and services with major export potential to the FRG is provided by *Focus Germany* published by the DTI (Department of Trade and Industry).

Strategies

Market strategy

To be successful in the German market, the British supplier must be not only as good as German or foreign competitors, but better. This means excelling in terms of product quality, new product technology, general technical competence, customer orientation, commercial competence, delivery performance, and after-sales service.

Before entering the market, the British supplier must adopt a strategic approach. The strategy should begin with in-depth market research, using both British and German sources of information: a quick visit to just one trade fair will not suffice.

The decision to go into the market must also be accompanied by one to allocate adequate resources: again, it is just not enough to have a representative on the road in the FRG if she or he is not backed up by staff at head office or if priority is constantly being given to domestic orders.

Market strategy must also embrace serious considerations of pricing policy. Products which command premium prices in the UK as market leaders will probably not command these same premiums in the FRG. Therefore, it is not enough to 'convert' sterling prices into DM. Nor should

the DM price of the product be allowed to drift upwards as a result of sterling fluctuations or UK inflation. A British exporter to the FRG, faced with rising domestic costs, might be advised to bite the bullet and trim profit margins rather than risk losing market share.

Conversely, a pricing strategy which sees prices pitched too low on the German market will not meet with success either. In the past, some British companies unable to meet German quality standards have entered the market with prices which were lower than German price levels. The outcome has been unsuccessful because the German purchaser has a habit of seeing prices which are too low as indicative of a lower-quality product, and with so much disposable income does not have to buy what is perceived as low quality. In the long term, there is no alternative but to take what the market defines as quality as given.

There is obviously no simple recipe available for successful distribution strategy in the FRG because circumstances vary from company to company. Depending on corporate policy, the size of the UK operation, the nature of the product concerned and a number of other variables, the decision will be taken to sell directly from the UK; to appoint a German agent or distributor; to operate from a warehouse in the FRG; or to set up a manufacturing facility there.

If it is decided to appoint an agent or distributor, great care should be taken in the final choice. The agent or distributor should not be given the contract just because he or she is available. Is he/she a quality agent? Who else does he/she represent? Is the quality of the other products handled commensurate with that from the British supplier? Where does the agent or distributor operate now? A German agent might agree to a franchise to sell all over the FRG when in practice the real trading area is one of the smaller states. In fact, different agents or distributors might be needed for different states or regions in order to cater for their distinctive and individualistic tastes. Indeed, German commercial law recognises this by allowing a supplier to appoint geographically exclusive distributors for different regions.

All technical products must be in metric units and in conformity with German safety and technical standards.

Sales literature should be accompanied at minimum by a good and accurate translation of the product's most important data.

No matter how good the market strategy, instant results should not be expected from an initial involvement in the FRG. A medium-term commitment to the market will be required, embracing strategic thinking, hard work and tenacity, before rewards are forthcoming in this demanding environment.

German companies feel that they have had to work hard and long to nurture their export markets: they perceive little reason to make life easy for their importers.

Visit strategy

The British business person travelling in the FRG can expect to encounter a high degree of professionalism in all dealings with German partners, from managing directors and purchasing managers to sales staff. Negotiations will be with people who have either studied a discipline which is related directly to business and management or who have taken an apprenticeship in their chosen function. Many will have done both. Quite naturally, Germans expect and appreciate professionalism from their business partners.

The success or failure of a business trip to the FRG will be determined by the thoroughness of the planning preceding the visit. It is essential for the British supplier not only to know in advance what he/she wishes to achieve from a business trip but how it is to be achieved. This means embarking on a visit with a clearly-defined visit strategy.

Appointments at individual companies must be confirmed in writing in advance: unannounced visits will not be welcomed. A good supply of visiting cards should be taken along (and not left behind in the other suit in the hotel bedroom). It should also be remembered that German purchasing managers are accustomed to being fêted, so a healthy expense account is an essential prerequisite.

The German businessman has a reputation for tough bargaining but also for straightforward bargaining. He will come to the negotiating table armed with a negotiating strategy, and it usually does not take long to deduce what his strategy is.

'Nicht seriös'

By contrast, the British businessman has acquired a reputation in the FRG, deserved or not, for 'playing it by ear'. This should be resisted as it tends to be dismissed by Germans as unprofessional (*nicht seriös*). However, the British habit of bringing humour into the toughest of negotiations is appreciated, so it is advisable not to leave one's sense of humour back at Heathrow!

The results of negotiations with German business partners should be confirmed immediately in writing. Often letters from German companies bear two signatures: the one at bottom left is from a so-called *Prokurist*, without whose signature the letter would not be binding on the German company; the other at the bottom right is from the *Sachbearbeiter*. Replies should be addressed to the latter because this is the person actually responsible for dealing with the matter in hand.

Finally, a word about language: it is just not true that all German businessmen speak English. Moreover, some German purchasing managers who do speak English have been known to adopt the attitude: 'Why should I put myself at a disadvantage in our negotiations by speaking your language? After all, you are trying to sell to me'. It would therefore appear obvious that the better the British supplier can speak German, the greater the chances of success in the market in the FRG. Courtesy alone surely dictates that the most monoglot Briton should be capable of producing *Guten Tag* and *Auf Wiedersehen*.

Collin Randlesome
Senior Lecturer in European Management
Cranfield School of Management

The trade fair

„Eine richtige Präsentation wollen wir doch geben."

The video sequence
Der Video-Abschnitt

This sequence shows you a typical slice of German business life – the trade fair. In fact, two slices: one from the Frankfurt consumer trade fair and the other from the Stuttgart CAD/CAM trade fair. British manufacturers were well represented at both and this sequence shows how some of them made use of the opportunities German trade fairs afford for introducing and promoting a product.

Trade fairs are a long-established feature of the German business landscape. Some towns, like Frankfurt, have been host to trade fairs for literally hundreds of years. Germany's position as a trading country at the crossroads of Europe gives a distinctly cosmopolitan flavour – a German trade fair will attract buyers from all over Europe.

In this sequence, we have concentrated on German interest in British products. The buyers obviously like to inform themselves very closely about a product. The message that comes over clearly is that if you want to get the most out of a trade fair as an exhibitor, it pays to prepare. For instance, make sure potential key customers know you are going to be there. Have all the relevant literature – product information, price lists – translated into the foreign language before you go.

In this sequence you will hear many Germans speaking, sometimes in strong regional accents. Some of them get quite carried away. This makes it difficult for you, as you struggle to follow what they are saying. In language learning terms, this sequence offers you excellent practice in *selective listening*. In a crowded environment, such as a trade fair, you have to select what you hear and you need to respond rapidly. This means learning to listen for the general sense of what is being said and developing a capacity for reacting quickly.

The German spoken by the British stand personnel is generally of high quality. As exhibitors, they need to know specialist terminology or constructions which really only come into play in circumstances like this. At the Stuttgart trade fair, for example, ICL used a German demonstrator to ensure an effective presentation.

Even if you are using a German demonstrator, it still makes sense to prepare yourself for the situation where the German demonstrator and/or interpreter is not available. This will give you the security of knowing that you can demonstrate the essential features of your product, system or service.

To prepare for that eventuality, make sure you have memorised the key words and phrases you need to demonstrate your product – write the key words on to sticky labels and fix them somewhere where you can refer to them easily, if necessary.

Your German sales and promotional literature is important as visual support – make good use of it. You can anticipate many of the questions that your German customers will ask – prepare the answers before you go. And, of course, work through this chapter: its main objective is to help you manage the trade fair effectively and successfully.

Key words

Here is a list of the key words in German used by the various people at the two trade fairs. Study the list and the meaning in this context, so that you can follow the video more easily. The words are listed in the order in which they occur.

die Messe (-n)	trade fair
der Verkaufspreis (-e)	selling price
der Markt (¨e)	market
die Werbung	advertising
die Zeitschrift (-en)	magazine
der Handel	trade
das Werbematerial (-ien)	publicity material
die Anleitung (-en)	instructions
im Verkauf	retail
die Preisliste (-n)	price list
das Sortiment (-e)	range
im Einkauf	wholesale
die Vertretung (-en)	agency
die Lieferzeit (-en)	delivery time
das Lager (-)	warehouse, stock
am/auf Lager	in stock
die Mehrwertsteuer	VAT
das Muster (-)	sample
der Rechner (-)	computer
das Handbuch (¨er)	manual
der Vertreter (-)	agent, representative
der Kunde (-n, -n)	customer
der Bildschirm (-e)	monitor

Practising listening and understanding
Hörvertständnisübungen

Normally you will be able to understand a lot more than you can say independently. There is, however, a direct correlation between listening/understanding and speaking. For most people, the better they are able to listen and understand, the better they are able to speak.

In this part of the video-based learning section we want to help you to understand more, and to understand more quickly, by asking you to answer three different kinds of question:
- questions which ask for **information** from the situation shown on the video,
- questions which ask you for a brief **summary** of key parts,
- questions which ask for highly specific **detail**.

The questions are based both on what the people say in German and on the order in which they say it.

We recommend you work through this part in the following way:
- **read the list of key words** which occur in the video sequence,
- **watch the video** and enjoy it, listening out for the key words. Do not look through the transcript yet. You may need to watch all or part of the video more than once. But do so without the transcript at this stage,
- **study the information questions** in Exercise A until you understand them,
- **watch the video again** listening carefully for the information you need to answer the questions. In this section, we are mainly concerned with understanding, so it does not matter whether you make a written or a mental note, nor whether you do so in English or German. You should decide this, based on your own needs and objectives,
- **compare your answers** with the answers given,
- **repeat this procedure** for the summary questions in Exercise B,
- **study the transcript** of the video carefully, using the Vocabulary Guide at the back of the book to help you,
- **look at Exercise C** and decide whether you find it helpful. It will be if you need to understand the very fine points of a business discussion. It requires close listening and aims to develop a high degree of understanding. You can do the exercise either as a listening comprehension or as a reading comprehension. If you do decide to

tackle it, we recommend you follow the above workplan,

● **revise the language** used in the sequence and

familiarise yourself with it by listening to the car cassette containing the German soundtrack of this sequence.

Information

Exercise A

What are they saying?

Bei Wedgwood

1. Was kostet Markum?

2. Für welche Märkte ist das Dekor?

3. Wem wird das Kaffeeservice gefallen?

4. Wie führt Firma Wedgwood das Dekor ein?

Bei Fräulein Taylor

5. Was für ein Geschäft hat der Herr?
6. Mit was für einer Anleitung kommt der Artikel?
7. Wie ist der Preis im Einkauf?

8. Und die Lieferzeit?

Bei der CAD/CAM-Ausstellung

9. Was ist außer den Befehlen in deutscher Sprache?
10. Was finden die technischen Zeichner schwer?

11. Arbeitet Dr Gründer nur für BYG?

12. Was hat man mit dem Arbeiter gemacht?

Answers

Bei Wedgwood

1. Es kommt auf einen Verkaufspreis von *siebenhundertzweiunddreißig Mark.*

2. Das Dekor ist *für viele verschiedene Märkte* gedacht.

3. Das Kaffeeservice wird *einer ziemlich breiten Masse* gefallen.

4. Wedgwood führt das Dekor *mit Werbung, auch in . . . Illustrierten* ein.

Bei Fräulein Taylor

5. Der Herr hat *ein Geschenkartikelgeschäft.*
6. Mit *deutscher Anleitung.*
7. (Jeder) Artikel im Einkauf . . . wäre *fünf Mark zwanzig . . .*
8. Wenn alles auf Lager ist, ist die Lieferung *eine Woche.*

Bei der CAD/CAM-Ausstellung

9. Es gibt *ein deutsches Handbuch* und *ein deutsches Nachschlagewerk.*
10. Die technischen Zeichner finden immer *das Lesen von Handbüchern* schwer.

11. Nein, er ist auch tätig *für andere englische Software-Entwicklungsunternehmen.*

12. *Man hat den Arbeiter durch einen Roboter ersetzt.*

Summary

Exercise B

Answers

What are they saying? Give a brief answer to each of the following questions:

1. Wie will Wedgwood Markum einführen?

1. Die Firma Wedgwood wird möglicherweise in

Illustrierten und in der örtlichen Presse Werbung machen, aber nicht sofort. Sie will nämlich warten, bis sie sieht, ob das Produkt erfolgreich ist.

2. Wie versucht Fräulein Taylor ihr Produkt zu verkaufen?

2. Sie macht den interessierten Kunden auf die Vorteile aufmerksam. Man braucht nichts mehr zu kaufen, weil man alles bekommt, was man braucht.

3. Warum ist es so wichtig für den CAD/CAM-Kunden, daß die Handbücher in deutscher Sprache sind?

3. Seine Leute sind technische Zeichner und verstehen meistens kein Englisch, deswegen finden sie das Lesen von Handbüchern in englischer Sprache schwer.

4. Welche Rolle spielt der Vertreter bei Hi-Tech-Produkten?

4. Er hat eine doppelte Rolle. Er muß sowohl Produkte verkaufen als auch seinem Partner helfen, seine Produkte für den deutschen Markt zu gestalten.

Close listening

Exercise C

Answers

We recommend that you only attempt this exercise if you need, or are keen, to understand the precise details of a discussion. Instead of doing the exercise as a listening comprehension exercise, you may like to try it as an exercise in reading comprehension. You are looking for what the words in italics refer to:

1. *das* ist für viele verschiedene Märkte schon gedacht

1. Ist das jetzt *ein Dekor*, das speziell für den deutschen Markt konzipiert ist? . . . Nee, *das* ist für viele verschiedene Märkte schon gedacht.

2. dann werden wir *das* schon machen

2. . . . und Sie führen das jetzt ein, *mit Werbung in Illustrierten* . . . ? . . . wenn wir sehen, daß es gut läuft, dann werden wir *das* schon machen.

3. *es* soll besonders scharf sein

3. Kennen Sie *unser Laser-Messer? Es* soll besonders scharf sein.

4. *an dem* die Firma ICL zu einem Teil beteiligt ist

4. Dieses Paket ist vom *CAD-Centre in Cambridge* entwickelt worden, *an dem* die Firma ICL zu einem Teil beteiligt ist.

5. sind *die* übersetzt worden ins Deutsche?

5. . . . *die Befehle* sind hier in deutsch; sind *die* übersetzt worden ins Deutsche?

6. *das* sind normale technische Zeichner

6. Weil *die Leute bei uns, das* sind normale technische Zeichner, . . .

7. *die* können also meistens kein Englisch

7. das sind normale *technische Zeichner – die* können also meistens kein Englisch . . .

8. *das* dürfte also kein Problem darstellen

8. . . . und sie finden immer *das Lesen von Handbüchern* ziemlich schwer . . . *das* dürfte also kein Problem darstellen.

9. wie *sie* ihre Produkte auch für unseren Markt weiterentwickeln . . . können

9. Darüber hinaus geben wir *unseren englischen Partnern* Anregungen, wie *sie* ihre Produkte auch für unseren Markt weiterentwickeln . . . können . . .

10. *das* wollen wir schließlich auch

10. line ?? so daß wir . . . eine Reihe von Aufgaben erfüllen, die *uns* – und *das* wollen wir schließlich auch – *bei unseren Kunden verankern* . . .

You should now feel confident that you have explored the text in depth and are ready to move on to consolidate your German. In the next part of this section you will find some specially-designed exercises for this. Remember to come back frequently to the video and the car cassette to remind yourself of the language you will hear and work with at a trade fair.

Consolidation
Konsolidierung

In this sequence, the language points for consolidation are:

- modal auxiliary verbs in main clauses
- prepositions
- adjectival endings (1)

Modal auxiliary verbs

When you are demonstrating a product, you need to be able to say what it *can* or *cannot* do, what people *want* it for, what your customer *must* appreciate about its special qualities and why your customer *should* look no further!

In German, how do you say:

I can . . .   he ought . . .
you may . . .   they want . . .
you must . . .

This sequence at the trade fair is full of examples. Here are some of them:

. . . eine richtige Präsentation *wollen* wir doch geben.
Kann ich Ihnen behilflich sein?
Man *muß* Kunden beraten . . .

In all there are six verbs like this. Here is the complete list:

müssen	**können**	**wollen**
sollen	**dürfen**	**mögen★**

★ *Mögen* is mostly used as *ich möchte*.

All of them are easy to handle. If there is anything you need to check, please refer to the Grammar Guide.

Practice A

Check through the German transcript of the trade fair sequence for modal auxiliary verbs. Which three are most commonly used?
Do you agree that they are:

können
müssen
wollen?

Practice B

Using modal auxiliary verbs how do you say the sentences below in the other language? You can approach this exercise either from English or from German depending on your own needs and confidence.

If you approach it from English, ask yourself how you would say the following sentences in German:

1. Can you translate the literature into German?

If you prefer to approach this exercise from German, ask yourself how an English speaker would say these sentences:

1. Können Sie die Literatur ins Deutsche übersetzen?

---

2. Do we have to wait a little while?

3. Can they advise our customers?

4. Do we want to develop our products for the German market?

5. Can he give a proper presentation?

6. Would you like to send him a price list?

2. Müssen wir ein bißchen abwarten?

3. Können sie unsere Kunden beraten?

4. Wollen wir unsere Produkte für den deutschen Markt entwickeln?

5. Kann er eine richtige Präsentation geben?

6. Möchten Sie ihm eine Preisliste schicken?

Practice C

Look at the German sentences in Practice B again. What do you notice about the way they are formed? The main feature is that you often need a second verb in the sentence to complete the meaning, e.g.:

Wollen wir unser Produkt für den deutschen Markt *entwickeln*?
Do we want to develop our product for the German market?

How do you say these sentences in the other language? Again, you can choose whether to approach this exercise from English or German depending on your own needs and confidence.

If you start with English, ask yourself how you would say these sentences in German.

If you prefer to start with German, ask yourself which of these verbs you would need to complete the sentence in German:

1. How can we improve this product for the German market?

2. Can you get this program in French too?

3. When do you want to send me a sample?

4. Can I see German literature as well?

5. Would you like to take a price list with you?

6. May I give you my card?

1. Wie können wir dieses Produkt für den deutschen Markt . . . . . ?

2. Kann man dieses Programm auch in französischer Sprache . . . . . ?

3. Wann wollen Sie mir ein Muster . . . . . ?

4. Kann ich auch deutsche Literatur : . . . . ?

5. Möchten Sie eine Preisliste . . . . . ?

6. Darf ich Ihnen meine Karte . . . . . ?

| (a) bekommen | (b) geben | (c) mitnehmen | (d) schicken | (e) sehen | (f) verbessern |

Key: 1. (f) 2. (a) 3. (d) 4. (e) 5. (c) 6. (b)

Practice D

You are a German agent for several British companies. You are advising a company wanting to enter the German market. Choosing the most appropriate modal auxiliary verb, ask for the following information about the company's:

1. willingness to exhibit at a trade fair.

2. ability to translate the sales literature.

3. ability to provide publicity material.

4. wish to find an agent.

5. need to develop products for the German market.

6. ability to send a sample.

1. Wollen Sie auf einer Messe ausstellen?

2. Können Sie die Verkaufsliteratur übersetzen?

3. Können Sie Werbematerial zur Verfügung stellen?

4. Möchten Sie einen Vertreter finden?

5. Müssen Sie die Produkte für den deutschen Markt entwickeln?

6. Können Sie ein Muster schicken?

Incidentally, when you checked through the German transcript for this sequence, did you notice these two examples:

Die Zeichner können meistens kein Englisch.
. . . und das wollen wir schließlich auch . . .

German sometimes leaves out a second verb when the meaning is already clear. In these examples, the verbs in brackets are understood.

Die Zeichner können meistens kein Englisch [verstehen].
und das wollen wir schließlich auch [machen].
Ich muß morgen nach Hamburg [fahren].
Ich soll heute zum Vertreter [gehen].

That's enough about modals for the moment – you can go on to the prepositions! (Try saying that in German . . .).

Prepositions

These are the (usually) short words which you use to say:

- **when** something happens (*at* ten o'clock)
- **where** something happens (*in* my office)
- **how** something happens (*with* our German agent)
- **why** something happens (*for* the quarterly review)

They come before a **noun** or a **pronoun**. In our mother tongue we tend not to be conscious of them. In German, however, they appear to us to present an inordinate problem because of those awful things called **cases**.

If you feel that prepositions are an area of the German language where you do not have too much of a problem, try the three exercises below. If, on the other hand, you feel that prepositions are an area where you need to revise, have a look at the Grammar Guide on page 174 first, before you attempt the exercises.

There are essentially two questions to ask about prepositions:

- which is the correct preposition?
- what, if anything, should I do to the words which follow it?

Practice A

Look through the German transcript of video sequence 1, pick out the prepositions and the accompanying noun or pronoun. Ask yourself why the speaker uses that particular preposition, and why he/she uses it in that particular way.

Practice B

Select the correct form of the words in brackets to follow the prepositions:

1. Wer hat das Handbuch in (die) (deutsch) Sprache übersetzt?
2. Das Handbuch können Sie in (alle) Sprachen bekommen.
3. Es gibt in (erste) Linie Literatur zu (jeder) Rechner.
4. Das ist die beste Lösung für (unser) (verschieden) Märkte.
5. Das geht über (das) (eigentlich) System hinaus.
6. Durch (die) (technisch) Beratung können wir unseren Kundenkreis weiter entwickeln.
7. Mit (dieser) Artikel erfassen wir (die) (breit) Masse.

1. Wer hat das Handbuch in *die deutsche* Sprache übersetzt?
2. Das Handbuch können Sie in *allen* Sprachen bekommen.
3. Es gibt in *erster* Linie Literatur zu *jedem* Rechner.
4. Das ist die beste Lösung für *unsere verschiedene* Märkte.
5. Das geht über *das eigentliche* System hinaus.
6. Durch *die technische* Beratung können wir unseren Kundenkreis weiter entwickeln.
7. Mit *diesem* Artikel erfassen wir *die breite* Masse.

8. Wir müssen es zwischen (der) Zeichner und (der) Bediener aufbauen.

9. Das Software-Unternehmen hat vor, ein genaueres System auf (der) Markt zu bringen.

10. Durch (die) (örtlich) Presse wollen wir es machen.

8. Wir müssen es zwischen *dem* Zeichner und *dem* Bediener aufbauen.

9. Das Software-Unternehmen hat vor, ein genaueres System auf *den* Markt zu bringen.

10. Durch *die örtliche* Presse wollen wir es machen.

Practice C

Choose the most appropriate preposition from the box to fill the gaps in these sentences:

an	auf	bei	durch	in	mit	von	zu

1. Ein Programm, ... dem die Firma beteiligt ist.

2. Der Vertreter versucht es . . . . . einem zweiten Rechner.

3. Die Leute . . . . . ihnen befinden sich . . . . . einer relativ neuen Situation.

4. Wenn man . . . . . sogenannten Vorab-Interessenten ist, muß man folgende Programme zeigen.

5. Wir stellen dem Handel Werbematerial . . . . . Verfügung.

6. Ich habe . . . . . diesem Messer schon gehört.

7. Als Vertreter beraten wir . . . . . der Entwicklung neuer Artikel.

8. Wir haben alles . . . . . Lager.

9. . . . . . dieses System erweitern wir schnell und preiswert unseren Markt.

10. Hier sehen Sie es . . . . . dem Bildschirm.

1. Ein Programm, *an dem* die Firma beteiligt ist.

2. Der Vertreter versucht es *auf/mit einem* zweiten Rechner.

3. Die Leute *bei/mit/von ihnen* befinden sich *in einer* relativ neuen Situation.

4. Wenn man *bei/mit sogenannten* Vorab-Interessenten ist, muß man folgende Programme zeigen.

5. Wir stellen dem Handel Werbematerial *zur* Verfügung.

6. Ich habe *von diesem* Messer schon gehört.

7. Als Vertreter beraten wir *bei der* Entwicklung neuer Artikel.

8. Wir haben alles *am/auf* Lager.

9. *Durch dieses* System erweitern wir schnell und preiswert unseren Markt.

10. Hier sehen Sie es *(an dem) am* Bildschirm.

Adjectival endings 1

Ask any German what is difficult about English and the answer will be tenses. Ask an English speaker what is difficult about German and the first thing to come to mind will probably be adjectival endings.

Adjectival endings are an important distinguishing feature in German but many people go round in something of a mental fog about them: every time they think they have the hang of them, up the adjectives pop with a different ending. In fact, adjectival endings are not as difficult as they may seem.

Orders are not lost or won on adjectival endings but making the effort to get them right will enhance your status in the mind of your customer. You will be making a good impression and the customer is more likely to take you seriously because of that. Knowing that you are getting them right will also boost your confidence enormously. Getting them right all the time is another matter – even the Germans make the occasional mistake – but with practice they will come more easily.

In German, there are three types of sentence where the endings on adjectives can cause confusion for the foreign learner. They are:

1. sentences where there is an **adjective and a noun**, such as:

New products are being developed.
Neue Produkte werden entwickelt.

2. sentences where there is an **indefinite article, an adjective and a noun**, such as:

A new design is being introduced.
Ein neues Muster wird eingeführt.

3. sentences where there is a **definite article, an adjective and a noun**, such as:

The new company is in Neuwied.
Die neue Firma ist in Neuwied.

In this sequence we shall concentrate on adjectives in sentences like the first one, e.g.:

Neue Produkte werden entwickelt.

If you already feel confident that you can handle the endings in sentences like these, go straight to the practice exercise. If you need to remind yourself of the pattern they follow, consult the Grammar Guide on pp. 172–4.

Sentences with an adjective and a noun

Some of the first expressions you encounter when you start to learn German follow this pattern. Simple greetings are one example:

guten Tag   gute Reise   schönes Wochenende
vielen Dank   gute Nacht   frohe Ferien

Items on a restaurant menu are another:

westfälischer Schinken   italienische Pizza
deutsches Bier   frische Erdbeeren

Forms of address in business correspondence are yet another:

sehr geehrter Herr Schmidt
sehr geehrte Frau Becker
mit freundlichem Gruß
mit freundlichen Grüßen

What comes over clearly from these examples is that the key to adjectival endings lies in knowing the gender of nouns i.e.:

| der Markt | die Firma | das Produkt |
| der Vertreter | die Messe | das System |

The first thing to remember is that an adjective takes its cue from the noun. Look at the restaurant menu again; the relationship between *der Schinken* and the adjectival ending in *westfälischer Schinken* is clear. In the same way, if you did not already know it was *das Bier*, you could probably recognise it from *deutsches Bier*.

But the problem is that these endings do not stay the same. You will hear *westfälische*, *westfälischen* or even *westfälischem*. So the second thing to remember is that these endings can change, even when the noun stays the same. The trick is to recognise the changes when you hear them and to make the right changes yourself when you are using adjectives. The practice exercises will help you.

Practice A

You have returned from a trade fair and are reporting on a company which has impressed you. You have made some notes, e.g.:

Literatur   deutschsprachig,
Kundendienst   gut,

and these form the basis of your report.

Using the adjectives and nouns taken from the lists below, construct the sentences to say what is available. Start each sentence with:

Wissen Sie, ...

and finish it with

. . . . . steht zur Verfügung

Examples:

Wissen Sie, guter Kundendienst steht zur Verfügung.
Wissen Sie, deutschsprachige Literatur steht zur Verfügung.
Wissen Sie, technisches Werbematerial steht zur Verfügung.

And in the plural

Wissen Sie, technische Zeichnungen stehen zur Verfügung.

Your notes read:

Item	Commentary	Answers
der Kundendienst	gut	Wissen Sie, guter Kundendienst steht zur Verfügung.
die Literatur	deutschsprachig	Wissen Sie, deutschsprachige Literatur steht zur Verfügung.
das Werbematerial	technisch	Wissen Sie, technisches Werbematerial steht zur Verfügung.
die Software	richtig	Wissen Sie, richtige Software steht zur Verfügung.
das Dekor	traditionell	Wissen Sie, traditionelles Dekor steht zur Verfügung.
die Zeichnungen	verschieden	Wissen Sie, verschiedene Zeichnungen stehen zur Verfügung.
die Preise	speziell	Wissen Sie, spezielle Preise stehen zur Verfügung.
die Vertreter	deutschsprachig	Wissen Sie, deutschsprachige Vertreter stehen zur Verfügung.
die Produkte	modern	Wissen Sie, moderne Produkte stehen zur Verfügung.
die Systeme	neu	Wissen Sie, neue Systeme stehen zur Verfügung.

Practice B

You are a German agent advising a British company how to approach the German market. Using the above list of adjectives and nouns, form your own sentences. Construct each sentence as follows:

Sie können ohne . . . . . nicht in den deutschen Markt gehen.

Examples:

Sie können ohne guten Kundendienst nicht in den deutschen Markt gehen.
Sie können ohne deutschsprachige Literatur nicht in den deutschen Markt gehen.
Sie können ohne technisches Werbematerial nicht in den deutschen Markt gehen.

And in the plural:

Sie können ohne gute Produkte nicht in den deutschen Markt gehen.

Answers

Sie können ohne guten Kundendienst nicht in den deutschen Markt gehen.
Sie können ohne deutschsprachige Literatur nicht in den deutschen Markt gehen.
Sie können ohne technisches Werbematerial nicht in den deutschen Markt gehen.
Sie können ohne richtige Software nicht in den deutschen Markt gehen.
Sie können ohne traditionelles Dekor nicht in den deutschen Markt gehen.
Sie können ohne verschiedene Zeichnungen nicht in den deutschen Markt gehen.
Sie können ohne spezielle Preise nicht in den deutschen Markt gehen.
Sie können ohne deutschsprachige Vertreter nicht in den deutschen Markt gehen.
Sie können ohne moderne Produkte nicht in den deutschen Markt gehen.
Sie können ohne neue Systeme nicht in den deutschen Markt gehen.

Practice C

This time you are giving your opinion of some of the companies and products you saw at the trade fair. Using the list of adjectives and nouns from Practice A above, complete the sentences we have started for you. Start each one with:

Das ist ein/eine . . . mit . . . . . .

Examples:

Das ist eine Firma mit gutem Kundendienst.
Das ist ein Produkt mit deutschsprachiger
Literatur.
Das ist ein Programm mit technischem
Werbematerial.

And in the plural:

Das ist ein Dekor mit kleinen Blümchen.*

Das ist eine Firma . . .
Das ist ein Produkt . . .
Das ist ein Programm . . .
Das ist eine Entwicklung . . .
Das ist ein Kaffeeservice . . .
Das ist eine Präsentation . . .
Das ist ein Geschenkartikelgeschäft . . .
Das ist eine Messe . . .
Das ist ein Center . . .
Das ist ein Geschäft . . .

Answers

Das ist eine Firma mit gutem Kundendienst.
Das ist ein Produkt mit deutschsprachiger
Literatur.
Das ist ein Programm mit technischem
Werbematerial.
Das ist eine Entwicklung mit richtiger Software.
Das ist ein Kaffeeservice mit traditionellem Dekor.
Das ist eine Präsentation mit verschiedenen
Zeichnungen.
Das ist ein Geschenkartikelgeschäft mit speziellen
Preisen.
Das ist eine Messe mit deutschsprachigen
Vertretern.
Das ist ein Center mit modernen Produkten.
Das ist ein Geschäft mit neuen Systemen.

Development
Erweiterung

In this sequence on describing a product or
service, the development exercises concentrate on

---

* (do not forget that sometimes you need an extra -n here!)

- demonstrating a product
- highlighting features of a product.

The main objective of the development section is
to extend your range of language skills by focusing
on two or three language points selected from the
video. It is important that you practise these
language points in conversation. To help you,
some of the exercises are included on the study
cassette as well as in the book. Make your own
choice about which to tackle first – but make sure
you try both.

Describing a product or service

First, we shall be looking at demonstrating a
product.

So far in this chapter, most of the exercises have
been based on short sentences which are direct, to
the point and easy to handle. But sometimes you
will want to express your ideas in longer sentences.
Take a simple sentence like this:

Sie *können* ihre Produkte für unseren Markt
verbessern.

Notice what happens to those two verbs when
Willi Gründer describes part of his job:

Darüber hinaus geben wir unseren englischen
Partnern Anregungen, wie sie ihre Produkte für
unseren Markt *verbessern können.*

Remembering what to do with the verbs can be
difficult when you are already trying to express
more than one idea, to grapple with the right
vocabulary and to listen attentively to your
German customer. But, of all these items, verbs
are probably the easiest to handle because they are
predictable. [See the Grammar Guide page 171 for
more information on word order.]

Let's look at getting the word order right when
you have a modal auxiliary verb to cope with as
well.

Exercises	Answers

1. You are demonstrating a software package. Tell your customer what you are demonstrating, by saying:

We are showing you how . . .
Wir zeigen Ihnen, wie . . .

Wir zeigen Ihnen, wie . . .

and change the word order.

- Sie können dieses Programm auch in französischer Sprache bekommen.

Sie dieses Programm auch in französischer Sprache *bekommen können.*

- Sie können sich weitere Menüs frei gestalten.

Sie sich weitere Menüs frei *gestalten können.*

- Wir können ein einfaches Teil produzieren.

wir ein einfaches Teil *produzieren können.*

- Sie können nicht nur vorgefertigte Zeichnungen machen.

Sie nicht nur vorgefertigte Zeichnungen *machen können.*

2. You are a colleague wanting information about this package. Say you want to know whether . . . , by saying:

Ich möchte wissen, ob . . .

Ich möchte wissen, ob . . .

and change the word order.

- Müssen wir unsere Literatur ins Deutsche übersetzen?

wir unsere Literatur ins Deutsche *übersetzen müssen?*

- Soll man ein neues Software-Paket entwickeln?

man ein neues Software-Paket *entwickeln soll?*

- Kann ich ein Beispiel ausprobieren?

ich ein Beispiel ausprobieren *kann?*

- Dürfte das ein Problem darstellen?

das ein Problem *darstellen dürfte?*

3. You are telling your boss why your software is selling well. Say the customers are buying the product because:

Die Kunden kaufen das Produkt, weil . . .

Die Kunden kaufen das Produkt, weil . . .

and change the word order.

- Sie wollen ihre Leistungsfähigkeit steigern.

sie ihre Leistungsfähigkeit *steigern wollen.*

- Die Zeichner müssen ein deutsches Handbuch haben.

die Zeichner ein deutsches Handbuch *haben müssen.*

- Man kann es für den französischen Markt entwickeln.

man es für den französischen Markt *entwickeln kann.*

- Man darf die eigenen Teile zeichnen.

man die eigenen Teile *zeichnen darf.*

Highlighting important points

How can you prepare yourself to highlight specific qualities of your product or service? One way is to use an introductory phrase such as:

Wir *achten in England sehr stark darauf*, unsere Produkte speziell für den deutschen Markt zu konzipieren.

In England *we pay very close attention to* designing our products especially for the German market.

The introductory phrase is made up of a verb *achten* (to consider) plus a preposition *auf*, two words which, when used together i.e. *achten auf*, and followed by the appropriate case, take on a new meaning.

There are a number of verbs that work like this in German:

auf etwas achten	to pay attention to something
an etwas denken	to intend, to think of doing something (an action)
auf etwas bestehen	to insist on something (an intention, a condition)
aus etwas bestehen	to consist of something (a material)
bei etwas bleiben	to keep to something (a decision, a habit)
sich auf etwas freuen	to look forward to something (an event)
sich über etwas freuen	to be pleased about something
auf etwas warten	to wait for something
an etwas liegen	to be due to, to depend on something

Here is the example again.

Wir achten in England sehr stark darauf, unsere Produkte speziell für den deutschen Markt zu konzipieren.

Notice how a comma separates the introductory phrase from the description. Notice the word order, too, and the use of *zu* in the description.

Exercise 1

Prepare yourself for talking about and/or demonstrating your products or service by saying that:

1. you are thinking of changing the pattern.
2. you insist on finding a new system.
3. you are keeping to using agents.
4. you are looking forward to receiving the manual in German.
5. you are pleased to be implementing the programme.

Answers

1. *Wir denken daran, das Dekor zu ändern.*
2. *Wir bestehen darauf, ein neues System zu finden.*
3. *Wir bleiben dabei, Vertreter zu benutzen.*
4. *Wir freuen uns darauf, das Handbuch auf deutsch zu bekommen.*
5. *Wir freuen uns darüber, das Programm einzuführen.*

Instead of giving so much detail, perhaps you just want to make a simple statement. The example above could have said:

In England achtet man sehr stark auf die Konzeption für den deutschen Markt.

In England we pay very close attention to design for the German market.

Exercise 2

How can you adapt the sentences in Exercise 1 to make them into simple statements?
Look at the above example again. Notice that, this time, there is no comma, no *zu* and no second verb.

Answers

1. *Wir denken an ein geändertes Dekor.*
2. *Wir bestehen auf ein neues System.*
3. *Wir bleiben bei Vertretern.*
4. *Wir freuen uns auf ein Handbuch auf deutsch.*
5. *Wir freuen uns über das Programm.*

Exercise 3

There is a similar construction which will give you equal flexibility and a higher level of sophistication in your German. It is of great value when demonstrating and explaining. You will, however, need to use two prepositions. You may feel that this is difficult but it will be made easier if your learn the phrases below as set phrases:

auf etwas an/kommen	to depend on something
von etwas ab/hängen	to depend on something
sich um etwas handeln	to be a question of something

For example:

Es kommt darauf an, wen wir als Partner nehmen.
It depends on whom we take as a partner.

Es hängt davon ab, ob die Literatur in deutscher Sprache ist.
It depends on whether the literature is in German.

Es handelt sich darum, den Vertreterstatus zu erweitern.
It's a question of extending the agency status.

Practise using these very useful introductory phrases by making the appropriate statements below. How would you say in German that:

1. it depends on how the programme functions.
2. it depends on how the draughtsman works.
3. it's a question of wanting to implement the new advertising.
4. it's because the software is being improved.

Answers

1. *Es kommt darauf an, wie das Programm funktioniert.*
2. *Es hängt davon ab, wie der Zeichner arbeitet.*
3. *Es handelt sich darum, daß wir die neue Werbung einsetzen möchten.*
4. *Es liegt daran, daß die Software verbessert wird.*

Exercise 4

As before, you can be more direct and avoid going into detail by saying:

Es kommt auf das Programm an.
Es hängt von dem Zeichner ab.
Es handelt sich um die Werbung.
Es liegt an der Software.

How would you say in German that:

1. it depends on the partner.
2. it depends on the literature.
3. it's a question of the agent's status.
4. it's because of the so-called hi-tech products.

Answers

1. *Es kommt auf den Partner an.*
2. *Es hängt von der Literatur ab.*
3. *Es handelt sich um den Vertreterstatus.*
4. *Es liegt an den sogenannten Hi-Tech-Produkten.*

Exercise 5

Examine your own products and/or services. Make sure that you can say:

● what a particular point depends on
● what it is a question of
● where the cause, solution, advantage lies.

Make sure that you can express these points in both a detailed and a simple way.

When you are the customer, you'll be asking the question. What question would you ask in German to find out:

1. what a particular point depends on.
2. what it is a question of.
3. where the cause, solution, advantage lies.

Answers

1. *Worauf kommt es an? Wovon hängt es ab?*
2. *Worum handelt es sich?*
3. *Woran liegt es?*

Practising speaking
Sprachpraktische Übungen

This section will help you to prepare for operating at a trade fair. You will find
- a scripted dialogue
- a dialogue chain
- dialogue practice.

Scripted dialogue

Stage 1: *Listen* to the scripted dialogue on the study cassette. It is a simple discussion between a prospective customer and someone presenting his product at a trade fair.

BESUCHERIN: Guten Tag! Hempel. Ich interessiere mich für selbstgesteuerte Lernprogramme.

AUSSTELLER: Guten Tag, Frau Hempel. Mein Name ist Rutt. Ja, wir haben solche Programme, und zwar sowohl für Schulkinder als auch für Erwachsene geeignet. Was suchen Sie genau?

BESUCHERIN: Ich leite ein Sprachzentrum für Geschäftsleute. Viele von unseren Kunden möchten auch allein studieren. Was können Sie mir zeigen?

AUSSTELLER: Unser Programm A ist sowohl für Gruppentraining als auch für Selbststudium geeignet.

BESUCHERIN: Mit welchen Computersystemen ist dieses Programm vereinbar?

AUSSTELLER: Selbstverständlich mit IBM und mit den meisten „desk-top" Computern. Darf ich Ihnen vielleicht das System zeigen?

BESUCHERIN: Aber gerne. Ich suche vor allem ein benutzerfreundliches Programm.

AUSSTELLER: Bitte schön. Sie sehen hier ein Obermenü. Sie können in diesem Obermenü blättern. Unter diesem Menü finden Sie weitere Menüs, die Sie sich auch frei gestalten können . . . Haben Sie sonst noch Fragen?

Dialogue chain

Stage 2: *Study* the plan below. It is a diagram of the dialogue, showing you the various stages of the conversation. You will see that the script follows this plan closely.

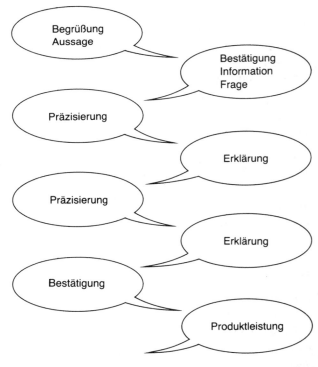

BESUCHERIN: Nein, danke. Darf ich vielleicht Ihren Prospekt mitnehmen?
AUSSTELLER: Selbstverständlich. Alle Prospekte sind mehrsprachig. Hier ist auch meine Karte.
BESUCHERIN: Danke. Auf Wiedersehen!
AUSSTELLER: Auf Wiedersehen! Danke für Ihr Interesse. Kommen Sie jederzeit wieder!

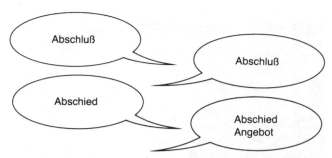

Stage 3: *Listen* to the dialogue while following the chain.

Stage 4: *Take* the role of the missing person on the study cassette. It will help you to practise speaking German in a trade fair situation.

Stage 5: You can *use* the dialogue chain as a guide to make sure that you can present your product or get the information you require from someone exhibiting at a trade fair.

Dialogue practice

Use the headings below to prepare what you might say if you were the demonstrator:

greeting	Begrüßung
confirmation	Bestätigung
information	Information
question	Frage
explanation	Erklärung
product performance	Produktleistung
closing	Abschluß
leave-taking	Abschied
offer	Angebot

Use these headings to prepare what you might say if you were the visitor:

greeting	Begrüßung
statement	Aussage
precision	Präzisierung
confirmation	Bestätigung
closing	Abschluß
leave-taking	Abschied

Well done, you are now at the end of the language exercises. Familiarisation is all-important, so do get into the habit of listening repeatedly to material which you have worked through. The next part will help you to put what you have seen, heard and worked at, into perspective.

Review
Überblick

Language comment

In this sequence, Willi Gründer is talking about his job. Clearly, he sees the relationship he is developing with BYG as long-term. It is also clear that he takes his responsibilities very seriously. He delivers his information as a mini-lecture. He is speaking spontaneously – he has not prepared his information specifically. In language terms, serious though he may seem, Willi Gründer is behaving the way most of us do when we speak off the cuff but as an expert in a familiar business situation.

So, some of his sentences are quite long – in the region of 30 words – and most sentences contain more than one idea. It would make life easier if he were using sentences of about 15–20 words and limiting each sentence to one idea. Well, it's not an ideal world and many Germans speak like him so you need to accustom yourself to hearing long

sentences but luckily for us he does speak slowly, clearly and deliberately. His regional accent is slight and does not intrude. He is the only speaker and there is not a lot of background noise.

Willi Gründer uses many sentences in which the verbs go to the end. The difficulty for you as the listener is that you have to hold on to a lot of information along the way.

It will be nearly impossible for the newcomer to German to understand every word Willi Gründer says – not first-time round, at any rate. And imagine trying to understand every word when you have to keep an eye on the next customer waiting to speak to you, to calculate discounts, keep smiling and make a mental note to cancel that hire car all at the same time.

What is the good news then? First, you can help yourself by acknowledging that such difficult language is normal. As the Germans say, *die deutsche Sprache ist eine schwierige Sprache*. Don't let that put you off though. At the end of the day – not to mention the end of the sentence – as long as you can pick up the gist and tone of what the speaker is saying, that is enough to keep the lines of communication open. If you are prepared, so is the path to a deal.

Pocket phrasebook

Some of the key phrases that will be useful to you when representing your company at a trade fair

have been recorded on to the study cassette. You can practise your pronunciation by repeating them in the pause provided or you can use the pause to supply your own version in English and then compare it with our suggestion.

These are the phrases selected from this video sequence for you to learn:

- Wir konzentrieren uns nicht nur auf einen Markt.
- Eine richtige Präsentation wollen wir doch geben.
- Kann ich Ihnen behilflich sein?
- Sie können selbstverständlich dazu auch deutsche Literatur bekommen.
- In erster Linie haben wir die Aufgabe, die Produkte zu verkaufen.

Sequence summary

In this sequence showing British exporters taking advantage of the opportunities afforded by German trade fairs, you have covered the following language points:

how to

- handle modal auxiliary verbs
- use prepositions
- put the right endings on adjectives without articles
- describe your products and services
- give and receive information at a trade fair.

Business guide — The trade fair

In video sequence 1, you see a number of British companies exhibiting at the twice yearly Frankfurt Consumer Fair. 'Messe Frankfurt' accommodates 30 International Trade Fairs a year, of which 12 are the largest of their kind in the world. Klaus Endres and John Collins have been the UK representatives of Messe Frankfurt since 1975 and are responsible for helping hundreds of British companies each year to plan their presence at Frankfurt. They have compiled this business guide to provide intending exhibitors and visitors to German Trade Fairs with the means to exploit successfully the business opportunities which Trade Fairs offer.

German trade fairs

The world-wide success of Germany's trade fairs is based upon the stability of the German economy, the country's buying power (Germany spends £20 million a day on British goods) and the fact that most of the German exhibition organisers also own their fairgrounds and exhibition halls. Such independent control over all exhibition services and amenities enables them to provide international trade and industry with both cost-effective exhibitions and a very stable marketing platform.

West Germany is the largest trade fair orientated country in Europe with purpose-built exhibition facilities in no less than 18 major cities. According to FKM, the German Society for the Voluntary Control of Fair and Exhibition Statistics, a self-managing organ of the German trade fair companies, the gross exhibition space normally

available at any one time is 1,720,000 square metres. To give some indication of the size of the exhibition facilities, Hanover, the largest centre, has a gross rentable exhibition area of approximately 471,850 square metres, followed by Frankfurt which, at the moment, has 261,775 square metres. This compares with 105,000 square metres at the National Exhibition Centre at Birmingham. In addition to this, numerous exhibitions are staged annually throughout the country in congress halls, sports halls and multi-functional buildings. The FKM draws its statistics from figures provided by 38 German trade fair companies which between them staged over 170 events in 1986.

Why participate in a trade fair?

Some manufacturers would argue that trade fairs are an expensive means of selling their products. This attitude stems mainly from a lack of

appreciation of the numerous other benefits which an international trade fair offers. As an exhibitor, you will be able to assess market trends and gain an insight into the international climate of your market. You will have the opportunity to assess your own products against the competition in terms of quality, design and price structure. The trade fair is also the ideal location for making contact with new overseas agents and distributors.

You will have the opportunity to participate in auxiliary events and symposia hosted by the exhibition organisers and can stage your own promotional activities, including dealer and distributor receptions and new product launches. If you select the right event and plan your participation thoughtfully, exhibiting should become one of the most cost-effective marketing instruments for your company's export business.

How to select the right trade fair

Firstly, ensure that your products conform to the technical standards of the country or countries to which you wish to export. This is done by checking with the British Standards Institute, (see Sequence 3). Secondly, bear in mind that most German exhibitions are for trade only. So, having established your own marketing aims, check with the organisers or their UK agents about the format of the fair in which you have a particular interest. Most German fairs are represented in the UK by specially-appointed representatives who are there to assist you through the planning stages.

It is also helpful to obtain from them the attendance figures and a breakdown of the statistics on visitors and exhibitors for previous events. These will give some indication of the internationality of the fair and provide you with useful information for your marketing strategy. Many exhibitions are divided into product groups. The fair's representative should also be able to advise you as to which event and product category would be most suitable. The names and addresses of such representatives can be obtained from the German Chamber of Commerce in London.

Should you consider participating in an event which is being held for the first time, safeguard your own interests by ensuring that it is being staged at an internationally-recognised trade fair

centre by well-established organisers. This can be verified either through the regional offices of the Department of Trade and Industry (Fairs and Promotions service), or the German Chamber of Commerce.

Other helpful information can be found in the monthly trade publication *Exhibition Bulletin*, which is updated regularly and is available on subscription. In there, you will find information on world-wide exhibitions, and a classified industrial and trade index listed by venue and date. This will enable you to see at a glance the international exhibition calendar relevant to your industry or trade. The *Exhibition Bulletin* also has useful lists of the organisers and/or their UK representatives. Another publication to consider is the yearly guide entitled *International Trade Fairs: Made in Germany*. This contains a quick reference section with all German fairs in any one month, together with the names of the German associations sponsoring each event. This is available through AUMA, the German Council of Trade Fairs and Exhibitions. (See 'Where to Go' Guide.)

In addition to the guidelines obtainable from the above sources, it may be beneficial for you to attend the fair as a visitor first before deciding whether to exhibit there. Other useful information can be gained from talking to exhibitors, distributors and retailers who may have visited previous fairs and who should have some useful comments to make. Of course, you should not forget to contact your own trade association for first-hand experience of the fair and its standing in your field.

A large number of the German exhibitions are sponsored by one or more trade associations and have been given Department of Trade and Industry financial support. Do check with the DTI (Fairs and Promotions service) to find out whether the event is supported in this way. Prospective exhibitors can obtain a copy of the quarterly DTI trade promotions guide, which gives detailed information on all sponsored fairs and exhibitions including cut-off dates and the names of the DTI desk officers handling each event.

DTI support scheme

As a newcomer, it is worth considering the DTI's

joint venture support system, which exists primarily to assist first-time exhibitors entering the international export market, by offering both technical and financial support. To participate in a joint venture, you must first make an application to the sponsoring trade association. Incidentally, it is not essential that your company be a member of that association. However, it is necessary for the firm to be registered in the UK and for the products to be of UK manufacture. A percentage of components of foreign origin may be included in the finished product and this should be clarified on application.

One of the main advantages of being accepted as a sponsored exhibitor by the DTI is that you will automatically become eligible for financial assistance in the following way: at present, first time exhibitors are charged only 40% of the actual stand rental, stand design and furnishing which includes carpeting, lighting, electrical installation and display costs. This percentage increases to 55% for the second and 75% for the third and subsequent exhibitions. In addition to those charges, you will be required to pay an administration fee to the sponsoring association. This will be slightly less if you are already an existing member.

The manufacturer should bear two things in mind: sponsored exhibitors are normally restricted to an exhibition stand of 15 square metres and will automatically become part of a uniform stand design emphasising a British presence at the exhibition.

Whether you ultimately decide to participate in a DTI joint venture or to exhibit independently it is important that you prepare well in advance, ideally 12 months before the event. There are two very helpful DTI publications to assist those doing business in Germany entitled *Hints to exporters – the Federal Republic of Germany and West Berlin* and *The export initiative*.

Planning your participation

If you have chosen a team, or an exhibition manager, from within your company to be responsible for planning and monitoring the work up to the exhibition, make sure they are all familiar with the sources of information available

to help them. Most important at this stage is the exhibition's UK representative. You will receive an exhibition space booking form from the organisers or their UK agency. A decision must now be made about the size of stand needed to give an adequate display for your products and to allow space for a hospitality area.

By now you should have some idea on stand design, since this can have a bearing on the location which you will ultimately be given within the exhibition hall. Some fairs divide their products into groups, allocating them to different exhibition halls or floors. Bear this in mind when booking space and ensure that you are being allocated a place in the most suitable hall for your product line. Also check the hall plan and give the organisers a choice of preferred locations.

You may wish to consider a *package* exhibition stand – one which is already furnished and carpeted – but first check the prices and determine exactly what such a package includes. Compare this with your own costings for the exhibition space plus stand design and furnishing. If you intend exhibiting heavy machinery or large structures, then check ceiling heights and load bearing. Check the type of flooring in the hall if your exhibits will require bolting down.

After your stand application has been processed, the organisers will send you a confirmation invoice and an exhibition manual which should be studied in detail. Apart from the do's and don'ts it contains order forms and information about support services and serves as a checklist for technical planning. A typical exhibitor's manual should give advice on the following: stand confirmation, stand rental, plans of halls and grounds, hall and floor regulations, regulations for the construction of stands, technical regulations, terms for support services, electrical and water installations, cleaning services, room reservations, exhibitors' tickets, personnel passes, parking permits, exhibition insurance, telephone connections, catalogue entries, vouchers for complimentary admission tickets, free advertising material, furniture and carpet hire.

Further points to add to your checklist are:

● Stand design and construction: If not carried out by your own company, obtain several quotes from both UK and German contractors. (Names can be supplied by the exhibition organisers or their UK agents).
● Shipping of exhibits: The fair's UK representative can recommend suitable shipping agents, but do obtain several quotes before making your final choice. If you intend to transport your goods to Germany personally, make sure that you check the transit countries' customs regulations first. This information is obtainable from the UK-based branch of the appropriate Chamber of Commerce. Also check German customs regulations – particularly if you intend leaving some of your exhibits in Germany.
● Insurance: As well as arranging adequate insurance cover for your goods in transit, make sure that they are insured on the exhibition site. Take out insurance against injury to any person, either visitors or personnel, while they are on your stand during the exhibition.
● Travel and accommodation: Accommodation is often at a premium during major exhibitions so it is advisable to book early. You can use the organisers' accommodation service or book a special travel and accommodation package through a UK travel operator. Special travel packages will save you money but check on possible travel restrictions if there is a chance that you may wish to change your bookings in any way.
● Translations and interpreters: When

participating in an international exhibition you will obviously need publicity material printed in several languages. There are numerous translation services which specialise in this but check beforehand that they are able to handle your specific technical needs. Ask the UK representatives or the German Chamber of Commerce for names and addresses. Have enough sales literature to last for the entire exhibition (any unused material is going to be useful for follow-up work). Interpreters can usually be hired through the exhibition organisers' office or, if you wish to book one in advance, through the British Consulate General nearest to the town in which the fair is being held. These are listed in the publication *Hints to exporters – The Federal Republic of Germany and West Berlin*.
● Advertising and PR: The whole purpose of advertising is to make sure that existing and potential clients know that you are there. Firstly, make sure that the name, date, venue and your stand number are included in your general media advertising during the months leading up to the exhibition. Sales literature should be printed in the languages of the countries to which you wish to sell. Mention in your advertising any technical specifications that comply with German standards. Do not print your stand number on the advertising literature as this dates it.

Advertise in the official exhibition catalogue as this tends to be used by visitors as a trade reference book long after the exhibition is over. Make use of any free publicity material offered by the exhibition organiser such as publicity postcards, invitations for your clients, posters, trade fair guides and promotional stickers.

Finally, do not forget to register for any congresses or symposia which may be taking place during the exhibition. Details will be supplied by the exhibition organisers or their UK agents.

On the exhibition stand

After all the time, money and effort spent on planning your exhibition, success will depend not only on the stand location and design but most of all upon your exhibition stand personnel. Always

use staff with proven sales ability, who are confident and competent sales negotiators. It's worth checking who, among your staff, is a good German speaker, and bringing them along. This might be the opportunity for a bright 'junior' to shine. Staff from your overseas agents will be a useful asset not only for their languages but also for their knowledge of local market trends. Stand staff should be able to quote up-to-date prices, including import duty, as well as precise delivery dates.

Product information conforming to the technical standards of the import country should also be to hand if possible. And do arrange for your stand personnel to arrive at least 24 hours before the exhibition opens, allow time to check last-minute details, including the correct stand layout, stand number and company logo, lighting, electrical points as specified, telephone installation.

Check on daily stand cleaning services if these are not provided by the organisers. Make sure that you know the location of the organisers' service office in the event of last-minute or emergency work on your stand. Finally, ensure that you have enough people to keep your stand manned at all times, otherwise you might just miss your most important sale!

Behaviour on the stand is critical too. Germans take their trade fairs seriously and expect to be dealt with professionally. Trade fairs in Germany are not the occasion for a company 'jolly'.

After the event

Apart from debriefing your stand personnel, requesting a report from your overseas agents and distributors and following up any sales leads, you will be adding up the financial costs of the venture. It is important to bear in mind that the results of trade fair participation are not always immediately apparent from the order book. They need to be judged long-term.

By participating, you will have established or widened your company's export potential to Germany and other foreign markets. You will also have gained the opportunity to assess the competition, to observe market trends and to note changes in order patterns. These are more difficult to evaluate as benefits, but are just as important in helping your company to make the right marketing decisions in the future.

The follow-up work after your first participation should form the basis of your planning for the next event. It is important to show commitment to the market and to exhibit several times in order to reap the full benefit from your efforts. This shows customers that your company and its products are a stable, long-term business.

For further information listen to the Business Magazine Track 1 where Chris Serle packs his bag and visits the Nuremburg International Toy Fair to quiz a cross section of British Exhibitors about their experience of trade fairs and the German market in general.

Presenting your company

„Darf ich Ihnen kurz meine Karte geben?"

The video sequence
Der Video-Abschnitt

Following up interest shown in your company is an important part of doing business, wherever you are. In this sequence, we see Marian Heller, export sales representative for Spenco Engineering, presenting her company and its products to Fähse, manufacturers of seed-drilling equipment. Marian has already had a little contact with Fähse's parent company but this is the first opportunity for Fähse to find out more about Spenco. In turn, it is also Marian's first opportunity to find out in detail about Fähse and its products, so in this sequence you will see both companies presenting themselves to each other. As such, this sequence offers a lot of practical advice in both language and business terms for the British exporter wanting to enter the German market.

Both companies describe their activities and business in some detail and this will give you some very useful terms to use when presenting your own company. Given the nature of Fähse's business, some of the vocabulary is quite specialised, but all the speakers, German and English, are easy to follow.

The main things to look out for in this sequence are the conventions associated with introductions and presentations. Making the appropriate greeting, introducing yourself, in person or on the telephone, shaking hands, exchanging business cards and, of course, knowing when to make your exit may be small things in themselves, but they all help to give your prospective German customer a good impression of you and your company.

Marian Heller has something of an advantage here. She knows Germany quite well and has experience of how German companies like to approach business. As a Modern Languages graduate, her German is very fluent, so she has few problems on the language side. But she also knows she can leave nothing to chance and this is why she places such a high value on thorough preparation. As she says herself, German buyers are very organised and so it is important to have very clear objectives when you are presenting your company and its products in Germany.

But there can sometimes be a disadvantage for people like Marian operating in situations like this and unless you know Germany well, it may not be immediately apparent. It is not that she is a woman operating in a man's world – although that is probably an extra reason for putting so much effort into getting all the elements of her presentation right. It has more to do with the differences in the educational systems of the two countries. As mentioned in the section on the business environment in Germany, German schoolchildren start school later than British schoolchildren. Degree courses generally last rather longer than in Britain, so Marian's German counterpart would be at least three or four years older. Some German companies could find it disconcerting to be dealing with someone younger than they would normally expect.

That did not seem to be a problem for Marian on this occasion but there were other difficulties to overcome. Above all, what this sequence shows is just how persistent you have to be sometimes. On the face of it, Marian would seem to have everything going her way: the meeting has been properly set up; she is received by Fähse's MD before going on to meet Herr Krahn, the prospective buyer. She is entirely professional in her approach and her company offers a product range and service which could well be of great interest to Fähse. Does she come out with a firm order? Well, study the list of key words, watch the video and see for yourself what happens.

Key words

Here is a list of the key words in German used in presenting a company and its products. Study the list and the meaning in this context, so that you can follow the video more easily. The words are listed in the order in which they occur.

der Termin (-e)	appointment
die Beobachtungsmöglichkeit	opportunity to observe
die Verstellbarkeit	adjustability
die Mutterfirma	parent company
die Standardproduktpalette	standard product range
die Zulieferung (-en)	supply
die Erstausrüstung	original equipment
der Sonderproduktionsauftrag	special order
der Auftrag ("e)	order
die Anfrage (-n)	enquiry
der Prokurist (-en, -en)	authorised signatory
die Verantwortung (-en)	responsibility
der Aufgabenbereich (-e)	area of responsibility
das Rechnungswesen	accounting
die Bestellung (-en)	order
die Einrichtung (-en)	facility
die Umstellung (-en)	changeover
die Verkaufsbedingung (-en)	conditions of sale
die Lieferung (-en)	delivery
der Hafen ("e)	port
der Auftragseingang ("e)	receipt of order
die Bezahlung (-en)	payment
die Zeichnung (-en)	drawing
der Überblick (-e)	overview
das Angebot (-e)	quotation

and one technical word

| die Einzelkornsaat | single-seed sowing |

Practising listening and understanding
Hörverständnisübungen

Information

Exercise A

What are they saying?

mit dem geschäftsführenden Direktor

1. Was für Maschinen baut die Firma Fähse?

Answers

mit dem geschäftsführenden Direktor

1. Die Firma Fähse baut *Maschinen für die Einzelkornsaat.*

2. Was ist das Besondere an ihren Maschinen?

2. Die Maschinen können zeigen, wo die Körner hängen, geben also *eine ideale Beobachtungsmöglichkeit*.

3. Wie steht es mit der Verstellbarkeit?

3. Die Verstellbarkeit *ist* bei jeder Maschine *gewährleistet*.

bei Herrn Krahn – die Einführung

bei Herrn Krahn – die Einführung

4. Wie wird die Firma Fähse in Großbritannien vertreten?

4. Die Firma Fähse wird *über einen Importeur* vertreten.

5. Worauf hat sich die Firma Spenco hauptsächlich spezialisiert?

5. Die Firma Spenco hat sich hauptsächlich *auf die Zulieferung von Erstausrüstung* spezialisiert.

6. Was für Aufträge übernimmt die Firma Spenco zusätzlich zu ihren Standardartikeln?

6. Die Firma Spenco übernimmt zusätzlich *Sonderproduktionsaufträge*.

bei Herrn Krahn – sein Aufgabenbereich als Prokurist

bei Herrn Krahn – sein Aufgabenbereich als Prokurist

7. Welche Leitung hat Herr Krahn?

7. Herr Krahn hat *die ganze kaufmännische Leitung*.

8. Wer macht die Bestellungen?

8. *Herr Krahn* macht die Bestellungen *selber*.

auf der Suche nach einem Auftrag

auf der Suche nach einem Auftrag

9. Was stellt die Firma Fähse selber her?

9. Fähse stellt *die Teile*, die sie *zum Bau der Maschinen* benötigt, selber her.

10. Was müßte Herr Krahn prüfen?

10. Herr Krahn müßte prüfen, *ob eine Umstellung* auf Spenco-Produkte für seine Firma *kostengünstiger wäre*.

die Verkaufs- und Lieferbedingungen

die Verkaufs- und Lieferbedingungen

11. Wie steht es mit der Lieferzeit bei Standardteilen?

11. Die Lieferzeit bei Standardteilen ist in der Regel *vier bis sechs Wochen*.

12. Welche Bezahlungsmodalitäten hat die Firma Spenco?

12. Es gibt nur eine Bezahlungsmodalität, und zwar *dreißig Tage netto per Scheck*.

Summary

Exercise B

What are they saying?

1. Marian Heller fragt, ob es möglich wäre, mit einem baldigen Auftrag von der Firma Fähse zu rechnen. Wie reagiert Herr Krahn darauf?

Possible answers

1. Herr Krahn will sich nicht festlegen, weil er in seinen Bestellungen noch nicht zu Ende ist. Er möchte zuerst prüfen, welche Standardteile Firma Fähse in ihre Fertigung einbauen kann. In ungefähr acht Wochen kann Firma Spenco eventuell mit einer Anfrage für diese Teile rechnen.

2. Wie steht es mit den Spezialteilen, die Herr Krahn eventuell bestellen könnte?

2. Spezialteile sind nicht in der DIN-Norm. Also muß die Firma Fähse Zeichnungen für die Firma Spenco kopieren, damit sie ein Angebot unterbreiten kann.

Close listening

Exercise C

What are they referring to?

im Hotel

1. *zehn Uhr*

mit dem geschäftsführenden Direktor

2. *Das* ist auch gewährleistet

bei Herrn Krahn – die Eröffnung

3. Dezember *sechsundachtzig*

4. *neun Filialen*

auf der Suche nach einem Auftrag

5. die Gruppen *A, B und C*

6. *das* würd' ich nicht so sagen.

die Verkaufs- und Lieferbedingungen

7. *vier bis sechs* Wochen

8. *dreißig Tage netto per Scheck*

der Abschluß

9. *in den nächsten Wochen*

10. *nicht in der DIN-Norm*

11. *acht Wochen*

12. *1988*

Answers

im Hotel

1. Marian Heller hat *einen Termin* mit Herrn Krahn *um zehn Uhr.*

mit dem geschäftsführenden Direktor

2. . . . *die Verstellbarkeit* das muß alles sein, *das* ist auch gewährleistet . . .

bei Herrn Krahn – die Eröffnung

3. Marian Heller hat Firma Fähse auf der *Royal Smithfield Show* schon gesehen. „Sie wurden *im Dezember '86* da repräsentiert."

4. Spenco ist ein Mitglied der *Sparex-Gruppe* . . . mit *neun Filialen in aller Welt.*

auf der Suche nach einem Auftrag

5. Herr Krahn sieht im Verzeichnis nach. Bei seinen Maschinen würden *Teile (aus) Gruppen A, B und C* verwendet (werden).

6. Marian Heller meint, daß es *keine Öffnung* für Spenco gibt. Herr Krahn antwortet: „*das würd' ich nicht so sagen . . .*"

die Verkaufs- und Lieferbedingungen

7. *Bei Standardartikeln* erfolgt *die Lieferzeit* in der Regel *vier bis sechs Wochen* nach Auftragseingang.

8. Es gibt nur eine *Bezahlungsmodalität* bei Spenco, und zwar *dreißig Tage netto per Scheck.*

der Abschluß

9. Es wird *nicht möglich* sein, *in den nächsten Wochen eine Anfrage* von der Firma Fähse *erhalten zu können.*

10. . . . *Spezialartikel, die nicht in der DIN-Norm* sind . . .

11. die Anfrage für *Standardteile*, etwa *acht* Wochen.

12. die Anfrage für die *Teile, die noch geprüft werden müssen.* . . . das wird *Anfang 1988* werden.

Consolidation
Konsolidierung

In this sequence the language points selected for consolidation are:

● reflexive verbs
● using the perfect tense.

Reflexive verbs

On the phone from her hotel, Marian Heller checks with the company she's about to visit. She needs to know exactly how to find her way from where she is at the moment, so she tells the company:

Ich befinde mich momentan im Hotel Germania.

Later, when presenting her company, Marian tells Herr Krahn about Spenco's specialist areas by saying:

Spenco hat sich hauptsächlich auf die Zulieferung von Erstausrüstung spezialisiert.

In both these statements Marian Heller uses a reflexive verb. In this and other sequences the speakers use a variety of reflexive verbs. Here is a list of them:

sich ab/zeichnen	to stand out clearly
sich befinden	to find oneself
sich bemühen	to take trouble
sich ein/stellen	to adapt/prepare oneself
sich ergeben	to be the result
sich erstrecken	to extend
sich erweisen	to turn out to be
sich freuen auf	to look forward to
sich freuen über	to be pleased with
sich heraus/stellen	to turn out to be
sich konzentrieren	to concentrate
sich senken	to drop down
sich spezialisieren	to specialise

sich stellen	to arise
sich überzeugen	to satisfy oneself
sich umhören	to make inquiries
sich unterhalten	to talk
sich verlagern	to transfer
sich verschärfen	to harden/intensify

As you can see, there are quite a lot of reflexive verbs so you need to know how to handle them. Here are some exercises to help you consolidate your ability to do this.

Practice A

You must first be sure about the correct reflexive pronoun. What is the word missing from these sentences?

1. Die Zulieferfirmen überlegen . . . . ., wie sie die Anfragen prüfen sollen.
2. Der Lagerbestand hat . . . . . auf Null gesenkt.
3. Bitte, überzeugen Sie . . . . . von der Qualität.
4. Wir wollen . . . . . auf den Importeur einstellen.
5. Das Problem hat . . . . . verschärft.
6. Die Möglichkeit hat . . . . . als machbar erwiesen.
7. Ich werde . . . . . bemühen, den Termin einzuhalten.
8. Meine Damen, hören Sie . . . . . auf der Messe um.

Answers

1. Die Zulieferfirmen überlegen *sich*, wie sie die Anfragen prüfen sollen.
2. Der Lagerbestand hat *sich* auf Null gesenkt.
3. Bitte, überzeugen Sie *sich* von der Qualität.
4. Wir wollen *uns* auf den Importeur einstellen.
5. Das Problem hat *sich* verschärft.
6. Die Möglichkeit hat *sich* als machbar erwiesen.
7. Ich werde *mich* bemühen, den Termin einzuhalten.
8. Meine Damen, hören Sie *sich* auf der Messe um.

Practice B

Next, check how to use reflexive verbs in questions, commands, statements, dependent clauses and with *nicht*.

How do you say the sentences below, in the other language?

This is an exercise which you can approach from the German or from the English, depending on your confidence and your need in German.

If you approach it from the German, ask yourself how you, as an English-speaking business person, would express yourself in this situation.

If you approach the exercise from the English, ask yourself how your German counterpart would express himself/herself in a similar situation.

1. Worauf erstreckt sich Ihr Aufgabenbereich?

2. Konnten Sie sich auf die Umstellung konzentrieren?

3. Warum wollten sie sich das Angebot überlegen?

4. Ich würde gern wissen, ob wir uns auf eine Anfrage freuen dürfen.

5. Meine Kunden wollen sehen, daß sie sich in guten Händen befinden.

6. Die Firma hat den Importeur gebeten, sich nach Spezialisten umzuhören.

7. Unterhalten Sie sich mit der Mutterfirma.

8. Bemühen Sie sich, die Zeichnung zu verwenden.

9. Stellen Sie sich auf eine andere Bezahlungsmodalität ein.

10. Ihre Verkaufsbedingungen haben sich verschärft.

11. Das Sonderteil erweist sich als zu teuer.

12. Unsere Mitglieder haben sich nicht darüber gefreut.

1. What does your area of responsibility extend to?

2. Were you able to concentrate on the changeover?

3. Why did they want to think over the offer?

4. I should like to know whether we may look forward to an enquiry.

5. My customers want to see that they are in good hands.

6. The company has asked the importer to make enquiries about specialists.

7. Talk to the parent company.

8. Try to use the drawing.

9. Prepare yourself for another means of payment.

10. Their sales conditions have hardened.

11. The special part is turning out to be too expensive.

12. Our members were not pleased with it.

Just before we leave reflexive verbs, let us have a closer look at three of the phrases which are particularly useful for business descriptions. They will be of most use to you when you use them as below to introduce findings:

es ergibt sich, daß . . .
the result is that . . .

es stellt sich heraus, daß . . .
it turns out that . . .

or to report questions:

die Frage stellt sich, ob . . .
it is a question of whether . . .

Look, for example, at such sentences as:

Es ergibt sich daraus, daß das Pfund sehr stabil ist.
The result is that the pound is very stable.
(Sequence 6)

Es stellt sich heraus, daß die Deutschen schwarz vorziehen.
It turns out that the Germans prefer black.
(Sequence 5)

Die Frage stellt sich, ob wir in Kanada oder in Deutschland herstellen sollen.
It is a question of whether we should produce in Canada or in Germany. (Sequence 6)

Expressing the past using the perfect tense

When Marian Heller is presenting her company to Herr Krahn, she says:

Wahrscheinlich haben Sie von uns vorher (noch) nicht *gehört* . . .
Probably *you have* not *heard* of us before . . .

English and German are often very similar when it comes to expressing the past. In both languages, the verb usually changes, e.g.:

ich höre	ich habe gehört
I hear	I have heard

Sometimes the similarity between English and German is very close, e.g.:

ich sehe	ich habe gesehen
I see	I have seen

Understanding the past tense when you hear it is not usually a problem, but most people have to practise before they feel confident in using it correctly and without too much difficulty.

What do we mean when we talk about **the past tense**? Like English, German has more than one form of the past. Take the verb *sagen* (to say) as an example. In both languages you can say:

ich sage	ich sagte	ich habe gesagt
I say	I said	I have said

These forms are called **tenses**:

ich sage	**is in the present tense**
ich sagte	**is in the imperfect tense**
ich habe gesagt	**is in the perfect tense**

You have come across the imperfect tense with:

sein	ich war
haben	ich hatte

and probably also with:

dürfen	ich durfte

können	ich konnte
müssen	ich mußte
sollen	ich sollte
wollen	ich wollte

but generally speaking it is the perfect tense which people use when they are **speaking** German. The imperfect is usually reserved for **written** or **more formal** German.

We shall now practise using the perfect tense. If you already feel confident about forming it, go straight on to the practices themselves. If not, let's run through the ways to form the perfect in German.

The vast majority of verbs in German form the perfect with *haben*. What you have to remember is the **form** of the **past participle**. There really is no reliable short cut here, but fortunately there is only a limited number of ways to form the past participle.

A. Verbs with *haben*

Example 1: *hören*　　*ich habe gehört*

This is the simplest way of forming past participles. Here are some other verbs which follow this pattern used in the video sequence:

bauen	gebaut
kaufen	gekauft
zeigen	gezeigt
fragen	gefragt
prüfen	geprüft
arbeiten	gearbeitet
machen	gemacht

This also applies to these verbs in their separable or reflexive form, e.g.:

zu/machen	zugemacht
ein/kaufen	eingekauft
vor/stellen	vorgestellt
sich fragen	ich habe mich gefragt

Example 2: *sprechen*　　*ich habe gesprochen*

This is also a common way of forming the past participle. There is often a change of vowel from the infinitive form and the past participle ends in *-en*. Some other examples are:

nehmen	genommen
schließen	geschlossen

geben	gegeben
sehen	gesehen

Again these forms are also used when the verb is part of a separable verb, e.g.:

an/nehmen	angenommen
ab/schließen	abgeschlossen
auf/geben	aufgegeben

The best way to cope with the perfect tense for all verbs is to learn the past participle at the same time as you learn the infinitive. Hardly a thrilling piece of advice but, to begin with, restrict your range to the verbs that are essential to you. Then, when you have gained confidence and experience in using them, you can widen the range. Do not try to take on too much to begin with, however.

The majority of verbs which take *haben* will follow one or other of the patterns mentioned so far. But there are some verbs which depart from these patterns slightly. For example, some do not take the prefix *ge-* to form the past participle. These verbs may already have a prefix, such as one of the following:

be-	beliefern	ich habe beliefert
ent-	entnehmen	ich habe entnommen
ver-	vergessen	ich habe vergessen
ge-	gebrauchen	ich habe gebraucht
er-	erhalten	ich habe erhalten

Another category of verb which does not take the prefix *ge-* is the one where the infinitive form ends in *-ieren*. Here are some examples:

produzieren	ich habe produziert
telefonieren	ich habe telefoniert
sich spezialisieren	ich habe mich spezialisiert

And there are also a few where the two basic patterns combine; they do have a vowel change (like some of the past participles ending in *-en*) but their past participles end in *-t*:

wissen	ich habe gewußt
bringen	ich habe gebracht
denken	ich habe gedacht
kennen	ich habe gekannt

We have not covered all the possibilities with *haben*, just the ones you are most likely to come across.

B. Verbs with *sein*

In English, we do not use the verb **to be** to form the perfect tense any more, though we used to with for example **to go**. Believe it or not, *he is gone* was once standard. But quite a lot of foreign languages do use their equivalent of the verb *to be* when forming the perfect tense.

It is worth remembering the example of **to go** because it gives us a clue to the kind of verbs that take *sein* in German. Like **to go**, these are nearly all verbs which express movement.

Marian Heller uses one of these verbs of movement when she first meets Herr Krahn:

Ich bin heute gekommen, um Ihnen Spenco vorzustellen.

Others that are frequently used are:

gehen	ich bin gegangen
fahren	ich bin gefahren
fliegen	ich bin geflogen
laufen	ich bin gelaufen

Separable verbs based on these verbs also take *sein* in the perfect:

aus/gehen	ich bin ausgegangen
durch/fahren	ich bin durchgefahren
ab/fliegen	ich bin abgeflogen
weg/laufen	ich bin weggelaufen

Unfortunately for you, the idea of motion is not a totally reliable one. This is best shown by the example of *bleiben*, whch means *to stay, to remain*. The perfect tense is:

bleiben	ich bin geblieben

and similarly

geschehen	*es ist geschehen*
to happen	it has happened

But though there is no hard and fast rule, at least there are not many verbs in the *sein* category. In fact, three are used in this video sequence – and only one of them in the perfect tense. They are:

kommen	ich bin heute gekommen, . . .
geschehen	jeder weiß, was geschieht
	jeder weiß, was geschehen ist
laufen	wie das bei uns läuft
	wie das bei uns gelaufen ist

Practice A

First go through the transcript of the video sequence and note all the examples of the perfect tense used. See if you can relate the past participles to the examples and notice their position in the sentence or clause.

Practice B

In this exercise, put these German sentences into the perfect tense. When you have done so, you will have a brief summary of the video sequence. Remember the position of the past participle at the end of the sentence or clause. (You can check the past participles in the Vocabulary Guide at the end of the book.)

1. Marian ruft vom Hotel an.

2. Auf dem Weg zur Firma prüft sie ihre Papiere.

3. Sie macht ihre Aktentasche wieder zu.

4. Sie spricht mit Herrn Gugenhan.

5. Er zeigt ihr die Maschinen für die Einzelkornsaat.

6. Sie stellt Herrn Krahn ihre Firma vor.

7. Ein Importeur vertritt die Firma Fähse in England.

8. Die beiden Firmen arbeiten zusammen.

9. Herr Krahn weist auf die Spezialteile hin.

10. Die Firma kauft einige Teile von Zulieferfirmen.

11. Herr Krahn schließt das Gespräch ab.

12. Marian meldet sich im Oktober wieder.

1. Marian hat vom Hotel angerufen.

2. Auf dem Weg zur Firma hat sie ihre Papiere geprüft.

3. Sie hat ihre Aktentasche wieder zugemacht.

4. Sie hat mit Herrn Gugenhan gesprochen.

5. Er hat ihr die Maschinen für die Einzelkornsaat gezeigt.

6. Sie hat Herrn Krahn ihre Firma vorgestellt.

7. Ein Importeur hat die Firma Fähse in England vertreten.

8. Die beiden Firmen haben zusammengearbeitet.

9. Herr Krahn hat auf die Spezialteile hingewiesen.

10. Die Firma hat einige Teile von Zulieferfirmen gekauft.

11. Herr Krahn hat das Gespräch abgeschlossen.

12. Marian hat sich im Oktober wieder gemeldet.

Practice C

In this exercise, put these German sentences into the perfect tense. The verbs are all taken from the video sequence.

1. Ein Importeur repräsentiert unsere Firma in Deutschland.

2. Wir spezialisieren uns auf dem Gebiet der Einzelkornsaat.

3. Sie kennt die Firma Fähse von der Messe her.

4. Der Aufgabenbereich erstreckt sich von der kaufmännischen Leitung zum Einkauf.

5. Die Firma Fähse verwendet Teile aus der Produktgruppe A.

6. Die Firma Fähse benötigt keine weiteren Spezialteile.

1. Ein Importeur hat unsere Firma in Deutschland repräsentiert.

2. Wir haben uns auf dem Gebiet der Einzelkornsaat spezialisiert.

3. Sie hat die Firma Fähse von der Messe her gekannt.

4. Der Aufgabenbereich hat sich von der kaufmännischen Leitung zum Einkauf erstreckt.

5. Die Firma Fähse hat Teile aus der Produktgruppe A verwendet.

6. Die Firma Fähse hat keine weiteren Spezialteile benötigt.

7. Die Firma Fähse erteilt die neuen Aufträge im November.

8. Die englische Firma beliefert den Kunden acht Wochen nach Auftragseingang.

9. Den genauen Liefertermin weiß sie nicht.

10. Sie erklärt ihm die Bezahlungsmodalitäten.

11. Er kopiert die Zeichnungen.

12. Die Firma unterbreitet ein Angebot.

7. Die Firma Fähse hat die neuen Aufträge im November erteilt.

8. Die englische Firma hat den Kunden acht Wochen nach Auftragseingang beliefert.

9. Den genauen Liefertermin hat sie nicht gewußt.

10. Sie hat ihm die Bezahlungsmodalitäten erklärt.

11. Er hat die Zeichnungen kopiert.

12. Die Firma hat ein Angebot unterbreitet.

Finally, here is a list of the examples of the perfect tense used in the video sequence. Did you note them all?

sein + past participle

Ich bin heute gekommen

haben + past participle . . .

1. *ge+ . . . +t*
Wahrscheinlich haben Sie von uns vorher noch nicht gehört.
Wenn wir das geprüft haben.
Wenn wir zu dieser Zeit nichts gehört haben.

2. *ge+ . . . +en*
Ich habe Fähse in London schon gesehen.
Ich habe mit Herrn Gutzenleuchter schon gesprochen.
Sobald wir also die Sache abgeschlossen haben.

3. past participle without prefix *ge* . . .
Spenco hat sich hauptsächlich auf die Zulieferung von Erstausrüstung spezialisiert.

Development
Erweiterung

Presenting your company

In this sequence on presenting your company the development exercises concentrate on

- expressing possibility and obligation
- introductions and presentations.

Remember, some of these exercises are included on the study cassette as well as in the book.

Expressing possibility and obligation

1. It cannot be done; it should not be done

Marian Heller pushes hard to get a commitment for a future order from Fähse. Herr Krahn, however, is either unable or unwilling to give one. When Marian says:

*Ja, aber Sie glauben dann schon, daß es einige Teile in Ihrem Programm gibt, die wir für **Sie** machen können.*

Herr Krahn counters with:

*Es **ist** im Moment noch nicht **abzusehen**.*

By using the verb *sein* (to be) with a second verb *absehen* (to foresee) and *zu*, he effectively says:

At the moment it cannot be foreseen yet (we cannot tell yet).

Herr Krahn has deliberately not allocated any responsibility for this situation. He simply presents his statement impersonally as 'something which cannot be done'.

This is not a difficult structure to handle, and it will help you to improve the sophistication of your German quickly, particularly in negotiations.

Exercises

1 How would you say these sentences in English? As you work the sentences out you will almost certainly feel that, in some cases, you want to put in a 'we' to make it sound natural. You are right to feel this. In English, we have a tendency to personalise things which, in German, are left impersonal.

Possible answers

1. *Die Zeichnung ist leider nicht zu verstehen.*

1. Unfortunately we cannot understand the drawing.

2. *Es ist einfach nicht zu glauben.*
3. *Ich bin nächste Woche nicht zu erreichen.*
4. *Unsere Spezialisten sind nicht zu sprechen.*
5. *Die Karte ist nicht zu lesen.*

2. It is simply unbelievable.
3. I am not available next week.
4. Our specialists are not free to meet.
5. We cannot read the card.

This is a flexible construction. In some situations you can use it to say what **should not be done**:

2 How would you say the preceding sentences in English? As you work the sentences out, feel free to put them into English in the most natural way possible. This will mean being more personal than the German.

Possible answers

6. *Diese Maschine ist nicht zu verkaufen.*

6. The machine should not be sold.

7. *Ich glaube, daß der Bediener nicht zu ersetzen ist.*

7. I do not think the operator should be replaced.

8. *Die Frage stellt sich, ob die Software nicht weiterzuentwickeln ist.*

8. The question arises whether we should not develop the software further.

9. *Wir fragen uns, ob das Nachschlagewerk nicht zu übersetzen ist.*

9. We wonder whether the reference book should not be translated.

10. *Der Kunde ist nicht so oft zu besuchen.*

10. We should not visit the customer so often.

2. It can be done; it has to be done

When you watch the Austin Rover sequence 'Supporting the market', you will see Herr Herrman introducing the company and its products to a prospective concessionaire, Herr Idelberger. At one point, Herr Herrman shows Herr Idelberger how the customer-care programmes **have to be** carried out:

. . . wie Kundendienstprogramme durchzuführen sind.

3 How would you say in English that the following tasks have to be done?

1. Der Vertrag ist hier zu unterschreiben.
2. Die Waren sind nach dreißig Tagen netto zu bezahlen.
3. Wir sind der Meinung, daß die Software weiterzuentwickeln ist.
4. Die Lieferbedingungen sind vorher festzustellen.
5. Die Aufträge sind diese Woche zu erteilen.

Possible answers

1. The contract has to be signed here.
2. The goods have to be paid for net within thirty days.
3. We think that the software has to be developed further.
4. The delivery conditions have to be established beforehand.
5. The orders have to be sent out this week.

In some situations you can use this construction to say that something *can be done*. Here, too, you will see that the German is more impersonal. Here are some examples.

4 How would you say in English:

6. Das Besondere an unseren Maschinen ist hier zu sehen.
7. Probleme sind hier zu finden.
8. Ja, die Umstellung ist zu machen.
9. Das Beispiel ist an dem Bildschirm klar zu erkennen.
10. Die Literatur ist in deutscher Sprache zu haben.

Possible answers

6. Here you can see the special feature of our machines.
7. This is where problems crop up.
8. Yes, we can make the changeover.
9. You can see the example clearly on the screen.
10. The literature is available.

Introductions and presentations: Exercises

The ability to talk about yourself, your company, its products and services is essential in a wide range of business and social situations. Yet, despite the familiarity of the subject matter, this can be an area where many people do not feel comfortable – perhaps because they feel the spotlight has been turned on them and what *they* really want to do is to turn it on someone else. Having a set of useful phrases 'up your sleeve' is a real asset in these situations. This exercise will give you a set of useful phrases.

We recommend you work through the exercise as follows:

- **read** the expressions and phrases through, section by section,
- **ask** yourself what an English person would say in the same situation. We have laid out the expressions and phrases in a way that will help you test yourself,
- **check** against our suggestion as to whether your version conveys the same message,
- **identify** the expressions and phrases which you feel you can handle confidently and accurately,
- **adapt** those expressions and phrases to your own situation,
- **check** that you are handling them appropriately. You may need a German speaker to help you here.

Stage 1

Introducing yourself

am Telefon

Guten Tag, hier Brown/Frau Brown von der
Firma . . . in England.
Kann ich bitte Herrn/Frau Schmidt sprechen?
Am Apparat.
Würden Sie ihm/ihr etwas ausrichten?
Ich rufe später wieder an,
Auf Wiederhören.

persönlich

Frau Heller von der Firma . . .
Ich habe einen Termin bei Herrn/Frau . . .
Darf ich Ihnen kurz meine Karte geben?
Ich habe Ihre Firma/ . . . auf der Messe in
Frankfurt schon gesehen.
Ich bin heute gekommen, um Ihnen meine Firma/
. . . vorzustellen.
Mein Aufgabenbereich erstreckt sich vom/von der
. . . zum/zur . . .

Stage 2

Presenting your company/product

Spenco ist ein Mitglied der Sparex-Gruppe von
Firmen.
Fähse-Accord ist unsere Mutterfirma.
Wir sind die Tochtergesellschaft von . . .
Unser Hauptsitz ist in Südwestengland/in der
Nähe von . . .
Dann haben wir auch neun Filialen weltweit/in
aller Welt.
Wir werden in Großbritannien über einen
Importeur vertreten.
Wir sind Spezialisten auf diesem Gebiet.
Das Besondere an unseren Maschinen ist . . .
Wir sind in der Lage, . . .
Spenco hat sich auf die Zulieferung von
Erstausrüstung spezialisiert.
Spenco beliefert mit ihrer Standardproduktpalette
. . .
Wir übernehmen Sonderproduktionsaufträge und
-anfragen.
Spezialteile kaufen wir von Zulieferfirmen.

Stage 1

Introducing yourself

on the telephone

Good morning, this is Michael Brown/Jane Brown
from . . . in England.
May I speak to Herr/Frau Schmidt please?
Speaking.
Would you give him/her a message?
I'll call again later.
Goodbye [*used on the telephone*]

in person

My name is Marian Heller, from Spenco . . .
I have an appointment with Herr/Frau . . .
May I give you my card?
I saw your company at the Frankfurt trade fair.

I have come to present my company.

My duties range from . . . to . . .

Stage 2

Presenting your company/product

Spenco is a member of the Sparex Group.

Fähse-Accord is our parent company.
We are the subsidiary of . . .
Our Head Office is in South West England/is near
. . .
We have nine branches throughout the world.

In Britain we are represented by an importer.

We are specialists in this area.
The particular feature of our machines is . . .
We are in a position to . . .
Spenco has specialised in supplying original
equipment.
Spenco supplies from its standard product range
. . .
We accept special production orders and enquiries.

We purchase special parts from suppliers.

Stage 3

Asking for information from your prospective customer

Darf ich mal fragen, . . .
Könnten Sie mir andeuten, welche Art von Teilen . . .
Was für Einrichtungen haben Sir hier im Hause, solche Teile selber zu machen?
Machen Sie die Bestellungen selber?
Sind Sie dafür verantwortlich, die Aufträge zu erteilen?
Wäre es möglich, daß wir eine Anfrage bekommen könnten?

Stage 4

Stating business terms

Darf ich kurz über unsere Verkaufsbedingungen sprechen?
Wir bieten normalerweise in DM an.
Lieferung ist entweder frei Haus oder f.o.b.
Lieferzeit erfolgt in der Regel . . . Tage/Wochen/Monate nach Auftragseingang.
Bei Spezialartikeln wird das etwas länger in Anspruch nehmen.
Unsere Bezahlungsmodalität ist 30 Tage netto per Scheck.
. . . damit Sie ein Angebot unterbreiten können.
. . . wie Sie es lieber haben möchten.

Stage 5

Rounding up – stalling and closing

Man müßte das im einzelnen prüfen.
Wenn wir das geprüft haben, können wir dazu Stellung nehmen.
Es ist im Moment nicht abzusehen.
In den nächsten Wochen wird das nicht möglich sein.
Wenn wir bis zu diesem Zeitpunkt nichts gehört haben, . . .
Sind Sie damit einverstanden?
Ich glaube, das wäre alles.
Ich bedanke mich für das Gespräch.
Ich melde mich bald/nächste Woche wieder.

Stage 3

Asking for information from your prospective customer

May I ask . . .
Could you tell me what kind of parts . . .

What facilities do you have in-house for making these parts yourselves?
Do you do the ordering yourself?
Are you responsible for placing the contracts?

Would it be possible for us to receive an enquiry?

Stage 4

Stating business terms

May I say a brief word about our sales terms?

We usually quote in Deutschmarks.
Delivery is either free domicile or f.o.b.
Delivery usually takes place . . . days/weeks/months after receipt of order.
It will take a bit longer for special parts.

Our payment terms are 30 days net by cheque.

. . . so that you can submit a quotation.
. . . as you prefer.

Stage 5

Rounding up – stalling and closing

We would have to look into that in detail.
When we have looked into it, we will have a better idea.
We cannot tell yet.
It will not be possible for a few weeks.

If we have not heard anything by then, . . .

Is that acceptable to you?
I think that is all.
Thank you for seeing me.
I will be in touch again soon/next week.

Practising speaking
Sprachpraktische Übungen

This section will help you to prepare for presenting your company.
You will find
- a scripted dialogue
- a dialogue chain
- dialogue practice

At the end of a long trip, the last thing you want to do is find yourself having a discussion with and presenting your company to the wrong person. Marian Heller was careful to make sure that Herr Krahn was, in fact, the right person to talk to.

This is a plan of how a discussion might well proceed when you need to establish areas of responsibility. The dialogue chain will help you to check this in a similar situation by providing you with a map.

Scripted dialogue

Stage 1 *Listen* to the scripted dialogue on the study cassette. It is a simple discussion between a visiting sales person and a manager.

BESUCHER: Guten Morgen, Harf, von der Firma, ALM.
LEITER: Rodert ist mein Name. Guten Morgen Herr Harf. Was kann ich für Sie tun?
BESUCHER: Darf ich Ihnen meine Karte geben?
LEITER: Danke. Hier ist meine. Ich sehe, Sie sind Projektleiter für Erstausrüstung.
BESUCHER: Jawohl. Ich bin heute gekommen, um Ihnen ALM vorzustellen. Ich möchte gern genau feststellen, in welchen Bereichen wir vielleicht in Zukunft zusammen arbeiten könnten.
LEITER: Ich habe von Ihrer Firma noch nicht gehört. Werden Sie vielleicht in Deutschland über einen Importeur vertreten?
BESUCHER: Richtig. Unsere Mutterfirma heißt RDE. Als Tochtergesellschaft der RDE haben wir uns hauptsächlich auf die Zulieferung von Erstausrüstung spezialisiert.
LEITER: Ich fürchte, Herr Harf, Sie sind bei mir nicht richtig. Ich bin für den Einkauf von Standardartikeln verantwortlich. Der Aufgabenbereich Erstausrüstung ist eine Abteilung für sich. Mein Kollege Dr. Dahms ist für diesen Bereich zuständig.
BESUCHER: Wäre es möglich, Herrn Dr. Dahms zu sprechen?
LEITER: Selbstverständlich. Er ist heute im Hause.

Dialogue chain

Stage 2 *Study* the plan below.

Stage 3 *Listen* to the dialogue while following the chain.

Stage 4 *Take* the role of the missing person on the study cassette.

Stage 5 Finally, *use* it as a guide to make sure that you can quickly and politely identify whether you are talking to the right person, or whether you are the person your visitor really needs to see.

Dialogue practice

Use the headings below to prepare what you might say when you are the visitor:

greeting	Begrüßung
identification	Identifizierung
presenting your card	Karte überreichen
aim	Ziel
explanation	Erklärung
request for help	Bitte um Hilfe

Use the headings below to prepare what you might say when you are receiving the visitor:

greeting	Begrüßung
offer help	Hilfe anbieten
observation	Feststellung
precision question	Präzisionsfrage
responsibility	Verantwortung
willingness to help	Hilfsbereitschaft

Well done, you are now at the end of the language exercises. Familiarisation is all-important, so do get into the habit of listening frequently to material which you have worked through. The next part of this section will help you to put what you have seen, heard and worked at, into perspective.

Review
Überblick

Language comment

In a situation where you are presenting your company to a prospective customer, usually you have to do a lot of the talking. In this sequence, we learn from Marian Heller that she has a format which she tries to follow. That obviously makes good business as well as good language sense. If you have a familiar routine, and one you know is acceptable in language terms, your own confidence will be boosted and every time you make a presentation in German, the quality will improve.

What is more difficult is gauging the reaction of your business partner. In this sequence, Herr Krahn comes over as a man of few words – he gives away very little and when he does speak, it does not always seem very encouraging. It is easy for a newcomer to the German market to feel quite downcast in circumstances like this but there are two points worth bearing in mind.

One is the reputation Germans have for efficiency – or at least, organisation. This company is no exception. Many parts are manufactured in-house and where non-standard items are required, its buying is planned well in advance and regular suppliers are used. So, what Marian is coming up against is an established timescale of operations rather than lack of interest in her company's products and services.

The other point is the differences there can be between the two languages in the way people express their views or impart information. The British are known for their apologetic manner:

'I'm afraid I'll have to ask you to come along with me', says the policeman to the motorist failing the breathalyser test; 'I'm sorry sir, you can't park your car here', says the traffic warden. To an ear accustomed to this way of saying things, the German way can seem too direct, sometimes even abrupt, or rude. But generally speaking, it is not – it is just different.

It can take some time to get used to this approach and only time and practice will make it easier. It will take even longer to adopt the same approach yourself and you would be well advised to steer clear until you are very confident, very proficient and very conversant with German and Germany. For now, try to listen for the meaning behind the words as well as the words themselves. Remember that listening is fundamental to understanding.

Pocket phrasebook

Some of the key phrases that will be useful to you when presenting your company have been recorded onto the study cassette. You can practise your pronunciation by repeating them in the pause provided or you can use the pause to supply your own version in English and then compare it with our suggestion.

These are the phrases selected from this video sequence for you to learn.

Ich habe einen Termin um zehn Uhr.
Hier sind einige unserer Maschinen.
Darf ich Ihnen kurz meine Karte geben?
Wir übernehmen Sonderproduktionsaufträge.

Lieferzeit erfolgt in der Regel 6 Wochen nach Auftragseingang.

Sequence summary

In this sequence showing Marian Heller presenting her company, you have covered the following language points:

- how to use reflexive verbs
- how to put verbs into the perfect tense
- how to express obligation and possibility
- how to introduce yourself and obtain information
- how to present your company, its products and services

Business guide – Presenting your company

This section has been prepared by Andrew Castley, Head of the Department of Languages at Nene College. Andrew has worked as an export sales manager in the automotive and electronics sector, and has published two business language books: *Business Situations, German* and *Business Situations, French*.

In the following business guide he suggests how best to prepare for a company presentation and offers advice on how to control the proceedings.

Video sequence 2 introduces you to Marian Heller of Spenco Engineering. When we meet Marian, she is coming to the end of a tiring three-week period of visits to potential customers – a period during which she averaged three meetings per day.

Being able to present your company and your products successfully at such meetings makes big demands on both your language ability and your business competence. But the meeting – the final face-to-face discussion – needs to be backed up by careful preparation to maximise the probability of a successful outcome. To make your visit a cost-effective one involves giving thought to the following:

- deciding exactly what you want out of each visit,
- carrying out background research,
- carefully planning an itinerary in the German market,
- preparing the information and samples you require,
- giving some thought to structuring the presentation and anticipating problems.

Taking all this into account, together with travel and personnel costs, the cost-per-minute of face-to-face contact is horrendous; you should therefore generally plan to make several visits on each trip and do everything you can to meet your aims.

Purpose

Your first decision will be to establish why you want to visit the market; this will then lead you to the most appropriate sources of information you need. Of course, market visits are made for many reasons; none of the following will be exclusive:

- looking for customers,
- establishing who your competitors are,
- establishing whether your product is compatible with what is currently on the market,
- establishing whether your product conforms to relevant German regulations (safety, foodstuffs, DIN, etc.),
- establishing whether your operation conforms to German custom and practice in the sector; for example, there might be generally accepted levels of discount and commission,
- finding out the situation on patents to cover your product,
- finding out where the geographical centres of demand are.

These are all areas which can and should be researched before you go into the market. You can probably think of more relating to your product.

Fact-finding

It is sometimes daunting to know where to start looking for this information but, without it, the presentation will suffer. If you think preparation is expensive, try not doing it!

First of all, look round. Has the company had any past contacts with the market? If so, are there any reports, names or sales literature tucked away in the files which relate to those contacts? You may have supplied a German customer in the past, which could provide a useful lead. Has anyone done any related market research in the past? If so, is there a report on file? Has anyone in the firm any experience in the market either currently or from a previous job? If you have any associated companies, ask the same question of them. Even anecdotal information can be extremely valuable.

This is what is called 'internal desk research'. You will be surprised how much information can be gleaned in this way. But now you have to move on to look outside your own organisation; this is 'external desk research'. Do not forget, always be guided by your purpose in visiting the market. The following will be of help:

- The DTI provides invaluable information on UK export markets. The introductory booklet *Hints to exporters* contains many useful leads, and specific information about the German market can be obtained from the Exports to Europe branch, telephone 01 215 7877. Alternatively, you can contact one of the DTI regional offices, the address of which appears in the reference section of this book.
- Trade associations in the FRG are very well established, for example, the Verein Deutscher Ingenieure in Frankfurt. Market information of a general nature, but also specific technical or legal information can be found through them. You will find the association relevant to your field through the German Chamber of Industry and Commerce in the UK, 12–13 Suffolk Street, London, SW1Y 4HG (01 930 7251).
- At the end of this book, you will find a list of further organisations which could be helpful in the same way in your particular field of interest.
- If you are looking for potential customers, competitors' trade fair catalogues can be a useful source of information. Trade fairs are an important means of establishing a market presence in the FRG and the major cities have full programmes of fairs throughout the year.
- If you are finding out about a particular company prior to visiting, you might request its sales literature by post. Larger companies

publish a house journal with information about new developments.

- Your local town or county library will have a business information service for the home and export markets. For company information you might refer to the Kompaß directory, which is probably the best known, but not the only one. Your librarian will be able to tell you the extent of local information services.

All these channels are very straightforward and inexpensive and can give you a clear idea of which potential business partners to contact, as well as the nature and scale of operations of these companies. They are all desk research channels. Field research designed and commissioned specifically for your own product will be expensive but might be appropriate for a large company. Again, the DTI will advise on this.

- For the smaller undertaking, the commercial section of the British Embassy in Bonn will provide useful assistance. It can be extremely useful to speak directly with staff there, but prior arrangements would have to be made initially via your local DTI office (you will find the address in *Hints to exporters* referred to above).
- The DTI also offers an 'Export marketing research scheme'; details from your regional office.
- Finally, you can pick up very useful leads via the Yellow Pages. Every post office in the FRG has a full set of classified telephone directories. This source of information would typically be used to supplement contacts established prior to a visit, using spare time in the market (there will inevitably be some) to maximum effect.

Planning the trip

By this point, having been guided always by WHY you want to visit the market, you will have established WHICH organisations to visit and therefore HOW to visit them, that is, by car, air, train and ship, or all four? You will know whether you wish to establish contact, elicit an enquiry, inform people of your company, your product and prices, elicit market information, or look around potential clients' factories. Depending on these

objectives it is useful to *anticipate issues likely to be confronted in your discussions and work out in advance your best response to them*. For example: price, quality, terms, reliability, legislation, sales record or (very important, this) flexibility. We shall return to these issues later in 'Structuring the presentation'.

It is important to plan your itinerary to ensure you arrive at each visit fresh and ready to do a day's work. Particularly if you speak the language, your German business partner will so appreciate the effort you have made to visit and contact him or her that you may fall into the trap of thinking you have achieved something by actually getting there. But the important part lies ahead; travelling must be done with minimum fuss and disruption.

Procedure

Plan your preferred itinerary. You may, if you have many potential business opportunities, divide the country into north and south and visit each on alternate trips. This might enable visits to, say, the Netherlands and Switzerland to be incorporated easily into each itinerary.

Having decided your preferred route, you might telex or, if it is a first meeting, write an introductory letter (in German!) with a proposed time for the meeting. Include the topics for discussion and request early confirmation of one or two alternative dates.

When all or most of the replies arrive you are sure to find your plan has been spoilt! Nevertheless, the itinerary should be altered to incorporate as many visits as possible but a few may have to be omitted each time round. Then it would be wise to confirm or cancel by telex or telephone, particularly if your business partner has proposed an alternative date.

While all this is going on, you could prepare samples and dossiers of all documentation relating to each visit, including a set of objectives or agenda, and a copy of your original letter might be useful to prove you have an appointment.

Some general points

At this point it is worth while mentioning some

useful hints on successful calling:

- Build the odd half-day free into your itinerary. Something could easily go wrong. If it doesn't, you can always browse through the Yellow Pages!
- In general, avoid cold-calling, except in some sectors like the fashion trade and smaller retailers. But it might be useful to telephone and ask for a meeting if you have half a day free.
- If you do this, be sure to obtain the name of the contact from the telephonist before you are put through: „Bitte, wie heißt der Herr/die Frau noch?" or „Wer ist für den Einkauf zuständig?".
- Remember that calling is generally possible from 8 a.m. (except in retail outlets). For a British representative, the day's workload should be brought forward between one and a half hours.
- Remember to be punctual, particularly if you are meeting senior management. This is extremely important; it is discourteous to be even slightly late in Germany.
- Your samples should be professionally presented. It should be a smooth process to use them as part of your presentation, whether in the form of components, or a pattern book. Remember to take extras so that you can leave some for testing. This is particularly important for a product with a high technical content. In this case, the lead time for the order to be placed may be longer than expected; your customer will be testing the samples!
- You should have a good supply of business cards; one should always be readily available.

Initial greeting and first steps

So, armed with everything you have meticulously prepared, you arrive punctually for your first meeting. You may, like Marian Heller in the video sequence, have telephoned to announce your imminent arrival. You have gone through the formalities at the gate, filling in an *Anmeldezettel*, and are awaiting your contact in the *Besucherzimmer*.

It is best to be formal, polite and cheerful; with senior management it is safest to be extremely

"... armed with everything you have meticulously prepared"

formal at first. It is not recommended to force the pace on to a 'matey' footing at any level.

We should always be wary of generalisations, but it is fair to say that it is more accepted in Germany to speak one's mind without the same degree of deference to the possible sensitivities of others than would be the case in a British context. The other person would naturally be expected to be equally frank. This is true, perhaps, more in a social than a formal business situation. Of course, politeness dictates in both countries that you try not to offend, and in our business meeting we should judge the situation as we would in the UK, but the British visitor would not be taken aback if confronted by a somewhat uncompromising and directly expressed view. „Ich sehe es etwas anders", or „Ich sehe es aber nicht so" might be a useful way to introduce a contrary view, if it is appropriate to state a contrary view.

Given this somewhat direct manner, we may possibly meet with an unwelcoming reception. How should we tackle this? The table below sets out a scheme which may help in deciding what course of action to take.

Reason for resistant or indifferent attitude	Strategy
1. Temporary mood on the part of the partner	Limit objectives of the visit initially at least.
2. Prejudice (strikes, quality).	Try to involve a colleague.

3. Anticipation of genuine problems.	Focus on the detail of the partner's misgivings.
4. 'Professional indifference.'	Professionalism; confidence in firm, product, self.
5. Talking to the wrong person.	Establish this quite openly and talk to the right person!

1. You will establish that this is the case only by eliminating 2 to 5. You might ask questions like: „Kaufen Sie überhaupt so etwas ein?" or „Gehört so etwas zu Ihrem Einkaufsprogramm?". If you are fairly sure you have hit a bad day, seek to finish the meeting promptly and hope for better luck next time. You may, for instance, be content with leaving samples for testing whereas you had hoped to talk about possible quantities and elicit an enquiry.

2. If, for example, the buyer is prejudiced against buying from abroad in general or the UK in particular (it is remarkably easy to see through an ostensibly objective argument against buying your product!), it is sometimes possible to involve a more genuinely objective colleague of theirs in the discussion. This might be someone on the technical or design side, for example. „Was halten Sie von unserem Produkt, Herr Tovar?" or „Wie beurteilen Sie die technischen Eigenschaften von diesem Produkt, Frau Dr. Wulf?" might help your case somewhat, but tact is of the essence here.

3. The buyer or technical expert might be anticipating genuine problems, in which case you should home in on these directly and deal with them in detail. This is where it will prove invaluable to have anticipated such problems in your planning.

4. Some buyers and technical people adopt a 'professional' indifference. Indeed, it would be strange if the buyer were to appear actually to want to buy the goods! This should not affect your presentation in the slightest. Remain professional and businesslike. You have the confidence in yourself and what you are there to do. Recognise the attitude for what it is and state your case fairly. In the end the buyer must decide whether it is worth his or her while to do business, and they will probably make that decision on very professional grounds!

5. Finally, you might be speaking to the wrong person, who is embarrassed to admit this is the case. You will have noted that Marian asked quite openly if Herr Krahn was responsible for buying the goods she was selling. Feel free to establish this, and ask if it is possible to see someone else if your fears are proved correct. „Sind Sie fur diesen Bereich zuständig?" or „Ich sollte vielleicht mit einem Ihrer Kollegen sprechen" might be useful here.

Structure of the presentation

In general terms, the UK enjoys no natural reputation on price, quality, design or technology. Clearly an individual product will possess characteristics in all these respects which we hope will be highly competitive. But the case has to be made clearly and professionally; there will be no predisposition to buy British.

Apart from ensuring that the product is competitive in the above respects – *and that is of primary importance* – there are a few general issues on which a positive stance can help establish a competitive edge:

- The buyer should be reassured that it is as easy to do business with a UK supplier as with the German competitor a few kilometres away. No buyer wants to place an order with a supplier with whom it is difficult to establish contact, even at a price advantage. It is always appropriate to emphasise that it is as easy to dial direct to a UK number as it is within the FRG; if your telephonist speaks German, say so: „Unsere Telefonistin kann auch gut Deutsch. Sie werden also keine Probleme haben, mich zu erreichen". Perhaps you employ a German agent who will be making frequent calls, or you yourself might be making visits at frequent intervals; if so, bring this out. Your procedures for exporting to the FRG will be as smooth as for supplying the home market; make the point that in this respect you treat the FRG as a home market: „Wir sind auf Export völlig eingestellt. Für uns ist das Exportgeschäft eine Selbstverständlichkeit".

- *Flexibilität* is a concept which continues to enjoy wide currency among buyers in Germany. The successful supplier can react swiftly to the demands made by customers, to accelerate or slow down deliveries, change specifications, or whatever. Of course, the supplier has legitimate interests and rights to represent and maintain in practice, but if your company is market-oriented, this flexibility will be inherent in its procedures. It is important to bring this out. „Flexibel sind wir auf jeden Fall." „Wir legen viel Wert auf Flexibilität."

Evincing a familiarity with the general factual background relating to the market is part of being a convincing, reliable business partner. If possible, a knowledge of the geography of the FRG (the Länder and major cities, the position of Berlin), some current affairs which can be gleaned from the British press before departure, and an awareness of custom and practice all make for a convincing presentation. It is a sign that a successful rapport has been established if the conversation ranges – perhaps during lunch – over broader issues than the business in hand.

Finally, a professional approach to time management, interpersonal relations, being informed about the customer and dealing with the business should be the order of the day.

The presentation itself

In the video sequence, Marian Heller describes how she structures her presentation in advance. Your preferred structure may be different, but it is important to plan what you want to achieve and how you want to achieve it. Marian's is a useful approach and we shall look at it in more detail here. It is worth recalling before we start that Marian did a last minute check of herself and her documents and plan before she arrived; this has much to commend it!

There will be language difficulties relating to technology and specialist terminology. Yet it is not usually difficult to get hold of the sales literature of, say, a German competitor or the catalogue of an appropriate trade fair and learn some of the vocabulary you will need. It is much easier to learn vocabulary relating to your product range than general vocabulary; it will not take long because of your familiarity with the subject.

Explain how and why you have made contact; present your firm – location, size, length of time established and product range. Perhaps you have the resources of a major group behind you. Emphasise your experience and track record (well-known customers) and your exporting experience. Keep this all fairly brief.

Move on to the product. Using samples or literature explain the benefits and features of the product. Make sure at this stage that your partner is 'in the market' for your product in principle: „Kaufen Sie überhaupt so etwas ein?". All this will have been a one-way flow of information, which should be broken. The question above might produce a good lead-in for your partner to describe his or her organisation; perhaps ask about:

- the end product
- the market
- whether they manufacture components in house: „Stellen Sie Bestandteile im Hause her?"
- broad buying policy (e.g. dual sourcing – „auf zwei Beinen stehen" – learn this!).
- the competition and competitive prices. Clearly, delicacy is needed here. As in the UK, the competition should not be criticised except by implication when you are emphasising the merits of your own product. You could ask outright about the competition's prices – „In welcher Preislage liegt die Konkurrenz?". „Welcher Preis entspricht Ihren Vorstellungen?" – but you may not get an answer!

An alternative, but no less direct way round, might be to ask by what percentage you should adjust your price to be competitive, but take the

answer with a pinch of salt! – „Um wieviel Prozent mußten wir den Preis herabsetzen . . . ?). Like Marian, you might ask to look round the factory to understand how the product will be used or assembled.

Having established a good, two-way flow of information you may perhaps now return to the product. Focus attention on potential business:

● Which of your products is a possibility?
● Is the technical specification in order?
● Is there anything else he/she needs to know?
● Would a trial order for a small test quantity be appropriate?
● What delivery times does he/she work to?
● What are their normal conditions?

It is important to test that both parties have fully understood terms and conditions, or the specification if this is complicated. You should be sure that the buyer can compare 'like with like' when your quotation is set against that of the competition. It is not unknown for orders to be lost because the buyer thought the UK offer was fob when it clearly stated *frei Haus verzollt*.

Focus on the next action:

● Will your partner place an enquiry?
● Will they take samples for testing?
● When will the enquiry arrive or the test results be known?
● Always confirm the meeting in writing. State that you will do this.
● if possible, arrange the date of the next meeting or telephone contact.
● This may be a suitable point to make or reiterate the point about your flexibility of response and 'nearness' as mentioned above.

● If significant business might ensue, you might consider inviting the buyer and/or technical personnel to your factory. They may prefer to wait until they have 'tried you out' before accepting, but the offer will be appreciated.

Know when to leave. This is vitally important. In Germany, „Zeit ist Geld". By outstaying your welcome, you are irritating the buyer, who has other things to do, and may be implying that you, yourself, are not so busy really. On the other hand, you should not rush off before the contact has been thoroughly developed. It might be useful to ask:

„Also, haben wir es erledigt?" or
„Also, wäre noch etwas zu besprechen?"

This allows the partner to indicate whether or not business is concluded as far as he/she is concerned.

Finally, it goes without saying that loyalty to the company is a must. There are times when it is tempting to lay the blame for some error where you know it lies – perhaps with quality control, production, or with accounts for insisting on stringent terms, and to distance yourself from the source of trouble. Yet to do so will severely diminish the credibility of your professionalism. It is in everyone's interest that you defend your company to the hilt – even though this can sometimes be difficult!

Confused by the many sources of advice available to would-be exporters to Germany? Don't be, listen to Business Magazine 2, where Chris Serle tracks them down to see what's on offer.

Taking an order

„Vertrauen ist gut – Kontrolle ist besser."

The video sequence
Der Video-Abschnitt

This is a selling situation. Mike and Pat Taylor import British kitchenware into Germany and, in this sequence, Mike Taylor is meeting one of his regular customers, Michael Hassenkamp, a buyer for a small chain of retail stores. Mike is hoping for an order for electric kettles from Michael Hassenkamp.

Mike Taylor has taken on a difficult task here. The electric kettle is not the everyday household item in Germany that it is in Britain, so he has to persuade Michael Hassenkamp of its practical advantages over other methods of boiling water that are more usual in Germany.

As if that were not enough, he cannot rely in this instance on the reputation for elegance, sophistication and class that British goods sometimes enjoy in Germany – *die feine englische Art*. Michael Hassenkamp is typical of many Germans in making mental associations between British goods and poor delivery dates, non-availability of spare parts and unreliable after-sales service.

A particularly interesting feature of this scene is the importance Michael Hassenkamp attaches to dealing with customer complaints. It is clear that he wants a mechanism which will satisfy his customers while making sure they know where the fault lies. The implication is obvious: German consumers do not expect to make complaints, and no self-respecting buyer wants to risk being held responsible should the unthinkable happen. We do not know whether this order was finally placed; if it was and the goods did not turn up on time, or turned out to be faulty, Mike Taylor stands to lose more than just an order for kettles.

Mike's German is far from perfect but he succeeds in conveying his message. The imperfect language does not seem to be a barrier. (By the way, the transcript has been corrected so you should take your cue from there.)

Does it matter? Probably not too much. The German buyer is not looking out for the quality of the language – he has other, more immediate concerns. You will see that Michael Hassenkamp is interested in reliable delivery, a good price, sound after-sales service and the game of not making it all too easy for Mike Taylor. The conversation continues at a rattling pace – language mistakes or no language mistakes.

But what about you, the learner? Well, of course it matters to you. The language in this sequence places high demands on you: you have to follow German that 'breaks the rules'. You see a situation where this might be acceptable, while at the same time having a metaphorical finger wagged at you if you do the same. If you think that's not fair, you are probably right.

But let's look at the other factors in Mike Taylor's favour. Well, he is based in Germany, in daily contact with German business colleagues and has been so for a long time. He has a 'feel' for the German way of doing business. He can tune in to broader concerns or areas of interest – it is easy to imagine Mike and Michael talking about last night's football match, say – and he has a very wide range of vocabulary at his disposal. Mike Taylor has at his fingertips all the polite turns of phrase, the useful idiom to inject into the conversation, as well as an extensive range of business vocabulary.

The chances are that you will not have this background and experience to draw upon. You will probably only get one chance to get your message across effectively and that will be your principal objective. It is important that you should recognise what can happen to your control of language if you are faced with similar pressures. Having done that, the next thing to do is to limit the damage that others can inflict upon your ability to communicate, by preparing for these eventualities. Think of the image of reliability, quality and attention to detail which good, accurate German will convey.

Key words

Here is a short list of the key words in German from the meeting between Mike Taylor and Michael Hassenkamp. Read the words and what they mean in this particular context. This will help you to follow the video sequence more easily. The words are listed in the order in which they occur.

die Einzelheit (-en)	detail
der Laden (″-)	shop
die Werbung	advertising
das Werk (-e)	factory
die Sicherheit	safety/security
der Haushalt (-e)	household
der Ärger	trouble
der Lagerbestand (″-e)	stock
der Kundendienst	after-sales service
der Ersatzteil (-e)	spare part
die Garantie (-n)	guarantee
die Reparatur (-en)	repair
die Vertretung (-en)	agency
der Mist	rubbish
das Vertrauen	trust
der Fehler (-)	mistake

Practising listening and understanding
Hörverständnisübungen

You will find a workplan to help you in Sequence 1, page 11.

Information

Exercise A

What are they saying?

die Eröffnung

1. Wann hat Herr Taylor sein Informationsmaterial losgeschickt?
2. Was hätte Herr Hassenkamp besser machen sollen?

Answers

die Eröffnung

1. Herr Taylor hat sein Informationsmaterial *vor einer Woche* losgeschickt.
2. Er hätte *das Informationsmaterial besser lesen* sollen.

3. Wie heißt das Thema der Swan-Werbung zur Zeit?

die Qualität

4. Wie steht es mit Fertigungstests bei Swan?

5. Worauf legt Firma Swan großen Wert?

6. Was für eine Garantie bietet Swan an?

7. Womit sind die Wasserkocher versehen?

der Kundendienst

8. Was hat Herr Taylor ausgedacht?

9. Wieviele Produkte verkauft Herr Taylor pro Jahr?

10. Wie steht es mit Ersatzteilen?

3. Das Thema der Swan-Werbung zur Zeit heißt: *„Wie oft täglich benötigen Sie kochendes Wasser?"*

die Qualität

4. *Jeder Kessel wird getestet*, bevor er das Werk verläßt.

5. Firma Swan legt großen Wert *auf Sicherheit.*

6. Swan bietet *ein Jahr Garantie* für die ganze Produktionspalette an.

7. Alle Wasserkocher sind *mit einer VDE-geprüften Schnur und einem Stecker* versehen.

der Kundendienst

8. Herr Taylor hat *die ganze Frage von Kundendienst und Garantieleistung* ausgedacht.

9. Herr Taylor verkauft *über eine Million Produkte* pro Jahr.

10. *THV hält Ersatzteile bis zu zehn Jahren.*

Summary

Exercise B

What are they saying?

1. Während der Diskussion sagt Herr Hassenkamp: „das ist leider nicht der Fall . . .". Dann meint er dazu weiter: „Zukunftsmusik für hier!" Wovon spricht er eigentlich?
2. Herr Hassenkamp hat etwas Bedenken wegen der Lieferzeiten. Herr Taylor versucht, ihn zu beruhigen. Welche Argumente bringt er an?

3. Herr Hassenkamp ist nicht dafür, daß seine Kunden sich mit Herrn Taylor direkt in Verbindung setzen. Warum nicht?

Possible answers

1. In fast jedem Haushalt in Großbritannien gibt es einen elektrischen Wasserkessel. In Deutschland ist das noch lange nicht der Fall.

2. Herr Taylor hat jetzt ein Lager in Neuwied und kann dadurch innerhalb einer Woche seine Kunden beliefern. Die Kontrolle liegt nun in seinen Händen.
3. Herr Hassenkamp möchte wissen, wenn etwas nicht in Ordnung ist. Dann kann er sich direkt bei Herrn Taylor beschweren.

Close listening

Exercise C

What are they referring to?

Eröffnung

1. *letzte Woche*

2. *das* ist für uns sehr wichtig

Answers

Eröffnung

1. . . . *Letzte Woche* habe ich *die (Sachen) (das Informationsmaterial) losgeschickt.*
2. . . . *Wie oft täglich* benötigen Sie kochendes Wasser? *Das ist für uns sehr wichtig . . .*

Qualität	*Qualität*
3. *ein* Jahr	3. Wir haben natürlich *ein Jahr Garantie* für die ganze Produktionspalette.
4. *zwoundneunzig Prozent*	4. *Zwoundneunzig Prozent aller Haushalte* in England haben einen Kessel.
5. *vierzig* Prozent	5. Aber wir gehen davon aus, daß sicherlich *vierzig Prozent des deutschen Marktes* an so etwas interessiert ist.
6. *VDE*	6. Für Deutschland sind alle Wasserkocher *mit so einem geprüften Schnur und einem VDE-Stecker versehen.*
Lieferzeiten	*Lieferzeiten*
7. *innerhalb von sieben Tagen*	7. Wir haben jetzt ein Lager in Koblenz, und da wird *alles* abgelagert, und nach Abruf *innerhalb von sieben Tagen* ausgeliefert.
8. etwa *hunderttausend Mark*	8. Wir haben *einen Lagerbestand von etwa hunderttausend Mark.*
Kundendienst	*Kundendienst*
9. *über eine Million*	9. Wir verkaufen *über eine Million Produkte.*
10. bis zu *zehn Jahren*	10. Und natürlich halten wir *Ersatzteile bis zu zehn Jahren.*

Consolidation
Konsolidierung

In this sequence the language points selected for consolidation are:
- modal auxiliary verbs in the past
- pronouns
- adjectival endings (2)

Modal auxiliary verbs in the past

In Sequence 1 you practised the way to say in German: I want, you may, she can, we must, they should. The examples we used there were all in the present tense. In this section we shall be revising the way to use them in the past.

Let's start with English and see what happens to modal auxiliary verbs when they are used in the past. Take a sentence such as:
He wants to test the kettle.

Simple – it becomes:
He wanted to test the kettle.

But what about this one?
We must test the kettle.

A little tricky – it becomes:
We had to test the kettle.

And what about:
Can you get spare parts?

This becomes:
Were you able to get spare parts?

Now you know why foreigners find English hard to handle . . . !

That is enough about English. Fortunately for us, this is one area where German operates more simply than English, as you can see when you put these sentences into the past:

Er will den Kessel testen. . . . . .
    Er wollte den Kessel testen.
Wir müssen den Kessel testen. . . . . .
    Wir mußten den Kessel testen.
Können Sie Ersatzteile bekommen? . . . . .
    Konnten Sie Ersatzteile bekommen?
Sollen Sie den Kessel testen? . . . . .
    Sollten Sie den Kessel testen?

Darf er den Kessel testen? . . . . . Durfte er den Kessel testen?

So, what is the problem? Well, it is really one of training yourself to think quickly so that you can use the German for:

he had to . . .
we were allowed to . . .
I was supposed to . . .

more or less automatically.

Practice

How do you say the following sentences in the other language? You can approach this exercise either from English or from German.

If you start from English, imagine that you are checking with a colleague on the following points. How would you make them in German?

1. I had to send you the information.

2. You were supposed to go on Monday.

3. Were you allowed to show them the whole range?

4. He wanted to talk about prices.

5. Were you able to meet your delivery date?

6. They were supposed to contact our warehouse.

7. We were not able to stock spare parts here.

8. My customers did not want to wait for repairs.

9. We were not allowed to test the kettle.

10. Were you able to deliver before the end of the month?

If you prefer to start this exercise from German, ask yourself how you would make these points in English:

1. Ich mußte Ihnen das Informationsmaterial schicken.

2. Am Montag sollten Sie gehen.

3. Durften Sie ihnen das ganze Sortiment zeigen?

4. Er wollte über Preise sprechen.

5. Konnten Sie Ihren Liefertermin einhalten?

6. Mit unserem Lager sollten sie sich in Verbindung setzen.

7. Wir konnten hier keine Ersatzteile auf Lager haben.

8. Meine Kunden wollten nicht auf Reparaturen warten.

9. Wir durften den Kessel nicht testen.

10. Konnten Sie vor Monatsende liefern?

Pronouns

In the heat of their discussion on kettles and customers, Mike Taylor and Michael Hassenkamp soon refer to their kettle(s) as 'it', 'they' and 'them', and to their customers as 'they' and 'them'. Each man refers to the other as 'you', to himself as 'I', 'me', 'we' and 'us'. They use these words, **pronouns**, to save repeating the corresponding nouns and making the discussion unnecessarily long and heavy. We all do the same in any discussion.

Why bother with pronouns anyway? Until you are confident about the level of your active command of pronouns, you would be well advised to go for accuracy and keep to nouns. They will almost certainly cause you less stress during the hunt because of the amount of processing it takes

to get the right form of the pronoun in the right place in time.

Look at the language comment on page 68 where Mike Taylor's German is analysed. This shows you what hunting for pronouns means in practice.

Remember that pronouns are essentially a short cut to a discussion subject that has already been identified and mentioned. Although you may not use them, your German partner certainly will. You have to be able to recognise them and what they refer to.

If you feel that pronouns are an area of the German language where you do not have too many problems, try the two exercises below. If, on the other hand, you feel the need to revise them, have a look at the Grammar Guide on page 167 first, before you attempt the two exercises.

Pronoun checklist

- is the noun *der*, *die* or *das?*
- what is there in the sentence to affect the pronoun in any way?
- which form of the pronoun should I use?

Practice

In the heat of discussion you would almost certainly change the words in italics to pronouns. What would you say then?

1. *Die Probezeit* kann drei Monate dauern.
2. *Das Werk in Neuwied* wird umgeändert.
3. *Der Kundendienst* läuft jetzt gut.
4. *Die langen Lieferzeiten* bedeuten Probleme für unsere Produktion.
5. Ich finde *die Anleitungen* zu lang.
6. *Der Hersteller* hat *diese Form* vorgeschlagen.
7. *Der hohe Lagerbestand* macht *das Problem* viel schwieriger.
8. *Herr Taylor* wollte *Herrn Hassenkamp* beruhigen.
9. *Der Vertreter* versichert *den Kunden*.
10. *Eine neue Farbe* wird von großem Vorteil für *den Konsumenten* sein.
11. *Der Hersteller* hat *der Werbeagentur* sein Sortiment vorgestellt.
12. *Eine gewisse Qualität* fehlt *diesem Produkt*.

1. *Sie* kann drei Monate dauern.
2. *Es* wird umgeändert.
3. *Er* läuft jetzt gut.
4. *Sie* bedeuten Probleme für unsere Produktion.
5. Ich finde *sie* zu lang.
6. *Er* hat *sie* vorgeschlagen.
7. *Er* macht *es* viel schwieriger.
8. *Er* wollte *ihn* beruhigen.
9. *Er* versichert *ihnen*.
10. *Sie* wird von großem Vorteil für *ihn* sein.
11. *Er* hat *ihr* sein Sortiment vorgestellt.
12. *Sie* fehlt *ihm*.

Two pronouns

Yes, but what if you are talking about two things? There will be times when you will be saying:

e.g. Let's send *the customers the samples.*

where 'the customers' strictly means 'to the customers'. In German this would normally be:

Schicken wir den Kunden die Muster.

You may want to replace either noun, or even both nouns, by a pronoun. How should you do this? Although it will feel complicated because of the search for the right pronoun and the right form, the natural word order is essentially the same as in English:

Let's send *them* the samples.
          *Schicken wir **ihnen** die Muster.*

Let's send *them* (to) the customers.
          *Schicken wir **sie** den Kunden.*

Let's send *them* (to) *them.*
          *Schicken wir **sie ihnen**.*

Sometimes there will be a preposition involved in what you are saying:

Mike Taylor says:

*Das ist **für unsere Kunden** auch sehr wichtig.*

*Wir haben natürlich ein Jahr Garantie **für die ganze Produktionspalette**.*

If he had wanted to replace the ideas in bold by a pronoun, Mike Taylor would have said:

*Das ist **für sie** auch sehr wichtig.*

*Wir haben natürlich ein Jahr Garantie **dafür**.*

In other words, if the idea is a **person**, you replace it by a **pronoun**. If the idea is a **thing** or an **event**, you add *da(r)* in front of the preposition.

Practice

Here are some statements which Hassenkamp and Taylor make during their discussion. Replace the ideas underlined with *damit, daran, darauf, daraus, darüber, davon, dazu*, as appropriate.

1. Wenn die Leute *an einen Kessel* denken . . .
1. Wenn die Leute *daran* denken . . .

2. Mike Taylor spricht *von den Vorteilen der Swan-Kessel.*
2. Mike Taylor spricht *davon.*

3. Swan legt großen Wert *auf Sicherheit.*
3. Swan legt großen Wert *darauf.*

4. Es gibt ein bißchen Geschichte *zu der Sache.*
4. Es gibt ein bißchen Geschichte *dazu.*

5. Unsere Werbung läuft *über dieses Thema.*
5. Unsere Werbung läuft *darüber.*

6. Wir können nicht alle Sachen *für alle Läden* nehmen.
6. Wir können nicht alle Sachen *dafür* nehmen.

7. Ich habe die Informationen *aus dem Material* entnommen.
7. Ich habe die Informationen *daraus* entnommen.

8. Wir müssen *über Preise* sprechen.
8. Wir müssen *darüber* sprechen.

9. Wir haben eine Werkstatt mit Ersatzteillager *für Reparaturen* in Neuwied.
9. Wir haben eine Werkstatt mit Ersatzteillager *dafür* in Neuwied.

10. Ich will wissen, was meine Kunden *mit den Kesseln* anstellen.
10. Ich will wissen, was meine Kunden *damit* anstellen.

Adjectival endings 2

Here, we shall be revising the endings which adjectives take after the **indefinite article**, i.e. in sentences such as:

A *new product* is being developed.
or
We have a *new agent* in Germany,
or
We buy our parts from *a small company* in Neuwied.

When we put the same sentences into German, this is what happens:

Ein neues Produkt wird entwickelt.
Wir haben *einen neuen Vertreter* in Deutschland.
Wir kaufen unsere Teile von *einer kleinen Firma* in Neuwied.

If you already feel confident about using adjectival endings after *ein/eine*, go straight on to the practice exercises. If you need to remind yourself of the pattern they follow, consult the reference tables on page 172.

Practice A

You have made some brief notes e.g.

Item	*Comment*
der Laden	groß
die Garantie	gut
das Produkt	neu

and now want to expand these into full sentences for a written report. Using the adjectives and nouns in the lists below, make full sentences. Start each sentence with:

Das ist ein/eine/ein . . .

Examples:
Das ist ein großer Laden.
Das ist eine gute Garantie.
Das ist ein neues Produkt.

Item	*Comment*
der Kessel	ausgezeichnet
der Laden	groß
der Prozeß	modern
die Garantie	schriftlich
die Lieferung	wichtig
die Qualität	gut
das Lager	traditionell
das Produkt	ideal
das Sortiment	wunderbar

Answers

Das ist ein ausgezeichneter Kessel.
Das ist ein großer Laden.
Das ist ein moderner Prozeß.
Das ist eine schriftliche Garantie.
Das ist eine wichtige Lieferung.
Das ist eine gute Qualität.
Das ist ein traditionelles Lager.
Das ist ein ideales Produkt.
Das ist ein wunderbares Sortiment.

Practice B

You are describing aspects of your business to a visitor. Using the above list of adjectives and nouns, form new sentences, changing the endings where necessary. Start each sentence with:

Wir haben einen/eine/ein . . .

Examples:

Wir haben einen großen Laden.
Wir haben eine gute Garantie.
Wir haben ein neues Produkt.

Wir haben einen ausgezeichneten Kessel.
Wir haben einen großen Laden.
Wir haben einen modernen Prozeß.
Wir haben eine schriftliche Garantie.
Wir haben eine wichtige Lieferung.
Wir haben eine gute Qualität.
Wir haben ein traditionelles Lager.
Wir haben ein ideales Produkt.
Wir haben ein wunderbares Sortiment.

Practice C

This time you are outlining your market plans. Using the list of adjectives and nouns from page 62, form new sentences, changing the endings where necessary. Start each sentence with:

Wir gehen mit einem/einer . . .
Complete each sentence with . . . *in den Markt.*

Examples:

Wir gehen mit einer guten Garantie in den Markt.
Wir gehen mit einem neuen Produkt in den Markt.

Answers

Wir gehen mit einem ausgezeichneten Kessel in den Markt.
Wir gehen mit einem großen Laden in den Markt.
Wir gehen mit einem modernen Prozeß in den Markt.
Wir gehen mit einer schriftlichen Garantee in den Markt.
Wir gehen mit einer wichtigen Lieferung in den Markt.
Wir gehen mit einer guten Qualität in den Markt.
Wir gehen mit einem traditionellen Lager in den Markt.
Wir gehen mit einem idealen Produkt in den Markt.
Wir gehen mit einem wunderbaren Sortiment in den Markt.

Development
Erweiterung

In this sequence on negotiating an order the development exercises concentrate on
- specifying times and dates
- clarifying details

Negotiating an order

Remember, some of these exercises are included on the study cassette as well.

Specifying times and dates

First, we shall be looking at *specifying times and dates*.

With a basic knowledge of German you can easily describe events in the order in which they take place:

Es wird getestet. Dann verläßt es das Werk.

When you are negotiating you need to be able to deal with the same point in a number of different ways. How much more emphatic you can be by linking the two points as Mike Taylor does:

Es wird getestet, bevor es das Werk verläßt.

Exercise A

Develop the habit of dealing with the same point from a different perspective by linking these points in the same way:

1. Die Werbeagentur studiert den Markt gründlich. Dann wählt sie die neue Werbung.
2. Der Kunde muß sich daran gewöhnen. Dann akzeptiert er das neue Material.
3. Die Waren brauchen einen VDE-Stecker. Dann können Sie sie in Deutschland verkaufen.

1. Die Werbeagentur studiert den Markt gründlich, bevor sie die neue Werbung wählt.
2. Der Kunde muß sich daran gewöhnen, bevor er das neue Material akzeptiert.
3. Die Waren brauchen einen VDE-Stecker, bevor Sie sie in Deutschland verkaufen können.

4. Der Hersteller hat mit seinem Vertreter gesprochen. Dann hat er seine Preise erhöht.

5. Wir wollen die Mengen besprechen. Dann können wir Ihnen einen Auftrag erteilen.

6. Der deutsche Konsument braucht Zeit. Dann kann er dieses Produkt aus Kunststoff akzeptieren.

7. Das Lager muß fertig sein. Dann können wir die Lieferzeiten bestätigen.

8. Wir werden drei Monate warten. Dann nehmen wir alle unverkauften Waren zurück.

9. Wir lassen unsere Literatur ins Deutsche übersetzen. Dann gehen wir zur Messe.

10. Wir mußten andere Bedingungen aushandeln. Dann war er mit dem Angebot zufrieden.

4. Der Hersteller hat mit seinem Vertreter gesprochen, bevor er seine Preise erhöht hat.

5. Wir wollen die Mengen besprechen, bevor wir Ihnen einen Auftrag erteilen können.

6. Der deutsche Konsument braucht Zeit, bevor er dieses Produkt aus Kunststoff akzeptieren kann.

7. Das Lager muß fertig sein, bevor wir die Lieferzeiten bestätigen können.

8. Wir werden drei Monate warten, bevor wir alle unverkauften Waren zurücknehmen.

9. Wir lassen unsere Literatur ins Deutsche übersetzen, bevor wir zur Messe gehen.

10. Wir mußten andere Bedingungen aushandeln, bevor er mit dem Angebot zufrieden war.

Exercise B

Here is another way to change the emphasis simply and effectively. This time you concentrate on the event or condition which precedes a point. You do so with the simple word *vorher*:

Die Waren kommen von unserem Werk in England, aber vorher werden sie alle getestet.

Imagine a situation in which the way you operate is under discussion. These are the words which might well be used. Note that the words *aber vorher* appear in each sentence. How do you say the following sentences in the other language? You can approach this exercise either from the German or from the English, depending on your confidence and/or your need in German.

If you decide to begin from the English, ask yourself what a German business person would probably say in the same situation.

1. The agency chooses the advertising, but before that they have to study the market thoroughly.

2. I am sure German customers will accept the product, but they have to get used to the material beforehand.

3. We can import these articles into Germany, but first (beforehand) they have to have an approved plug.

4. The manufacturer wants to raise his prices, but before he does that he ought to talk to his agent.

If you approach this exercise from the German, ask yourself how you would say these sentences in English.

1. Die Agentur entscheidet sich für die Werbung, aber vorher muß sie den Markt gründlich studieren.

2. Ich bin sicher, daß die deutschen Kunden das Produkt akzeptieren werden, aber vorher müssen sie sich an das Material gewöhnen.

3. Wir können diese Waren nach Deutschland importieren, aber vorher müssen sie einen geprüften Stecker haben.

4. Der Hersteller möchte seine Preise erhöhen, aber vorher müßte er mit seinem Vertreter sprechen.

5. We would like to give you an order, but before that we want to discuss delivery.

6. The market will accept a product made of plastic, but before it does we still need a little more time.

7. We can guarantee delivery dates, but first the new warehouse has to be ready.

8. Come to the trade fair, but first have your literature translated into German.

5. Wir möchten Ihnen gern einen Auftrag erteilen, aber vorher wollen wir die Lieferzeit diskutieren.

6. Der Markt wird ein Produkt aus Kunststoff akzeptieren, aber vorher brauchen wir etwas mehr Zeit.

7. Wir können die Lieferzeiten garantieren, aber vorher muß das neue Lager fertig sein.

8. Kommen Sie zur Messe, aber vorher lassen Sie Ihre Literatur ins Deutsche übersetzen.

Take a look at your own products and services, see to what extent you can explain your own points in the same way. When you feel confident about handling *bevor* and *vorher*, it is a simple step to add *seitdem/seither*, *nachdem/nachher* to your active language ability. What a range of negotiating and presentation possibilities you will then have at your disposal!

You use *seitdem/seither* and *nachdem/nachher* in the same way that you use *bevor/vorher*:

Seitdem wir das neue Lager haben, können wir die Lieferzeiten garantieren.

Since we have had the new warehouse, we have been able to guarantee delivery dates.

Wir haben letztes Jahr ein neues Lager eröffnet, und seither können wir die Lieferzeiten garantieren.

We opened a new warehouse last year and since then we have been able to guarantee delivery dates.

Nachdem Sie die Waren drei Monate lang gehabt haben, werden wir alle unverkauften Artikel zurücknehmen.

After you have had the goods for three months we will take back all unsold articles.

Sie behalten die Waren drei Monate lang, und nachher werden wir alle unverkauften Waren zurücknehmen.

You keep the goods for three months and afterwards we will take back all unsold articles.

Negotiating an order – clarifying details

When you are negotiating an order, you will want to give or ask for very specific information. This is what Michael Hassenkamp says:

Ich hätte noch eine Frage, *die mich ein bißchen nickelt.*
There is another question *which is bothering me a bit.*

Later, he wants to make a specific comment about Mike Taylor's prices which he considers too high:

Ja, bei den Preisen, *die Sie mir berechnen,* . . .
Well, at the prices *which you are charging me* . . .

In this part of the development section we shall be looking at some ways of clarifying details. We shall build longer sentences, using the correct form of *der/die/das* to link two short sentences.

This is not a very difficult undertaking but many people shy away from attempting it because they feel that sticking to short sentences is so much easier. As so often with German, the key to success lies in knowing how *der/die/das* change. You will find a full list of the changes under **relative pronouns** in the Grammar Guide, page 175.

First, look at these two sentences:

Ich habe den Katalog mitgebracht.
Sie wollten den Katalog sehen.

To make these two sentences into one longer, clearer sentence, you simply rearrange the order of the second one:

Ich habe den Katalog mitgebracht, *den Sie sehen wollten.*

Exercise A

Now join these pairs of sentences using the correct form of *der/die/das*:

1. Ich habe den Wasserkocher gekauft.
Ich habe den Wasserkocher letzte Woche gesehen.

2. Wir müssen die Maschine reparieren.
Wir haben die Maschine erst dieses Jahr installiert.

3. Ich habe das Informationsmaterial gelesen.
Sie haben mir das Informationsmaterial geschickt.

4. Er hat die Broschüren bekommen.
Die Broschüren wurden gestern bestellt.

5. Das ist der Prozeß.
Wir wollen Ihnen den Prozeß zeigen.

6. Das ist die neue Maschine.
Wir wollen mit der Maschine in den deutschen Markt gehen.

7. Hier ist unser Produktsortiment.
Wir haben mit dem Produktsortiment in Deutschland sehr viel Erfolg.

8. Das ist der traditionelle Wasserkocher.
Sie haben von dem Wasserkocher schon gehört.

9. Wir haben eine Tochtergesellschaft in Holland.
Ich war letzte Woche zu Besuch bei der Tochtergesellschaft.

10. Hier sind die neuen Maschinen.
Wir sind dieses Jahr zu den Maschinen übergegangen.

1. Ich habe den Wasserkocher gekauft, *den ich letzte Woche gesehen habe.*

2. Wir müssen die Maschine reparieren, *die wir erst dieses Jahr installiert haben.*

3. Ich habe das Informationsmaterial gelesen, *das Sie mir geschickt haben.*

4. Er hat die Broschüren bekommen, *die gestern bestellt wurden.*

5. Das ist der Prozeß, *den wir Ihnen zeigen wollen.*

6. Das ist die Maschine, *mit der wir in den deutschen Markt gehen wollen.*

7. Hier ist unser Produktsortiment, *mit dem wir in Deutschland sehr viel Erfolg haben.*

8. Das ist der traditionelle Wasserkocher, *von dem Sie schon gehört haben.*

9. Wir haben eine Tochtergesellschaft in Holland, *bei der ich letzte Woche zu Besuch war.*

10. Hier sind die neuen Maschinen, *zu denen wir dieses Jahr übergegangen sind.*

Exercise B

How do you say the following sentences in the other language? You can approach this exercise either from English or from German depending on your own needs and ability.

If you approach it from English, ask yourself how to say the following sentences in German:

1. We have received the brochures which you sent off last week.
2. The prices which we talked about are too high for me.
3. The kettle has a plug which the VDE has tested.
4. We have a warehouse from which we can deliver to the whole of Germany.
5. The company which we work with has an Italian subsidiary.

If you approach this exercise from German, ask yourself how you would say these sentences in English.

1. Wir haben die Broschüren bekommen, die Sie letzte Woche abgeschickt haben.
2. Die Preise, von denen wir gesprochen haben, sind mir zu hoch.
3. Der Kessel hat einen Stecker, den der VDE geprüft hat.
4. Wir haben ein Lager, von/aus dem wir ganz Deutschland beliefern können.
5. Die Firma, mit der wir zusammenarbeiten, hat eine italienische Tochtergesellschaft.

6. The customers he visited this morning were at the trade fair as well.

7. I will show you the product with which my company wants to enter the German market.

8. The agent you recommended has already given us some ideas.

9. The delivery which we ordered last week is already here.

10. The market share which we are reckoning on is 40%.

6. Die Kunden, bei denen er heute morgen zu Besuch war, waren auch auf der Messe.

7. Ich zeige Ihnen das Produkt, mit dem meine Firma in den deutschen Markt gehen will.

8. Der Vertreter, den Sie uns empfohlen haben, hat uns schon einige Anregungen gegeben.

9. Die Lieferung, die wir letzte Woche bestellt haben, ist schon da.

10. Der Marktanteil, mit dem wir rechnen, ist 40%.

Practising speaking
Sprachpraktische Übungen

This section will help you to prepare for taking an order.

You will find
- a scripted dialogue
- a dialogue chain
- dialogue practice.

Scripted dialogue

Stage 1 *Listen* to the scripted dialogue on the study cassette. It is a simple discussion between a seller and a prospective buyer.

VERKÄUFER: Guten Tag, Frau Rohr. Nett, Sie wiederzusehen.
KUNDE: Tag, Herr Gagsch. Wir haben uns lange Zeit nicht gesehen. Was haben Sie für mich heute?
VERKÄUFER: Wir haben Ihnen am Anfang des Monats den neuen Katalog geschickt. Ich hoffe, Sie haben Zeit gehabt, ihn durchzulesen. Haben Sie dazu Fragen?
KUNDE: Ja. Ich finde die neuen Waren in der Form sehr schön, sehr modern von der Form her. Aber das Material! Ich bin nicht sicher, wie unsere Kunden auf Kunststoff reagieren werden.

Dialogue chain

Stage 2 *Study* the plan below. It represents in diagrammatic form how a simple discussion between a seller and a prospective buyer might proceed when the buyer has objections to raise. The dialogue chain will help you to prepare, to present and to handle objections in a similar way by providing you with a map.

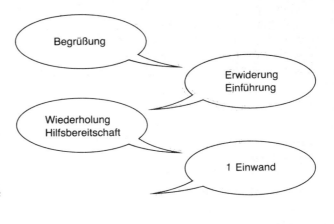

VERKÄUFER: Unsere Tests haben gezeigt, daß Kunststoff erstens länger hält, zweitens in der Form flexibler ist, und drittens von der Sicherheit her leistungsfähiger ist. Außerdem erlaubt er mehr Auswahl in den Farben.

KUNDE: Noch etwas, Herr Gagsch. Sie bestehen jetzt darauf, daß wir von jedem Modell jeweils zehn Stück nehmen. Das ist aber für einige Läden entschieden zu viel.

VERKÄUFER: Unsere Verpackungseinheit ist zwar zehn Stück. Wir sind aber gerne bereit, das Sortiment zu mischen. Ich darf auch einen weiteren Vorschlag machen. Wenn Sie unsere Waren innerhalb von drei Monaten immer noch am Regal haben, sind wir bereit, diese auf unsere Kosten zurückzunehmen.

KUNDE: Das scheint mir eine sehr gute Lösung zu sein. Ich nehme Ihr Angebot an. Ich habe für heute keine weiteren Fragen. Ich darf mich jetzt von Ihnen verabschieden. Auf Wiedersehen, Herr Gagsch.

VERKÄUFER: Gut. Ich bestätige alles nächste Woche schriftlich. Auf Wiedersehen, Frau Rohr. Vielen Dank.

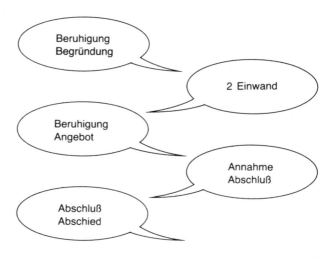

Stage 3 *Listen* to the dialogue while following the chain.

Stage 4 *Take* the role of the missing person on the study cassette. This will help you to practise speaking German in a negotiating situation.

Dialogue practice

Stage 5 Use the headings below to prepare what you might say if you were placing an order:

greeting	**Begrüßung**
reply	**Erwiderung**
introduction	**Einführung**
objections	**Einwände**
acceptance	**Annahme**
closing	**Abschluß**
leave-taking	**Abschied**

Use these headings to prepare what you might say if you were taking an order:

greeting	**Begrüßung**
repetition	**Wiederholung**
goodwill	**Hilfsbereitschaft**
reassurance	**Beruhigung**
substantiation	**Begründung**
offer	**Angebot**
closing	**Abschluß**

Review
Überblick

Language comment

Mike Taylor has learnt his German mainly by living and working in Germany. Although this is excellent for learning fluency and confidence, it does mean that you also risk acquiring bad habits. These become embedded and are very difficult indeed to break. We have seen that with Mike Taylor these 'bad habits' exist largely at the level of genders and pronouns. We can see how, under pressure, bad habits come to the fore.

What about Mike Taylor's 'good habits', though? What are they? They are his vocabulary and the phrases and fillers which enable him to stay with the conversation and contribute to cordial relations.

Have a look at the kind of phrase Mike Taylor, and of course, Herr Hassenkamp, use. Push yourself to use these and/or similar phrases in a similar way at every suitable opportunity.

lange nicht gesehen – I haven't seen you for a long time
nett, daß Sie mich empfangen haben – good of you to see me
es geht mir gut – I'm well
ja, das gehört dazu – that's all part of it
ja, genau – exactly
selbstverständlich – of course
da kann ich Sie eigentlich beruhigen – well, I can actually set your mind at rest on that one
das kann ich Ihnen versichern – I can assure you
ich würde mal vorschlagen – I'd just suggest
da kann ich Ihnen nur sagen, daß – all I can say is
das werde ich überhaupt nicht tun – I certainly will not do that at all

Pocket phrasebook

Some of the key phrases that will be useful to you when taking an order have been recorded on to the study cassette. You can practise your pronunciation by repeating them in the pause provided or you can use the pause to supply your own version in English and then compare it with our suggestion.

These are the phrases selected from this video sequence for you to learn:
Nett, daß Sie mich empfangen haben.
Ich wollte Sie nicht unterbrechen.
Wir haben ein Jahr Garantie für die ganze Produktionspalette.
Wir müssen dann über Preise sprechen.
Vertrauen ist gut, Kontrolle ist besser.

Sequence summary

In this sequence showing Mike Taylor, an importer of British kitchenware, negotiating an order for electric kettles, you have covered the following language points:

- how to use modal auxiliary verbs in the past tense
- how to make sense of pronouns
- how to handle adjectival endings after *ein*, the indefinite article
- how to specify times and dates
- how to clarify details
- how to negotiate an order.

Business guide – Fit for sale

In this section we draw your attention to some of the technical barriers to trade which could affect your approach to the German market. Like most developed countries, Germany has a complex set of standards and means of certifying goods, which intending exporters need to understand.

The section draws on interviews conducted with Bill Leicester, who is manager of engineering services with Technical Help to Exporters – based at Milton Keynes.

In video Sequence 3, Taking an order, Mike Taylor of THV conducts a negotiation with Herr Hassenkamp who is a buyer from a German retail store. Mike Taylor wants to sell Swan kettles, but the store buyer raises a number of questions for which Mike Taylor must have ready and convincing answers. Chief amongst these questions are reliable delivery, good after-sales service, assured quality, the right price and compliance with German technical standards. It's the last point, compliance with technical standards, that we're going to deal with in this section.

Broadly speaking – technical barriers can be identified as 'national technical requirements which occur in laws, regulations and standards, together with conformity certification schemes, which affect the design, manufacture, making and use of products in the country concerned'. Many of these so-called technical barriers to trade have not been erected consciously to keep exports out but are either an inherent part of the structure of the importing country, or the outcome of an historical situation. In the majority of cases, these barriers are not in any sense new, and have existed for decades and even centuries. They have become more apparent in the last fifteen or twenty years with the massive increase in trade between industrialised nations and the associated increase in competition for the markets involved.

Essentially there are two aspects of conforming to technical requirements that need to be understood.

1. Meeting national standards – these may or may not be legally binding but represent the nationally accepted standards for a product in a given industry.

2. Obtaining certification – this involves achieving formal recognition for a product which may then display the relevant certification mark. Certification does not automatically imply that national standards have been met.

Understanding how standards work in Germany is vital for any exporter intending to make an impact in the market. As you will discover, getting it right can be like finding your way through a maze. Very often UK companies leave compliance with standards to the production or engineering departments with sales and marketing paying very little attention to this area. In Germany, if your goods don't meet the relevant standard, they simply don't sell. Understanding German technical standards, therefore plays a vital part in your marketing strategy.

German law

There are no laws in Germany saying that technical equipment must be tested or certified in Germany by a German organisation – that would be an offence against EEC legislation. But there are laws which establish required safety standards, with respect to a wide range of products. The *Gerätesicherheitsgesetz* (Technical Equipment Safety Law) which was first promulgated on the

1 December 1968 makes the provision that 'all technical equipment must be safe'. It makes reference to compliance with 'recognised rules of technology' and published accident prevention regulations as a means of abiding by the law.

German employers are required to conform to these regulations so that their employees are covered by accident insurance.

The German insurance institutions, *Berufsgenossenschaften* – BG for short – are the equivalent of our National Insurance Scheme operated by the DHSS.

In Germany there is a BG for all types of industry: building, quarrying, gas and water, iron and steel, chemical, brewing, textile and leather, general engineering and so on. These organisations (BGs) publish the accident prevention regulations referred to in the law. These regulations, referred to generally as UVVs, can refer to the design of equipment, referenced VBg, VBg1. VBg1.1 or VBg6.3 etc. or be in the form of guidelines and rules for the use of equipment, referenced ZH1, ZH15, ZH27 etc. Germans in all areas of industry are likely to ensure that the equipment and tools they use in their work conform to the relevant standards. Companies selling products which don't conform will therefore find that their market potential is considerably reduced.

The Equipment Safety Law does not cover all products, but there are other laws and regulations which apply to specific subjects, the road traffic regulations and the building regulations being two obvious examples. Almost without exception, these laws and regulations also indicate that goods made to German Standards and safety requirements will be acceptable.

Standards

In Germany, many different organisations create and publish standards which have national status. Electrical Standards emanate from VDE, the German association of electrical engineers, mechanical standards from VDI, the association of mechanical engineers, gas equipment standards from VBGW, and TÜV for car MOTs, pressure vessels etc. There are many others besides. These standards, once accepted through a committee process, are incorporated into the DIN catalogue to become *Deutsche Industrie-Normen* – German Industrial Standards. In the UK we commonly find the DIN standard in connection with goods such as wall plugs and photographic film, where the German DIN standard has achieved international recognition.

If a manufacturer wishes to produce goods in compliance with German DIN standards there are two approaches which can be adopted. The first is to obtain a translation of the relevant DIN standards, and produce goods strictly in compliance with these. Copies of such translations can be obtained from Technical Help To Exporters at Milton Keynes. It should be remembered that a product might have to comply with a variety of different DIN standards depending upon the number of component parts and complexity of manufacture. If a manufacturer decides to make a declaration with respect to DIN standards in this way, it is essential that compliance is exact. If at a later stage a competitor is able to prove non-compliance, the company could become involved in costly litigation.

A safer alternative route is for a company to have its products tested by one of the organisations licensed to do this in Germany.

In this case the company will be permitted to display one of the marks of approval to show that the product has been tested. This carries much more weight with German buyers and consumers than does a simple declaration by the manufacturer. For electrical products the normal approval comes through VDE – the German Association of Electrical Engineers – who both publish and test for compliance with electrical standards. These standards are incorporated into the DIN catalogue and therefore goods displaying the VDE sign are deemed to have satisfied the national standards.

Certification

In Germany, this type of third party certification, and the subsequent use of certification marks, is traditionally considered much more important than in the UK where until about 1960 self-certification was the most widespread practice. In the UK one organisation publishes the national standard, and that is the BSI. Various nationalised and other large organisations such as the CEGB, British Rail, British Telecom and ICI issue their own purchasing or test specifications, but these are usually based on British Standards with additional requirements added. But in Germany, because there is a wide range of organisations offering certification of different products, the choice of certifying body will depend on a range of factors, such as normal practice in the industry, cost, degree of market penetration required, and even geographic location. Buyers in the Southern *Länder* may prefer goods which have been approved by a locally based organisation, as opposed to a distant one – only research can provide the answer.

Some products of course will combine both electrical and mechanical parts, and as such may require more than one type of certification, for example an electric lawnmower. Research of competitors' products can provide the information you need to decide what certification your product requires. Alternatively Technical Help to Exporters have comprehensive lists which you can consult.

A mark which has become very common in Germany is the GS mark. This mark means 'Tested for Safety' (Geprüfte Sicherheit) and can be awarded by over 80 government authorised bodies. The GS mark normally carries the logo of the testing organisation in the top left-hand corner. If a product carries a GS mark, it doesn't necessarily imply that it fulfils the entire DIN specification for that category of product. For this reason obtaining GS certification may be cheaper than producing to a DIN specification, and for a wide range of products, safety may be the most important element of certification as far as the market is concerned.

Some of the larger German mail order companies have their own testing laboratories and certification marks. 'Quelle' is one of the better known. If your product is accepted for sale through the Quelle catalogue some testing of the product may be done in their own laboratories and you may find their tests could be very stringent, as one British manufacturer found when he discovered sand bags being dropped on the roof of the shed he hoped to sell into Germany.

New marks or forms of certification which affect your product may appear. The latest is the 'Blue Angel' symbol, which can be awarded to goods using recycled products. The green or environmental lobby is a force to be reckoned with in West Germany, so the Blue Angel may be worth watching.

The types of certification dealt with so far, deal mostly with aspects of safety and technical specifications. However, one range of certification schemes also embraces elements of quality control. These are the RAL scheme, RAL standing for 'German Institution For Quality Assurance And Marketing'. RAL was founded in 1925 to 'establish technical terms of delivery and exact definitions of products and services' but has now broadened its brief to include the coordination of 'quality programmes and testing methods'. RAL is best known in the UK for its colour coding specifications, which are accepted throughout Western Europe. Under the RAL system, groups of companies within an industry get together and form a *Gütegemeinschaft* (quality association) and become a member of the RAL. Then a common quality programme is agreed and published by RAL for the industry and the members of the group are allowed to sign their products with a 'quality label RAL' which for each group is officially registered. Membership of RAL is only open to German companies, but understanding what RAL means may help UK exporters to

forearm themselves with answers about quality in the face of persistent questions from German buyers.

Obtaining a certificate

Having led you into the maze of German standards and specifications – it's time to help you find a way out. The first stage we've discussed already, and that is to identify the certification which applies to your product. The answer will come either from your own market research and/or with the assistance of Technical Help To Exporters. From this point there are two routes you might follow. The first is to seek BSI certification of your product in this country through the BSI test centre at Hemel Hempstead. Once a product has been approved and awarded the BSI Kite mark, a company can apply to a German testing authority for recognition of the product under German standards. This is facilitated under the Cenelec Certification agreement which allows test reports on electrical goods to be accepted in most EEC and EFTA countries. The foreign certifying authority still retains the right to test for deviations from the specified standards, but the big advantage is that the main testing is done in the UK with English speaking testers and English documentation.

If a company decides that full BSI certification is unnecessary, for example wanting only a GS certificate, direct application can be made to the relevant authorising body in Germany i.e. VDE, TÜV etc. (Addresses from THE). The cost of certification is not cheap. An applicant's factory has to be inspected to ensure adequate quality control, and the product itself has to be tested. A company should be prepared to make modifications to a product during this test period to comply with the findings of the test authority.

If a company does decide to make direct application to a German certifying authority, there are a number of hints which will ease the passage of the application through this process:

(a) Be prepared to respond to all questions fully. Some British manufacturers refuse to disclose all the information sought, sometimes on the basis of confidentiality, sometimes considering the question unwarranted. If a German tester finds unanswered

"... remarkable performance for watery sheep ..."

questions, time will inevitably be wasted as correspondence about the missing information is exchanged.

(b) Respond in accurate German. As we hope this course has suggested, it is a fallacy to think that all Germans speak English, and a German laboratory technician is certainly not guaranteed to speak English. Again time could be wasted obtaining translations. Also ensure that information in German is technically accurate. Much damage can be caused by errors. One company produced their technical specification in several foreign languages only to find eventually that they were claiming remarkable performance for their 'watery sheep', which is how the non-technical translator had dealt with 'hydraulic rams'. Also how many translators know that the German word 'Stickstoff' which literally translated means 'sticky material' is not glue but nitrogen? The list of similar mistranslations in the technical field is endless, and although amusing, they can cause serious delays, and expense.

(c) Use metric weights and measures. Sizes expressed in feet and inches, and weight expressed in pounds, will not put the German tester in a good mood.

(d) Consider using an agent or 'product champion' to support your application. If your company has already appointed a German agent, he or she should liaise closely with the testing authority. However, beware that the certification does not end up in the name of the agent. If at a later date you and the agent part company, you

may be required to go through the whole process of certification for your product again.

Some technical translators also specialise as 'product champions' and will see an application through the entire process of certification. Your regional DTI office will advise.

Conclusion

It is difficult to escape the conclusion that meeting technical specifications is a barrier which has to be tackled head on. In the long term, it is to be hoped that harmonisation of standards on an international basis will ease matters for exporters. In the short term the only solution is to cope with each market on an individual basis. It may well be that the product you sell to Germany, will be different from the product you sell to France, which will be different from the product you sell to the USA. You will inevitably need a commitment to the German market, and will need to monitor closely changes in legislation and technical requirements.

You will find much valuable help and support available from Technical Help To Exporters at Milton Keynes. They have available a range of consultant services, as well as specialist publications and updating services dealing with a wide range of products. German Standards can be obtained through the BSI sales department at Milton Keynes, where the translations section has a collection of over 2000 German standards translated into English, and will undertake translation of any nationally significant document in Germany into English.

For further information contact Technical Help To Exporters, Linford Wood, Milton Keynes, MK14 6LE, Tel. 0908 22022, Telex 825777 BSIMKG.

Business Magazine

They like quality, they like a bargain, and they don't like late deliveries. Who are these people that make up the 'German Market'? Chris Serle finds out on Business Magazine 3.

Operating in the market

„Bleiben Sie bei der Qualität, und wir bleiben Ihr Kunde.”

The video sequence
Der Video-Abschnitt

In these days of fast foods, meals on the move, takeaways, how does the caterer enable you, the customer, to enjoy hot food hot and cold food cold? By using the appropriate food container. *Fibracan* is one of the companies supplying polystyrene containers to the catering industry, Peter Cobbett is their Export Sales Manager. His agent in the FRG is Peter Rehberger, owner of *Rehberger – Fast Food Artikel* based in Kleve, north-west of Cologne. Peter Cobbett aims to visit Peter Rehberger at least twice a year to make sure that he keeps in close personal contact with an important customer in an important market.

During their meeting, the two Peters discuss prices, raw materials, design and packaging. They have a well-established relationship and their discussion is free of constraint. Peter Rehberger makes some suggestions for increasing the sales of drinking cups in the German market and takes Peter Cobbett on a tour of the warehouse so that he can inspect the packaging of *Fibracan* products. What you will hear in this sequence is a good range of vocabulary – especially nouns – drawn from these areas. You will also hear well-structured German. Peter Rehberger is a confident and clear speaker. He finishes his sentences; his meaning is always clear.

In the evening, business over, Peter Cobbett has invited Peter Rehberger and his wife Astrid to dinner and we join them in the restaurant. In language terms, Peter Cobbett is on more shaky ground here; in a business meeting he can direct the conversation into familiar areas but his ability to do so in a social situation is limited. He has to do his best to stick to the topics he can handle but also be flexible in responding to the unexpected. He relies on comprehension to get through – with very successful results, as you will see.

In learning terms, the most important thing to look out for in this sequence is the way Peter Cobbett remains in control of the situation without necessarily doing a lot of the speaking. He is in a position to do this for two reasons: firstly, his understanding of German is very good; secondly, he has prepared a number of topics for conversation, as well as comments and questions, which he can call on at any moment to keep the conversation going.

The situation is a help, of course. He is not in a selling situation as such and he has established a climate of trust with his opposite number in Germany. So he is fostering a business relationship rather than establishing or developing it.

What are the implications for the learner? How can you benefit from Peter Cobbett's approach? First and foremost, whatever your language level at the moment, copy Peter Cobbett's proven strategy. Listen carefully, listen attentively. In other words, train your listening. Develop your comprehension and it will pay off in effective and accurate communication.

Secondly, prepare for the situations you can anticipate and rehearse them. So, if you are going to be in a social situation next time you go to Germany, work out some possible topics for conversations before you go. If you can, try them out with your tutor, your colleagues or with a sympathetic German speaker. This will help you to keep a conversation going, knowing that what you are saying will be accurate in language terms and acceptable in communication terms.

Key words

Here is a list of the key words in German used in negotiations between agents and distributors. Study the list and the meaning in this context, so that you can follow the video more easily. The words are listed in the order in which they occur.

die Verkaufsziffer (-n)	sales figure
der Umsatz ("e)	turnover
die Preissituation (-en)	pricing situation
die Konkurrenz	competition
die Preiserhöhung (-en)	price increase
die Verkaufszahl (-en)	sales figure
die Gestaltung	design
die Ausführung (-en)	model
die Neuentwicklung (-en)	new development
der Erfolg (-e)	success
die Niederlassung (-en)	branch
das Verkaufsbüro (-s)	sales office
der Bereich (-e)	product area
die Beanspruchung (-en)	stress
die Raumersparnis (-se)	space saving

Practising listening and understanding
Hörverständnisübungen

You will find a workplan to help you in Sequence 1, page 11.

Information

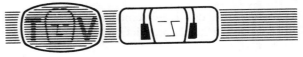

Exercise A

What are they saying?

die Vorstellung

1. Bei wem arbeitet Peter Cobbett?
2. Für wann ist sein Termin?
3. Wie war sein Flug?

die Einführung

4. Wie steht es mit den Verkaufsziffern?
5. Womit ist Peter Rehberger sehr zufrieden?

Answers

die Vorstellung

1. Er arbeitet bei *Fibracan* in England.
2. Er hat einen Termin *um vierzehn Uhr*.
3. Er war *sehr gut, sehr angenehm*.

die Einführung

4. Sie sind *im Moment sehr gut*.
5. Er ist *mit den Umsätzen in Deutschland* sehr zufrieden.

6. Was bereitet Peter Rehberger Schwierigkeiten?

7. Was kann Probleme geben?

die Produkte

8. Wie steht es mit den Food-Containern?

9. Wie steht es mit den Trinkbechern?

10. Was für eine Niederlassung hat Peter Rehberger in Berlin eröffnet?

beim Rundgang

11. Wie steht es mit den Kartons aus Griechenland?

im Restaurant

12. Warum sind Peter Rehberger und seine Familie glücklich?

6. *Das Wetter* bereitet ihm Schwierigkeiten.

7. *Die Preiserhöhung* kann Probleme geben.

die Produkte

8. Mit den Food-Containern *macht Peter Rehberger relativ gute Umsätze.*

9. *Peter Rehberger hat Probleme* bei den Trinkbechern.

10. Er hat *ein Verkaufsbüro* in Berlin eröffnet.

beim Rundgang

11. Sie sind *sehr schwach und fallen leicht zusammen.*

im Restaurant

12. Diese Woche gibt es *zwei Feiertage* hintereinander.

Summary

Exercise B

What are they saying?

1. Peter Rehberger hat ein Problem mit den Trinkbechern – welches Problem?

2. Warum findet Peter Rehberger Berlin geschäftlich so interessant?

3. Im Restaurant sprechen Astrid und Peter Rehberger über den Unterschied zwischen dem Norden Deutschlands und dem Süden. Was sagen sie darüber?

Possible answers

1. Im Vergleich zu den Bechern aus Holland oder aus Deutschland sehen die Trinkbecher von *Fibracan* etwas altmodisch aus. Die Kunden kaufen lieber die Becher von der Konkurrenz.

2. Obwohl Berlin nur eine Stadt ist, gibt es dort viele Touristen. Die Stadt ist ein großer Markt für seine Produkte.

3. Die neuesten Industrien sind in Süddeutschland, wie zum Beispiel die Automobilindustrie und die Computerindustrie. Es geht den Leuten im Süden besser.

Close listening

Exercise C

What are they referring to ?

die Eröffnung

1. *das* ist wohl in ganz Europa so

Answers

1. Was uns Probleme bereitet, ist so'n bißchen *das* Wetter, aber *das* ist wohl in ganz Europa so.

2. gegen *die* wir verkaufen müssen

die Produkte

3. *das* kann mit der Form zu tun haben

4. *die* von der Gestaltung her schöner aussehen

5. *die* dann zu unseren Ungunsten sich entwickeln kann

6. aus *dem* Grunde ist es höchste Zeit, daß wir mit diesen neuen Modellen auch in den Markt gehen

beim Rundgang

7. daß *er* bei der kleinsten Beanspruchung zusammenfällt

8. man kann *es* also praktisch verschrotten

9. wir sind also zufrieden *damit.*

10. alles, was *damit* zusammenhing

2. Einerseits haben wir natürlich *die Konkurrenz aus Holland und auch aus Deutschland*, nicht zu vergessen, gegen *die* wir verkaufen müssen.

3. . . . während wir *bei den Trinkbechern Probleme haben. Das* kann mit der Form zu tun haben.

4. . . . *in Holland* werden also *Becher* produziert, *die* von der Gestaltung her schöner aussehen.

5. . . . sonst gibt das auch wieder ein, eine *Konkurrenzsituation, die* dann zu unseren Ungunsten sich entwickeln kann.

6. weil . . . *die Konkurrenz dieses Design bereits hatte.* . . . *aus dem* Grunde ist es höchste Zeit, daß wir mit diesen neuen Modellen auch in den Markt gehen.

7. . . . aber *der Karton* ist dermaßen schwach, daß *er* bei der kleinsten Beanspruchung zusammenfällt.

8. . . . und *das Material* ist unverkäuflich, man kann *es* also praktisch verschrotten.

9. Wir können also sehr *hoch stapeln. Raumersparnis* kommt dann dazu, und wir sind also zufrieden *damit.*

10. Früher dominierte *das Ruhrgebiet mit der Schwerindustrie*, Kohle und Stahl und alles, was *damit* zusammenhing.

Consolidation
Konsolidierung

In this sequence, the language points selected for consolidation are:

● positive/comparative/superlative
● separable verbs.

Positive/comparative/superlative

When they review developments that have taken place since their previous meeting, the two Peters make a statement (positive):

mit diesen neuen Modellen
or, a comparison (comparative):
die angenehmere Seite
best/worst of its kind (superlative):
bei der kleinsten Beanspruchung

Practice

Here are twelve statements you might make during a normal business discussion. How would you express each of the descriptions as a comparative and as a superlative?

1. positive	die bekannte Gegend	1. positive	die bekannte Gegend
comparative		comparative	die *bekanntere* Gegend
superlative		superlative	die *bekannteste* Gegend
2. positive	die hohe Arbeitslosigkeit	2. positive	die hohe Arbeitslosigkeit
comparative		comparative	die *höhere* Arbeitslosigkeit
superlative		superlative	die *höchste* Arbeitslosigkeit
3. positive	unser teueres Modell	3. positive	unser teueres Modell
comparative		comparative	unser *teureres* Modell
superlative		superlative	unser *teuerstes* Modell
4. positive	der neue Bereich	4. positive	der neue Bereich
comparative		comparative	der *neuere* Bereich
superlative		superlative	der *neueste* Bereich
5. positive	ihre gute Niederlassung	5. positive	ihre gute Niederlassung
comparative		comparative	ihre *bessere* Niederlassung
superlative		superlative	ihre *beste* Niederlassung
6. positive	sein langer Flug	6. positive	sein langer Flug
comparative		comparative	sein *längerer* Flug
superlative		superlative	sein *längster* Flug
7. positive	die starke Ausführung	7. positive	die starke Ausführung
comparative		comparative	die *stärkere* Ausführung
superlative		superlative	die *stärkste* Ausführung
8. positive	ihr schwacher Umsatz	8. positive	ihr schwacher Umsatz
comparative		comparative	ihr *schwächerer* Umsatz
superlative		superlative	ihr *schwächster* Umsatz
9. positive	unsere große Preiserhöhung	9. positive	unsere große Preiserhöhung
comparative		comparative	unsere *größere* Preiserhöhung
superlative		superlative	unsere *größte* Preiserhöhung
10. positive	das kleine Lager	10. positive	das kleine Lager
comparative		comparative	das *kleinere* Lager
superlative		superlative	das *kleinste* Lager
11. positive	die interessanten Zahlen	11. positive	die interessanten Zahlen
comparative		comparative	die *interessanteren* Zahlen
superlative		superlative	die *interessantesten* Zahlen
12. positive	die kapitalkräftigen Firmen	12. positive	die kapitalkräftigen Firmen
comparative		comparative	die *kapitalkräftigeren* Firmen
superlative		superlative	die *kapitalkräftigsten* Firmen

Separable verbs

A separable verb probably sounds like the kind of verb you could do without and just the sort of trap German lays for the unwary learner. Well, we have them in English too, for example:

Please *take* your coat *off*.
Why don't you *sit down*?

In other words, a separable verb is one which has an extra integral part – usually a preposition. Here are some examples taken from the video sequence:

Das Flugzeug ist pünktlich *angekommen*.
Wollen Sie bitte *durchgehen*?

Separable verbs are frequently used in German and are simple to handle. If you feel confident about using them, go straight to the exercises.

If not, there are two things to remember about separable verbs:

1. There are two parts, i.e. a verb and (usually) a preposition.
2. The two parts separate in **main** clauses in the present and imperfect tense, e.g.:

Das Flugzeug *kommt* pünktlich *an*.
Er *ging* mit zu Herrn Rehberger *durch*.

Look at some other separable verbs taken from previous scenes:

Die Verkaufszahlen *reichen* nicht *aus*.
Wir *stellen* in Frankfurt *aus*.
Sie *führt* das neue Dekor *ein*.
Der Kessel *sieht* sehr gut *aus*.
Er *nimmt* die unverkauften Waren *zurück*.
Wir stellen ein Problem *fest*.

Practice A

Now look at the video sequence again and note the separable verbs with their English meanings in this context.

Check against this list:

an/fangen	to begin
an/kommen	to arrive
an/nehmen	to assume
sich an/siedeln	to settle
aus/drucken	to print out
aus/sehen	to look (as in: that looks good)
durch/gehen	to go through
vor/gehen	to go ahead
sich ein/bürgern	to become established
her/stellen	to manufacture
mit/teilen	to tell . . . about
zusammen/fallen	to collapse
zusammen/hängen	to be connected with

Practice B

Using the appropriate separable verb from the list, can you express these English sentences in German:

1. She *has printed out* the sales figures,
2. Would you like *to go through* please?
3. This traditional shape *looks* nicer.
4. *Have we* already *told you about* the price increase?
5. *We are beginning* to improve our packaging.
6. *I assume* you know our office in Berlin?
7. New industries *have become established* in the South.
8. When *does* your flight *arrive* in Cologne?
9. *Does* the competition *manufacture* food containers
10. These cartons *are collapsing*.

Answers

1. Sie *hat* die Verkaufsziffern *ausgedruckt*.
2. Möchten Sie bitte *durchgehen*?
3. Diese traditionelle Form *sieht* schöner *aus*.
4. *Haben* wir Ihnen die Preiserhöhung schon *mitgeteilt*?
5. Wir *fangen an*, unsere Verpackung zu verbessern.
6. Ich *nehme an*, Sie kennen unser Büro in Berlin?
7. Neue Industrien *haben sich* im Süden *angesiedelt*.
8. Wann *kommt* Ihr Flug in Köln *an*?
9. *Stellt* die Konkurrenz Food-Container *her*?
10. Diese Kartons *fallen zusammen*.

Development
Erweiterung

In this sequence on planning a course of action the development exercises concentrate on
● weighing up factors
● putting forward suggestions.

Planning a course of action

Remember, some of these exercises are included on the study cassette as well as in the book.

Weighing up factors

It is perfectly acceptable for you to speak in simple sentences – subject, verb, object – 'who does what'. You are communicating clearly when you do so. But you can improve the quality of your language discussion considerably by looking for introductory phrases. These announce your intention and prepare the listener to receive the message.

Notice the way Peter Rehberger says:

Was uns Probleme bereitet, *ist so'n bißchen das Wetter.*

An English speaker would probably have said something like:

Something that is causing us a few problems is the weather.

In the same way, Peter Rehberger says:

Was mir ein bißchen Kopfzerbrechen bereitet, *ist aber auch die Preissituation.*

An English speaker would probably have said:

Something that's causing me a bit of a headache as well is the pricing situation.

By using the introductory phrases in bold you sound more business-like. It is worth while making an effort to learn and use this type of phrase.

Exercise A

Here are some key words taken from the discussion. How would you say that they are causing you problems?

1. die Verkaufsziffern

2. die Preiserhöhung

3. der Umsatz
4. die Ausführung
5. die Konkurrenz

1. Was mir Probleme bereitet, sind die Verkaufsziffern.
2. Was mir Probleme bereitet, ist die Preiserhöhung.
3. Was mir Probleme bereitet, ist der Umsatz.
4. Was mir Probleme bereitet, ist die Ausführung.
5. Was mir Probleme bereitet, ist die Konkurrenz.

Here are some more key words taken from the discussion. How would you say that they are causing you a headache?

6. das Werk

7. der Markt

8. die Zukunft

6. Was mir ein bißchen Kopfzerbrechen bereitet, ist das Werk.
7. Was mir ein bißchen Kopfzerbrechen bereitet, ist der Markt.
8. Was mir ein bißchen Kopfzerbrechen bereitet, ist die Zukunft.

9. die Raumersparnis

9. Was mir ein bißchen Kopfzerbrechen bereitet, ist die Raumersparnis.

10. das Stapeln

10. Was mir ein bißchen Kopfzerbrechen bereitet, ist das Stapeln.

Using the key words below, how would you say that they are causing your company (die Firma) problems?

11. das Nord-Süd-Gefälle

11. Was meiner Firma Probleme bereitet, ist das Nord-Süd-Gefälle.

12. die Neuentwicklung

12. Was meiner Firma Probleme bereitet, ist die Neuentwicklung.

13. das Design

13. Was meiner Firma Probleme bereitet, ist das Design.

14. der Computer

14. Was meiner Firma Probleme bereitet, ist der Computer.

15. die Software

15. Was meiner Firma Probleme bereitet, ist die Software.

Using the key words below, how would you say that they are causing your boss (der Chef) a headache?

16. die Qualität

16. Was meinem Chef ein bißchen Kopfzerbrechen bereitet, ist die Qualität.

17. die Paletten

17. Was meinem Chef ein bißchen Kopfzerbrechen bereitet, sind die Paletten.

18. der Stahl

18. Was meinem Chef ein bißchen Kopfzerbrechen bereitet, ist der Stahl.

19. die Automobilindustrie

19. Was meinem Chef ein bißchen Kopfzerbrechen bereitet, ist die Automobilindustrie.

20. die Kunden

20. Was meinem Chef ein bißchen Kopfzerbrechen bereitet, sind die Kunden.

Expressing two areas of concern

If there are two areas of concern, you can express yourself more impressively by using:

einerseits . . . andererseits
on the one hand . . . on the other hand

Peter Rehberger does so when he says:

„Einerseits haben wir natürlich die Konkurrenz aus Holland . . . andererseits bekommen wir jetzt eine Preiserhöhung von Ihnen mitgeteilt.”

On the one hand we have the competition from Holland . . . on the other hand we have had notice from you of a price increase.

Exercise B

Here are pairs of key words from the discussion. How would you say that they both pose a problem for your department (die Abteilung)?

1. die Verkaufsziffern	die Qualität	1. Was meiner Abteilung Probleme bereitet, sind einerseits die Verkaufsziffern und andererseits die Qualität.
2. die Preiserhöhung	der Markt	2. Was meiner Abteilung Probleme bereitet, ist einerseits die Preiserhöhung und andererseits der Markt.
3. der Umsatz	die Zukunft	3. Was meiner Abteilung Probleme bereitet, ist einerseits der Umsatz und andererseits die Zukunft.
4. die Ausführung	die Raumersparnis	4. Was meiner Abteilung Probleme bereitet, ist einerseits die Ausführung und andererseits die Raumersparnis.
5. die Konkurrrenz	die Neuentwicklung	5. Was meiner Abteilung Probleme bereitet, ist einerseits die Konkurrenz und andererseits die Neuentwicklung.

Exercise C

Here are pairs of key words from the discussion. How would you say that they both create headaches for your colleagues (die Kollegen)?

6. das Nord-Süd-Gefälle	das Werk	6. Was meinen Kollegen Kopfzerbrechen bereitet, ist einerseits das Nord-Süd-Gefälle und andererseits das Werk.
7. das Stapeln	die Paletten	7. Was meinen Kollegen Kopfzerbrechen bereitet, sind einerseits das Stapeln und andererseits die Paletten.
8. das Design	der Stahl	8. Was meinen Kollegen Kopfzerbrechen bereitet, ist einerseits das Design und andererseits der Stahl.
9. die Kunden	die Automobilindustrie	9. Was meinen Kollegen Kopfzerbrechen bereitet, sind einerseits die Kunden und andererseits die Automobilindustrie.
10. der Computer	die Software	10. Was meinen Kollegen Kopfzerbrechen bereitet, ist einerseits der Computer und andererseits die Software.

Exercise D

Peter Rehberger uses an interesting phrase which will enable you to be more definitive and active in any conversation. Talking about the problems with the drinking beakers, he says:

Das kann mit der Form *zu tun haben*. It may be to do with the shape.

Practise explaining by using this phrase with the following words taken from the discussion:

1. der Termin	1. Das kann mit dem Termin zu tun haben.
2. das Wetter	2. Das kann mit dem Wetter zu tun haben.
3. die Gestaltung	3. Das kann mit der Gestaltung zu tun haben.
4. die Zeit	4. Das kann mit der Zeit zu tun haben.
5. die Ferien	5. Das kann mit den Ferien zu tun haben.
6. das Geschäft	6. Das kann mit dem Geschäft zu tun haben.
7. der Behälter	7. Das kann mit dem Behälter zu tun haben.
8. der Stil	8. Das kann mit dem Stil zu tun haben.
9. das Essen	9. Das kann mit dem Essen zu tun haben.
10. das Büro	10. Das kann mit dem Büro zu tun haben.

Putting forward suggestions

Peter Cobbett and Peter Rehberger have established a close working relationship and their conversation reflects this. Peter Rehberger expresses opinions, criticisms and comments freely.

Making suggestions, putting forward ideas and making proposals are important elements in any business discussion and as such you will want to feel confident that you have the right language at your disposal. Peter Rehberger has some ideas to put forward to Peter Cobbett. This is one expression he uses to introduce them:

Es wäre ganz gut, . . .
It *would be* quite good . . .

In this section, we shall be practising four ways to make suggestions, using this useful phrase. We shall start by making some simple suggestions following this pattern:

It would be quite good to find an agent.
Es wäre ganz gut, *einen Vertreter zu finden.*

Exercise A

Here are some suggestions in English, followed by the German version. Try to work out the German for yourself. Start each sentence with:

Es wäre ganz gut, . . .

It would be quite good . . .

1. — to change the design.	1. Es wäre ganz gut, *die Form zu ändern.*
2. — to print out the sales figures.	2. Es wäre ganz gut, *die Verkaufszahlen auszudrucken.*
3. — to visit the customer.	3. Es wäre ganz gut, *den Kunden zu besuchen.*
4. — to look round the warehouse.	4. Es wäre ganz gut, *einen Rundgang durchs Lager zu machen.*
5. — to open an office in Berlin.	5. Es wäre ganz gut, *ein Büro in Berlin zu eröffnen.*

6. — to stack the cartons.	6. Es wäre ganz gut, *die Kartons zu stapeln.*
7. — to improve the quality.	7. Es wäre ganz gut, *die Qualität zu verbessern.*
8. — to deliver on time.	8. Es wäre ganz gut, *pünktlich zu liefern.*
9. — to send sample cartons.	9. Es wäre ganz gut, *Musterkartons zu schicken.*
10. — to demonstrate the new model.	10. Es wäre ganz gut, *das neue Modell vorzuführen.*

Exercise B

Now let's vary the pattern a little. This time you want to make more specific suggestions, such as:

It would be quite good *if we had an agent in Germany.*

Es wäre gut, *wenn wir einen Vertreter in Deutschland hätten.*

Now use the construction to practise making this kind of suggestion. Start your answers with:

Es wäre ganz gut, wenn . . .

and end them with:

. . . hätten.

It would be quite good, . . .

1. — if we had a more modern design.	1. Es wäre ganz gut, *wenn wir eine modernere Form hätten.*
2. — if we had the sales figures.	2. Es wäre ganz gut, *wenn wir die Verkaufszahlen hätten.*
3. — if we had an office in Berlin.	3. Es wäre ganz gut, *wenn wir ein Büro in Berlin hätten.*
4. — if we had stronger packaging.	4. Es wäre ganz gut, *wenn wir eine stärkere Verpackung hätten.*
5. — if we had sample cartons.	5. Es wäre ganz gut, *wenn wir Musterkartons hätten.*

Exercise C

So far, so good. But supposing you wanted to make a slightly more detailed suggestion. For example, you might want to say:

It would be quite good *if we could improve the quality.*

Es wäre ganz gut, *wenn wir die Qualität verbessern könnten.*

Let's practise making this kind of suggestion using the construction. Start your answers with:

Es wäre ganz gut, wenn . . .

and end them with:

. . . könnten.

It would be quite good . . .

1. — if we could change the design.	1. Es wäre ganz gut, *wenn wir die Form ändern könnten.*
2. — if we could print out the sales figures.	2. Es wäre ganz gut, *wenn wir die Verkaufszahlen ausdrucken könnten.*
3. — if we could visit the customer.	3. Es wäre ganz gut, *wenn wir den Kunden besuchen könnten.*
4. — if we could look round the warehouse.	4. Es wäre ganz gut, *wenn wir einen Rundgang durch's Lager machen könnten.*
5. — if we could open an office in Berlin.	5. Es wäre ganz gut, *wenn wir ein Büro in Berlin eröffnen könnten.*
6. — if we could stack the cartons.	6. Es wäre ganz gut, *wenn wir die Kartons stapeln könnten.*
7. — if we could improve the quality.	7. Es wäre ganz gut, *wenn wir die Qualität verbessern könnten.*
8. — if we could deliver on time.	8. Es wäre ganz gut, *wenn wir pünktlich liefern könnten.*
9. — if we could send sample cartons.	9. Es wäre ganz gut, *wenn wir Musterkartons schicken könnten.*
10. — if we could demonstrate the new model.	10. Es wäre ganz gut, *wenn wir das neue Modell vorführen könnten.*

Exercise D

Finally, it is easy to vary this pattern slightly so that you can make a different kind of suggestion. Instead of saying:

. . . if you could. . . .

you could use the same pattern with *würde/würden* to say:

. . . if you would . . .

Here is an example:

We would be grateful if you would change the design.

Wir wären dankbar, wenn Sie die Form ändern würden.

Let's use the construction to practise making this kind of suggestion. Start your answers with:

Wir wären dankbar, wenn . . .

and finish them with

. . . würden.

We would be grateful . . .	Answers
1. — if you would change the design.	1. Wir wären dankbar, *wenn Sie die Form ändern würden.*
2. — if you would print out the sales figures.	2. Wir wären dankbar, *wenn Sie die Verkaufszahlen ausdrucken würden.*
3. — if you would visit the customer.	3. Wir wären dankbar, *wenn Sie den Kunden besuchen würden.*
4. — if you would look round the warehouse.	4. Wir wären dankbar, *wenn Sie einen Rundgang durch's Lager machen würden.*
5. — if you would open an office in Berlin.	5. Wir wären dankbar, *wenn Sie ein Büro in Berlin eröffnen würden.*
6. — if you would stack the cartons.	6. Wir wären dankbar, *wenn Sie die Kartons stapeln würden.*
7. — if you would improve the quality.	7. Wir wären dankbar, wenn *Sie die Qualität verbessern würden.*
8. — if you would deliver on time.	8. Wir wären dankbar, *wenn Sie pünktlich liefern würden.*
9. — if you would send the sample cartons.	9. Wir wären dankbar, *wenn Sie die Musterkartons schicken würden.*
10. — if you would demonstrate the new model.	10. Wir wären dankbar, *wenn Sie das neue Modell vorführen würden.*

You should now feel confident about your ability to make suggestions in a variety of ways and in an acceptable fashion. Some of these exercises are on the study cassette too, so come back as often as you can to practise them. Then try them out in conversation.

For practice in a social situation as host or guest, move on to the next section.

Practising speaking
Sprachpraktische Übungen

This section will help you to prepare for entertaining your business partners.

You will find ● a scripted dialogue
● a dialogue chain
● dialogue practice.

Scripted dialogue

Stage 1 *Listen* to the scripted dialogue on the study cassette. It is a simple discussion between two business partners over a meal.

Dialogue chain

Stage 2 *Study* the plan overleaf. It represents a simple discussion between two business associates talking over a meal. One person is the host, the other the guest. The dialogue chain will help you to anticipate and prepare for your role as host or guest in a similar situation by providing you with a map.

PETER C: Herr Rehberger, guten Abend, nett daß Sie gekommen sind. Wie geht's?

PETER R: Herr Cobbett, guten Abend. Es geht mir gut. Vielen Dank für die Einladung.

PETER C: Nichts zu danken. Unser Tisch ist gleich hier am Fenster. Bitte, nehmen Sie Platz. Sie gestatten – die Speisekarte? Möchten Sie 'was trinken?

PETER R: Danke, für mich nur ein Mineralwasser. Ich muß fahren, und die Polizeikontrollen sind inzwischen leider sehr streng geworden.

PETER C: Ich verstehe, bei uns in England ist es auch nicht anders. Wollen wir gleich bestellen? Als Vorspeise nehme ich Krabbencocktail, und als Hauptgericht hätte ich gerne Rumpsteak mit Salzkartoffeln. Oder vielleicht können Sie mir 'was empfehlen?

PETER R: Sie haben eine sehr gute Wahl getroffen. Ich nehme als Vorspeise die französische Zwiebelsuppe und danach Wiener Schnitzel und Spätzle.

PETER C: So, Sie fahren nächste Woche auf Urlaub, nicht wahr?

PETER R: Ja, richtig. Wir machen dieses Jahr eine Campingfahrt nach Südwestfrankreich. Das machen wir zum ersten Mal – letztes Jahr, zum Beispiel, waren wir in einem Hotel auf der Insel Mallorca. Das war sehr schön; herrliches Wetter hatten wir und das Hotel liegt direkt am Strand. Dort gibt es auch viele Sportmöglichkeiten, auch für die Kinder, aber eben weil dort so viel angeboten wird, kommen massenweise die Touristen – aus allen Ländern.

PETER C: Und Sie wollen dann diesmal einen Ort finden, wo es ein bißchen ruhiger ist?

PETER R: Ja genau, und vor allem wollen wir auch die Freiheit haben, den Ort zu wechseln, wenn es uns nicht gefällt oder wenn wir mal Lust haben, eine andere Gegend näher kennenzulernen. Und Sie, was haben Sie in diesem Sommer vor?

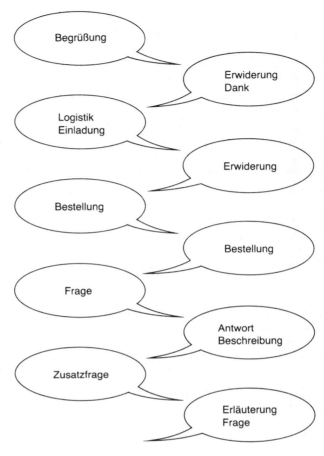

PETER C: Tja, wenn es nach mir ginge, würde ich gerne wieder mal nach Skandinavien fahren. Aber wissen Sie, wir sind dieses Jahr zu Ostern in unser neues Haus eingezogen – das heißt, es ist ein älteres Haus und wir müssen viel renovieren. Sie kennen das auch aus Ihrer Erfahrung, glaube ich?

PETER R: Sicher – ein Haus ist ein teurer Spaß, nicht wahr? In welcher Gegend wohnen Sie dann jetzt?

PETER C: Wir wohnen jetzt ein bißchen außerhalb der Stadt, landschaftlich sehr schön gelegen – und doch ist die Stadtmitte innerhalb von 20 Minuten mit dem Auto zu erreichen. Das ist für mich sehr praktisch und für unsere Kinder sehr schön, weil wir einen sehr großen Garten haben. Vielleicht besuchen Sie uns das nächste Mal, wenn Sie in England sind? Haben Sie da schon einen Termin?

PETER R: Nein, noch nicht. Normalerweise aber fahre ich jedes Jahr im November, kurz nach der Messe.

PETER C: Ach ja, die Messe – die wollte ich bei Gelegenheit mit Ihnen besprechen. Aber da kommt schon Ihre Suppe.

PETER R: Und auch Ihr Krabbencocktail. Ich wünsche guten Appetit.

PETER C: Danke schön. Ich wünsche auch.

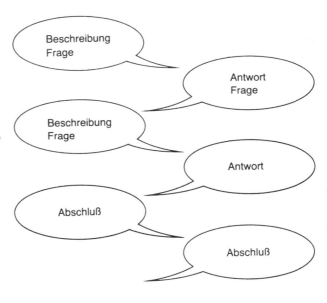

Stage 3 *Listen* to the dialogue as you follow the chain.

Stage 4 *Take* the role of the missing person on the study cassette.

Dialogue practice

Stage 5 You can *use* the dialogue chain to make sure that you can entertain and/or be entertained over a meal.

Use the headings below to prepare what you might say if you were the host:

greeting	Begrüßung
logistics	Logistik
invitation	Einladung
order	Bestellung
questions	Fragen
supplementary questions	Zusatzfragen
descriptions	Beschreibungen
closing phrase(s)	Abschluß

Use these headings to prepare what you might say if you were the guest:

reply	Erwiderung
thanks	Dank
order	Bestellung
answers	Antworten
descriptions	Beschreibungen
explanations	Erläuterungen
questions	Fragen

Language comment

Towards the end of the restaurant scene Astrid Rehberger and Peter Cobbett start to talk about the North-South divide in Britain and Germany, Peter's awareness of the German situation enables him to make a direct input into the conversation. Peter Rehberger responds very fully by giving a clear picture of the current situation and a useful insight into the growth of the leisure industry in Germany – *die für den Freizeitwert interessanten Plätze*.

What he means by the use of the word *interessant* may not be immediately clear. He is talking about the general attractions of the southern part of Germany for potential investors in the leisure industry as well as for the industry's consumers. And what attractions they are: skiing in the Bavarian Alps, all sorts of water sports on the many lakes in the area, some excellent wines, good food and superb communications to a number of desirable European capital cities. Who would not invest if they had the means? Who would not consume if they were able to? Of course though, there is a price to pay – do not forget the reputation the Germans have for hard work. This is said particularly of the Swabians, the inhabitants of the Stuttgart region. Perhaps this is why Stuttgart, with its Black Forest hinterland, has

attracted so many IT-related industries and is emerging as one of West Germany's fastest-growing areas. Perhaps too this is why public holidays are so highly prized; and when there are two holidays together – as was the case in mid-June 1987 – you can see why Peter Rehberger decided to tack on a long weekend.

This is all in great contrast to the traditional picture of the wealth being centred on the manufacturing industries based in the North, or as Peter Rehberger puts it:

„was früher das Nord-Süd-Gefälle – aber im anderen Sinne – war,"

Those industries have suffered disproportionately by comparison with the South, and it is those industries that Astrid Rehberger may well have in mind when she introduces the topic of unemployment in the Greater Manchester area.

All this is implied and referred to in Peter Rehberger's response and, as he warms to his subject, he addresses Peter Cobbett as though he were a native speaker of German, too. He makes no concessions on the language side and uses vocabulary and constructions which make heavy demands on the language learner.

How does Peter Cobbett cope with this situation?

Well, what comes over most clearly is the way he has worked hard to develop his listening comprehension ability to a high level. He is an attentive listener and is able to keep up with the conversation – as his contribution about BMW shows.

And it pays off for him in terms of market intelligence. Peter Cobbett knows the German market well so he fully understands what Peter Rehberger means when he says:

„im Süden wird jetzt das gute Geld verdient"

But this statement is interesting in language terms too.

When you have seen the literal meaning, ask yourself how you would have expressed the same idea in English. Would you have used the passive voice? Probably not because, in English, we tend not to use the passive voice when speaking informally. In fact, you may well have said something quite different, possibly 'the South is where the money is'. So what we learn from this sequence is to listen, and to listen out for the idea *behind* the words rather than working out the exact translation. Listening attentively is hard work but most people like a good listener and the Germans are no exception.

Pocket phrasebook

Some of the key phrases that will be useful to you when meeting your agent or distributor have been recorded on to the study cassette. You can practise your pronunciation by repeating them in the pause provided or you can use the pause to supply your own version in English and then compare it with our suggestion.

These are the phrases selected from this video sequence:

- Unsere Verkaufsziffern sind im Moment sehr gut.
- Einerseits haben wir die Konkurrenz aus Holland.
- Andererseits bekommen wir jetzt eine Preiserhöhung von Ihnen mitgeteilt.
- Das kann mit der Form zu tun haben.
- Bleiben Sie bei der Qualität, und wir bleiben Ihr Kunde.

Sequence summary

In this sequence showing a British company operating in the German market you have covered these language points:

- how to listen effectively
- how to use positives, comparatives and superlatives
- how to handle separable verbs
- how to weigh up factors
- how to put forward suggestions
- how to play an active role in a social situation as host or guest.

Business guide — Operating in the market

Getting the right representation for a product or company in the German market is a vital part of any company's market entry strategy. In the following business guide, Andrew Castley looks at some of the factors which can help a company select the right form of representation.

There is one guiding principle to help the exporter choose his or her channel of distribution correctly; that is the question:

What degree of control do I want over the distribution of my product in the overseas market?

This question of control might be considered from a variety of angles:

- How do I want to control physical distribution and stocking in the market?
- Do I need to maintain direct contact with the buyers or technical people?
- Do I need to retain control over sales negotiations, to ensure consistency with other overseas markets?
- Do I need to provide technical advice and customer service direct?

Depending on the answer to these questions, the exporter has a number of alternatives. But the golden rule applies: the greater the degree of control, the more it costs.

Sales and distribution channels open to the exporter

- Export merchants, who would buy the goods in the UK and re-sell abroad.
  In this case, the exporter exercises no control over marketing the product overseas. This type of operation is suitable for the small firm with few or no resources for exporting.
- Buying offices in the UK.
  Some of the larger companies like multiple chain stores, have buying offices in London. The exporter targeting these companies has the

Cretschmar Cargo

Die Leistung macht den Unterschied.

less difficult task of selling within the domestic market.

● Importer.
The UK company sells to an importer who re-sells the goods within Germany. Again there is no control over marketing the product in the FRG.

● Licensing.
This is a possibility which does not require intensive resourcing, but the exporter will have no control over the marketing of the product in the FRG.

● Joint venturing.
Here significant investment is involved, and would only be appropriate for a major undertaking. Extensive advice and guidance on both joint ventures and licensing are available from the DTI. Note that these two are 'non-selling' approaches.

● Overseas agent or distributor.
This is traditionally a popular way of exporting for British firms. Agents can do an excellent and highly professional job, but great care must be taken in ensuring that the agent selected is the best suited to represent the product in question.

● Selling direct.
This is clearly the most expensive way of operating, but it offers the advantage that the exporting company retains control over the marketing of the product. The exporter must

have the resources in terms of trained staff and generous sales budgets to make this a success.

Note that in 'Presenting your company', Marian Heller sells direct into the FRG whereas in this sequence, Peter Cobbett's firm uses an agent, Peter Rehberger. The respective decisions of the companies involved will have been based on considerations such as the above.

In general, there is greater openness to direct selling in the FRG than say, in France. Nevertheless, there are regional differences which might influence the decision to employ an agent or not. For instance, Northern Germany, particularly in the neighbourhood of Hamburg, tends to be *englandfreundlich*, whereas Southern Germany understandably looks more to Southern Europe for design, fashion and, perhaps, its trading partners. We should not over-emphasise this, but the tendency is there.

If you are exporting to the FRG, these quite strong regional differences may mean that your product is acceptable in one area, but not in another. Moreover, if you intend to deal through an agent or distributor, as Peter Cobbett is doing, you should be looking for agents who will each cover a region; one agent per *Land*, perhaps, or one agent to cover two or three adjoining *Länder*. If you decide that your product is to be sold in the whole country, notwithstanding regional differences in buyer profile, you might be using between four and seven agents. In some sectors, notably foodstuffs and textiles, German agents organise themselves into *Interessengemeinschaften* (associations); you might approach one member of an *Interessengemeinschaft* initially to promote your product in one area and, in time, through the association, gain access to the whole market. Your initial contact would be your key person, and the associates, sub-agents.

By using agents for each area, you will be taking the strong regionalism of the FRG into account in your marketing plan.

Finding an agent

The usual practice in dealing with the FRG is to work with a commission agent rather than one who buys on his or her own account. A greater degree of control can be retained by working through a commission agent rather than through someone who is free to operate his or her own marketing policy.

So where do you start looking for an agent to represent your product? The DTI, through its Export Intelligence Service, operates an agency-finding service. Contact your nearest DTI office or telephone The Export Intelligence Service, 01 866 8771 ext 266. The advantage of using this service is that potential agents at least carry the credibility of having been included on an official British list of business partners.

Further possibilities are offered by:

- Your bank's international service.
  The advantage of using your bank is that you are no doubt a valued customer, and you are keeping your bank abreast of your developing business operations. Moreover, the bank might well be able to provide credit and trade references on any agent they put you in contact with.
- The German Chamber of Industry and Commerce in the UK, 12–13 Suffolk Street, London, SW1Y 4HG, tel. 01 930 7251. The Chamber produces a journal called 'Business Opportunities in Germany' which carries advertisements from agents offering their services.
- Zentralvereinigung Deutscher Handelsvertreter- und Handelsmaklerverbände, Geleniusstraße 1, 5000 Köln 41, tel. 0221 514043. This organisation represents around 70,000 agents in the Federal Republic.
- The Chamber of Commerce of the Land or Länder in which you are interested.
  The address of the appropriate Chamber can be obtained from the German Chamber of Industry and Commerce in the UK.
- Advertising in the appropriate trade journal or in the bulletins of the local Chambers of Commerce. Again, relevant information on these can be obtained from the German Chamber of Industry and Commerce in London.
- The trade association relevant to your industry or product.
- Trade fair catalogues.
  Agents often manage stands for their principals and they can be identified in the fair catalogue. The Agents' Federation mentioned above has a stand at the principal fairs and often acts as intermediary between a principal and a prospective agent.

Selecting an agent

From various sources you may have put together a list of several possible agents. You will want to visit them to make an appraisal prior to making a choice. So what will you be looking for?

- Financial position and standing.
  Obviously you will want to know that the agent is well thought of and enjoys good standing in the market. The usual procedure is to ask for a bank reference and two or three references from clients who themselves enjoy a good reputation. It is worth mentioning here that The Exports to Europe Branch of the DTI in London can provide status reports on agents.
- Resources.
  The agent should have the financial, physical and staff resources to represent your company both now and in circumstances of future growth. So you will probably want to ask about or see some or all of the following:
  — The company balance sheet or turnover figures.
  — The records of market coverage. These will tell you the frequency with which customers are visited and the market covered.
  — Length of time in (related) market. The agent should be fully conversant with all aspects of the market as it relates to your product.
  — Storage facilities. Customers might need prompt deliveries or replacements, in which case your agent should have adequate space and conditions of storage.
  — Staff. Has the agent the strength to represent you properly? You might be looking at the number and quality of sales personnel, or the qualifications of technical staff.
  — Attitude. Does the firm have an aggressive attitude to marketing? Or do you get the impression it is resting on its laurels? You might consider that a young firm makes up in dynamism for what it lacks in experience.
- Commitment
  Here you are looking for evidence of the potential concentration of activity:
  — If there are too many portfolios, can you be

sure that he or she will devote enough attention to your interests?

— If there are too few portfolios, doesn't this suggest that other suppliers have decided against using him or her? It may, of course, be that the new, young agency has not yet built up its operation. On the other hand, it may emerge that the agent is also a manufacturer and takes on the agency for complementary products to enhance the range. This might be all right, but there might be a temptation to manufacture a competing product. You might check whether there is, in fact, a manufacturing facility.

— The agent should, of course, not be carrying any competing products; there would be an impossible conflict of interest in this case.

— On the other hand, your product should fit neatly into the agent's overall range and be complementary to the other goods. Otherwise your product will be the odd-one-out in the portfolio and not be part of a coherent range.

● Competence.

— Does the agent have the marketing knowledge and experience to formulate a marketing strategy for your product? Does he or she have sufficient technical background to make sensible decisions during negotiations? There must be sufficient credibility with the customer not to have to refer back to you, the principal, at every turn.

— Does the agent have sufficient technical knowledge to carry out after-sales servicing of your product?

— Is the agent willing to undergo product training, or to carry it out for the customer if this is appropriate?

— If you have a technical product you should satisfy yourself about the agent's confidence.

In summary, you need to satisfy yourself that the firm's resources, commitment and competence are adequate to generate and cope with future expansion. Do you have enough information to forecast this expansion? To set targets? The less knowledge you have about the market, the less control you have; the more dependent you are on the agent. This is not necessarily a good thing. Generally, the agent should not feel indispensable to you. In this connection, think back to the video sequence: Peter Rehberger tells Peter Cobbett that he is satisfied with sales. But is Peter Cobbett

satisfied? Does Peter Cobbett have enough information to know whether he should be satisfied?

● What are you offering?

But the interrogation is not all one-way! If you are dealing with a good potential agent, you will find that you will be asked for assurance on a number of questions:

How marketable is your product? The agent will not want to devote resources to marketing a product which will bring little return. To attract the good agent, you would be well advised to have amassed what evidence you can of the viability of your product, and to have an idea of the market.

You will also have checked that your product conforms to the relevant safety or food regulations, or quality standards. The DTI Exports to Europe branch can help here, or the Technical Help to Exporters at Milton Keynes. If these obstacles have still to be surmounted, your product will not be so attractive to the potential agent.

What are your terms and conditions? What is the rate of commission? How often will you settle accounts? Are expenses payable in addition? Will the agent have exclusivity? You should be prepared with firm proposals before you visit.

How reliable are you in terms of quality and regularity of supply? Like any buyer, the agent will want to be reassured on those points.

What level of support are you offering in terms of advertising materials, training and technical assistance?

So, part of the job of selecting a good agent is actually *attracting* that agent to your organisation.

The agreement

In drawing up an agreement you should always be conscious of two guiding factors: the level of control you wish to maintain, and the fact that, in case of doubt, German law will generally favour the agent.

The agreement should specify the period of time

for which it is valid. Generally it is advisable to agree a short term initially, of perhaps nine months or a year, to see how things go. But bear in mind that your agent will need time to build up your clientele; this argument will be used to extend the initial period.

The agent might want exclusive rights of representation of your product within an agreed territory. Your response to this will depend on your assessment of how thoroughly he or she can cover the territory and cope with developing business. If your negotiating position is strong, you may wish to hold out the prospect of exclusivity at the end of an initial period, during which time a number of agents have the rights. But you need a shrewd assessment of the value of your account to the agents concerned, and bear in mind that the status of the agent in Germany is quite high; cynical manipulation of a competitive situation would not be well received.

Clearly the agreement should spell out the level of commission and the frequency with which this is paid. The agent will want short accounting periods, whilst it is in your interests to agree longer ones. The agent will expect to be paid a commission on all business emanating from the territory, irrespective of whether he or she had a hand in winning it; this would be the usual arrangement.

You should clearly agree the limits placed upon the agent's jurisdiction in terms of the product range to be represented and the territory covered.

If you are serious about establishing yourself in the market in the longer term, you might require the agent to provide you with market information and advice, for example on pricing policy, or target-setting. You might want research carried out into your market share. In this case, the type and extent of information required should be clearly spelled out, but bear in mind that the agent has a vested interest in the information supplied. Again, your own informed assessment of the market is important to establish your organisation's interests vis-à-vis the agent.

The agreement might include the level of advertising and technical support to be provided by you. This will vary considerably from operation to operation, and you should formulate your policy on this in advance.

If you wish the agent to hold consignment stocks, the level of these stocks should be specified, as it will cost the agent to run these stocks.

You should also agree the role of the agent as intermediary. Will orders be placed without your having sight of the original order from the customer, or will the customer pass the order to you with the agent retaining a copy for records? Your own position on this will depend on the level of confidence you have in the agent, or on company policy in overseas markets generally.

The agreement should also carry a provision for cost recovery on, for example, after-sales servicing and visits to clients on the part of the agent.

Finally, it is important to specify the terms under which the contract may be terminated. As mentioned above, German law will apply and this will favour the interests of the agent in cases of dispute. You might specify these terms with reference to sales targets, agreed number of visits, the supply of market information, or the satisfactory completion of key tasks, such as after-sales service.

If you decide to terminate an agreement with one agent, and appoint a new one, under German law, the former agent may be eligible for compensation based on the size of the market and degree of goodwill that he or she has established. So beware, terminating an agreement can be expensive.

Agency Agreement
Handelsvertretungsvertrag
(englisch-deutsch)

1. Messrs.: .... (principal) of .... entrust Messrs.: .... (commercial agent) of ....

....

with their sole agency for the territory

....
....
....

for the sale of the following products:

....
....
....
....

1. Die Firma .... (vertretene Firma) in .... betraut die Firma .... (Handelsvertreter) in ....

....

mit ihrer Alleinvertretung für den Bezirk ....

....
....
....

zum Verkauf folgender Waren:

....
....
....
....

2. The agent shall endeavour to obtain business for the principal and is bound to serve the interests of the said principal to the best of his ability. He will do his best to provide all information necessary for the purpose of promoting business, and especially inform the principal immediately about every order received. He may not deviate from the prices, delivery and payment conditions of the principal without his consent.

2. Der Handelsvertreter hat sich um die Vermittlung von Geschäften zu bemühen und ist verpflichtet, hierbei das Interesse der vertretenen Firma mit der Sorgfalt eines ordentlichen Kaufmannes zu wahren. Er wird der vertretenen Firma nach besten Kräften alle für die Förderung des Geschäftes erforderlichen Nachrichten geben, namentlich ihr von jedem Auftrag unverzüglich Mitteilung machen. Er darf nicht von den Preisen sowie Lieferungs- und Zahlungsbedingungen der vertretenen Firma abweichen.

3. The principal will provide the agent with all necessary samples as well as printed and advertising matter free of charge, Customs duties and carriage. The samples remain the property of the principal, provided that they are not intended for consumption, and will be returned by the agent on request and at the expense of the principal.

The principal will supply the agent currently with all information of importance for the conduct of business, furthermore he will inform him without delay especially of the acceptance or refusal of orders. He will also inform the agent, if there is a possibility that he can only accept orders to a limited extent.

3. Die vertretene Firma wird dem Handelsvertreter Proben, Muster, Drucksachen, Werbematerial usw. in ausreichender Menge ohne Berechnung sowie zoll- und frachtfrei zur Verfügung stellen. Die Gegenstände bleiben, soweit sie nicht zum Verbrauch bestimmt sind, Eigentum der vertretenen Firma und werden auf deren Wunsch und ihre Kosten vom Handelsvertreter zurückgesandt.

Die vertretene Firma wird dem Handelsvertreter alle für den Verkauf wichtigen Informationen laufend übermitteln, ihm ferner insbesondere die Annahme oder Ablehnung eines Auftrages unverzüglich mitteilen. Sie wird den Handelsvertreter auch unterrichten, wenn sie Aufträge voraussichtlich nur in begrenztem Umfang annehmen kann.

The agent will be supplied with copies of correspondence with firms in his territory and of all invoices.

4. The agent is only entitled to collect money from the customers in the case of express authorisation.

5. The commission will be .... %
(in words .... %)
....
....
....
....

of the invoice amount for all business, both direct and indirect, transacted with customers in the territory mentioned under no. 1.

The principal will furnish the agent with a statement of commission due upon all deliveries made during the month/quarter of the year not later than the 15th of the following month. The commission, to which according to such statement the agent is entitled, falls due on the day the statement is forwarded.

The agent's claim to commission expires only in respect of any delivery for which it is certain, that the customer will not pay; commission amounts that have already been received by the agent will be taken into account in the next commission statement.

The agent is also entitled to commission if it is certain that the principal has failed to complete a transaction or has not executed it in the manner agreed upon. This shall not apply if the principal can show that he is not responsible.

6. The principal will reimburse the agent for the following expenses:
....
....
....

7. The contract shall come into force on the ....
and is concluded for an indefinite period/for a period of
.... years.

8. All claims that might be brought against the agent because of a violation of a patent, a utility model, a trademark or a copyright shall be the exclusive responsibilty of the principal. He has to make available to the agent the necessary advances of the costs of the case, and at the agent's request to advance them and to give all such information as may be required for the defence of the case. The principal has also to reimburse the agent for his own expenses. He

Von dem Schriftwechsel mit Firmen seines Bezirks und von den Rechnungen erhält der Handelsvertreter Kopien.

4. Der Handelsvertreter ist zum Inkasso von Kundengeldern nur berechtigt, wenn er von der vertretenen Firma dazu ausdrücklich bevollmächtigt ist.

5. Die Provision beträgt .... %
(in Worten .... %)
....
....
....
....

vom Rechnungsbetrag für alle direkten und indirekten Geschäfte, die mit Abnehmern des in Ziffer 1 angegebenen Bezirks abgeschlossen worden sind.

Die vertretene Firma erteilt dem Handelsvertreter für jeden Kalendermonat/jedes Kalendervierteljahr, spätestens bis zum 15. des folgenden Monats, eine Provisionsabrechnung über die in dem Kalendermonat/Kalendervierteljahr erfolgten Lieferungen. Der hiernach dem Handelsvertreter zustehende Provisionsbetrag ist mit der Abrechnung zahlbar.

Der Anspruch auf Provision entfällt nur bezüglich der Lieferungen, von denen feststeht, daß der Kunde sie nicht zahlt; Beträge, die der Handelsvertreter bereits empfangen hat, werden bei der nächsten Provisionsabrechnung angerechnet.

Die Provision ist auch zu zahlen, wenn das Geschäft nicht oder nicht so ausgeführt wird, wie es abgeschlossen worden ist. Dies gilt jedoch dann nicht, wenn die vertretene Firma nachweisen kann, daß sie insoweit kein Verschulden trifft.

6. Die vertretene Firma vergütet dem Handelsvertreter folgende Kosten:
....
....
....

7. Der Vertrag tritt am .... in Kraft
und ist auf unbestimmte Dauer/auf die Dauer von
.... Jahren abgeschlossen.

8. Alle Ansprüche, die etwa gegen den Handelsvertreter aus Verletzung von Patent-, Musterschutz-, Warenzeichen- und Urheberrechten erhoben werden sollten, fallen ausschließlich der vertretenen Firma zur Last, die dem Handelsvertreter die nötigen Prozeßkostenvorschüsse bereitzustellen und auf Verlangen vorzulegen sowie alle für die Prozeßführung erforderlichen Unterrichtungen zu erteilen hat. Die vertretene Firma hat in solchen

warrants to the agent his compliance with those legal provisions for the protection of end-users in force in the contractual territory relating to the nature, labelling or packaging of the products. The principal shall be exclusively responsible for all claims and obligations arising in the event of violation of such provisions.

9. This agreement can be terminated by either party thereto giving .... months notice by registered letter. Should the contract have been concluded for a definite period then it shall be prolonged automatically for a further like period provided that notice of termination has not been given within the agreed time to take effect at the end of the period contracted for.

10. In other respects the law valid at the domicile of the agent is applicable to this agreement.

11. Any disputes arising out of or in connexion with this agreement shall be decided by the court in the area of which the plaintiff has his residence or registered offices.

12. Amendments and supplements to this contract must be confirmed in writing in order to have validity.

....
....
Place: .... Date: ....
....

....
(Signature of principal)
(Unterschrift des vertretenen Unternehmers)

Fällen dem Handelsvertreter auch alle eigenen Aufwendungen zu ersetzen. Sie sichert dem Handelsvertreter zu, die zum Schutz des Endabnehmers im Vertretungsbezirk geltenden rechtlichen Bestimmungen über die Beschaffenheit, Kennzeichnung und Verpackung der Waren zu beachten. Die in Fällen der Verletzung dieser Vorschriften erhobenen Ansprüche und entstehenden Verpflichtungen fallen ausschließlich der vertretenen Firma zur Last.

9. Dieser Vertrag kann von jedem Vertragspartner unter Einhaltung einer Kündigungsfrist von .... Monaten durch eingeschriebenen Brief gekündigt werden. Ist der Vertrag für eine bestimmte Dauer abgeschlossen, so verlängert er sich für den gleichen Zeitraum, wenn er nicht zum Ende der Vertragsdauer mit der vereinbarten Frist gekündigt wird.

10. Maßgebend für das Vertragsverhältnis ist im übrigen das am Sitz des Handelsvertreters geltende Recht.

11. Gerichtsstand für etwaige Rechtsstreitigkeiten ist der Sitz des Klägers.

12. Änderungen und Ergänzungen des Vertrages bedürfen zu ihrer Rechtswirksamkeit der schriftlichen Bestätigung.

....
....
Ort: .... Datum: ....
....

....
(Signature of agent)
(Unterschrift des Handelsvertreters)

Motivating the agent

Formally agreeing a working relationship is only the beginning. It is important to give attention to motivating the agent throughout the whole period of the agreement so that maximum time and effort are devoted to marketing your product. These are some possible strategies:

- Pay regular visits; find out how things are going and ask about any problems you could help with.
- Suggest you visit some of the major customers as well. This is useful support, but bear in mind the resistance; the less you visit customers, the more dependent you are, so he or she may not

"It is important to feel an integral part of a team effort"

wish you to come too close to the customer. For the same reason, you should get to know the customers themselves as much as possible.

- You might invite the agent to your factory or office for any of a number of reasons: for product training; to make contact with company personnel and to get to know the company at first hand; to get to know other agents at an agents' conference. It is important to feel an integral part of a team effort.
- An agreed system of target setting, together with an attractive reward package, will encourage commitment. For this, you need independent knowledge of the market so that the targets will be realistic yet demanding.
- You should maintain regular correspondence with your agent with news of latest developments and perhaps relevant sales literature.

Developing a good working relationship with your agent can be a rewarding experience. You will share common goals, and in the process of achieving them, will acquire much knowledge about each other's culture and way of life. Treat your agent as a partner, rather than as an employee or subcontractor, and you and your company will benefit.

In the process of developing this relationship, you are bound to find yourself in social situations as Peter Cobbett did when he invited Peter Rehberger and his wife Astrid to dinner. Entertaining your business partners is always an important feature of business life and entertaining in Germany is no exception. Overall, the practice in Germany is much the same as in any other country but there are a few minor differences worth knowing about, especially if you are a newcomer to the German market.

Marianne Howarth offers some practical advice.

Entertaining – the role of host

Germany offers a wide selection of hotels, restaurants, *Gasthäuser* and other places to eat. Hotels and *Gasthäuser* will often specialise in German cuisine, restaurants come in all flavours – Italian, Yugoslav, Greek – and all price ranges. Service and cleanliness are generally reliable; portions are often substantial. Booking is not

"Your guest may well have already had a long day . . ."

always necessary, unless you have chosen somewhere small or very smart.

There are two basic points to remember about eating out in the evening in Germany. The first is that the German working day starts early; 7.00 a.m. is not uncommon, 8.00 a.m. is standard and so the main meal of the day is often taken around midday. In the evening, at home, many Germans will have an early cold meal. Consequently, many restaurants – especially traditional German ones in smaller towns – will stop serving hot food by 9.30 p.m. Your guest may well have already had a long day by the time he joins you for dinner and might appreciate an invitation for 7.00 p.m. rather than 8.00 or later.

The second point is the attitude the Germans have to hard cash. By comparison with Britain Germany is very far from being a cashless society. Credit cards, the mainstay of business entertaining here, are by no means unknown in Germany, but they tend to be unused. Do not rely on the restaurant to take any of your credit cards – you could be disappointed and very embarrassed. (Incidentally, the same also applies to petrol stations.) The problem for the business traveller is the difficulty of getting to a bank during opening hours, especially if you need to replenish cash stocks during a trip. One generally reliable solution is to take a supply of Eurocheques. These can be used to settle bills and as a way of acquiring cash quickly. Because each Eurocheque is guaranteed, many hotels will cash a Eurocheque for you and you would have to be very unlucky for a restaurant not to accept Eurocheques in payment. Having said that, there is the true story of the German railway booking clerk who refused to accept a Euro-traveller's cheque in D-Mark in payment for a railway ticket . . . So, you never can tell and, if you can, take cash.

Nearly all restaurants make good provision for their guests to hang their coats and it is considered polite to help women guests with their coats. However, experience of women business travellers in Germany tends to be a bit mixed. Outside the large cities, Germany does seem to be rather slow to recognise the role played by women in business and some hotels and restaurants do not always make it comfortable for a woman travelling or eating on her own.

Most British business people enjoy German food. The quality of the ingredients is good and food is usually attractively presented. But don't expect the Germans to eat Black Forest gateau for dessert; they don't. Indeed don't expect a groaning sweet trolley in every restaurant. Often, a standard meal will only be two courses – a *Vorspeise* and a *Hauptgericht* – and coffee is seldom drunk after a meal. If you want to try German coffee and cakes, take a little time in the afternoon and go to a *Konditorei*, if you have ever been in Germany on a Sunday afternoon, you will have seen that the trip to the *Konditorei* is something of a national pastime.

Service and VAT are usually included in the bill but it is customary to round it up to the next mark or two, especially if you are paying cash. This saves fiddling around for very small change. If service is not included, add 10%.

Entertaining – the role of guest

Until very recently, nearly all business entertaining was done in public and it could take many years of fostering a business relationship before an invitation to a German home was forthcoming. After the war, there was an acute housing shortage and many German families lived in quite small flats. This may have been one reason for preferring to entertain in restaurants. Another may have been that, as mentioned before, many German families do not have a cooked meal in the evening – just a selection of cold meats and cheeses, eaten with bread and usually taken earlier than one would eat in a restaurant. Providing a cooked meal for a guest at home was not always easy under these circumstances.

Things are changing now and it is certainly possible that you will be invited to a German home. It may not necessarily be an invitation to eat though – *Abendbrot*, the cold evening meal, is still the norm for most families and, if you have not checked, you could find that everyone else has eaten before you get there. There is no reliable guide, except that if you are invited to someone's home for 8.00 p.m. or later, the chances are that it's for drinks and nibbles.

Again, there are two things to remember if you are invited to a German home. The first is to be on time: the Germans are generally very punctual and if you are invited for a set time, that is when they are expecting you. The second thing to remember is not to go empty-handed. A bottle of wine for your host – why not take an English wine? – or flowers for the hostess are firm favourites. There is no shortage of excellent flower shops in Germany and some stay open quite late. With flowers, there are some funny little rituals to observe. It is customary to take an odd number, say seven, with a bit of greenery for decoration, and to present them to your hostess without the wrapping paper. This either means finding a convenient litter bin near your host's front door, or a large and empty pocket to conceal the paper in or making an early acquaintance with the kitchen bin. Very often, the gift of flowers is swiftly followed by the gift of wrapping paper.

Flowers are about the only thing that do not get wrapped. Other gifts, like wine, are usually wrapped to present to your host or hostess and nearly every shop will gift-wrap your purchase at no extra charge. If you are in Germany over a weekend, you will find that shops are closed from 2.00 p.m. on Saturdays (except for the first Saturday in the month) so don't leave your shopping to the last minute.

If you are invited for a meal, your evening will be spent in much the same way as in Britain. If you have been invited for drinks, it is likely that you will sample several different German wines. It is not the done thing in Germany to top up a glass that still has some wine in it. This is useful to know if you want to control your drinking, because your host will either wait for you to finish your glass or ask your permission to replenish – *darf ich nachschenken?* Likewise, a good host will not allow a guest to sit with an empty glass in front of him. An empty glass is a silent request for a refill. It's an easy way to drink more than you bargained for. An evening spent drinking German wine is also something of a tour of your host's wine cellar. There will be a selection and often the one your host considers his best will be saved until last.

Knowing when to make your exit is another point to bear in mind. German drink-driving laws are very strict. As we saw in the video sequence, Peter Rehberger was sticking to mineral water because of that. If your host has had anything to drink, it is very unlikely that he will offer to drive you back to your hotel at the end of the evening. He may offer to call a taxi for you; he may wait for you to suggest he does so. Taxi services in Germany are fast and reliable and usually not expensive. Even if you have hired a car, it still could make sense to travel by taxi to and from your host's home. It will save you getting lost and avoid any risk of a brush with the police.

It is in a social situation that a knowledge of German can be most appreciated. You will know from your own experience that business entertaining, however enjoyable, can also be something of a strain at the end of a long day. By making the effort to use German, especially in a private house, you will be doing your host and yourself a favour – even more of one if he has been making the effort to speak English all day. Germans make good hosts and, with a little help from you, they will probably do a lot of the talking. All you have to do is relax, listen and enjoy your evening. *Guten Appetit* and *zum Wohl!*

Business Magazine

Vertreter gesucht – How do you find one? How do you treat them? What do they want from you? Chris Serle enquires in Business Magazine 4.

Extending your market

„Wir haben 'was Schönes für Sie.”

The video sequence
Der Video-Abschnitt

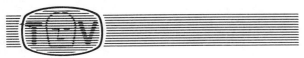

This sequence features two British companies already established in the German market who now want to introduce more of their products. Marley Tiles have developed a new gutter system which should appeal to the DIY enthusiast and Bernhard, the Rugby-based gardening supplies company, hopes to make a splash with a new garden pond. We follow representatives of both companies on their visits to possible retail outlets.

As ever, questions of quality, technical standards, price and customer preference are well to the fore. Once again, the message comes over clearly that Germany is a highly sophisticated and competitive market.

At the same time, it is good to see that the Germans can learn something from British retailing practice. There is also an interesting insight into differences in consumer preference in the two countries.

The myth is scotched that the British are no good at languages. Although in this sequence we only hear one British businessman, Mike Evans, speaking German, it is flawless, native-speaker level. He is very good indeed – but not unique. The sequence also features John Herbert, whom we only hear speaking English but who is equally proficient. They are both living proof that, with determination and effort, extremely high standards can be reached. Of course, they both have very strong incentives to do so – they are both Managing Directors of their respective companies and it would be a pretty poor show if their German was not up to scratch. In Britain, more and more companies are recognising that they can improve their image abroad if their staff, especially sales and marketing staff, can operate in a foreign language. It takes time as well as motivation but the rewards in terms of confidence and ease of operation are clearly seen.

Because of the high standard in this sequence, you will effectively be hearing the kind of everyday business German used between Germans. More than any other sequence, this one will test the listening skills we hope you have been able to develop by now. All the speakers speak clearly, but not all of them speak slowly. Then there are all the usual features of any conversation: unfinished sentences, false starts, repetition, change of direction. See if you can keep up with the Evanses!

This sequence is equally informative about the business side. It sheds light on the efforts needed to develop a product for the German market. Ulrich Kayser, Bernhard's German agent, describes the process in detail to his prospective customer and in so doing, boosts her confidence in the product. She knows that it conforms to all the necessary standards and that it comes with proper guarantees of safety and durability.

Bernhard's Grünhaus

Ulrich Kayser

Heinrich-Zille-Straße 1
Am Neuen Meßplatz
6800 Mannheim 1
Telefon 06 21 / 30 45 91
Telex: 463745 BERNX

So, confidence boosted all round, study the list of key words and watch the video sequence.

Key words

Here is a list of the key words in German used in meetings and presentations. Study the list and the meaning in this context, so that you can follow the video more easily. The words are listed in the order in which they occur.

das Programm (-e)	range
der Gartenbereich (-e)	garden sector
der Abverkauf	sales turnover
der Austausch	exchange
der Anteil (-e)	share
der Vorschlag (¨e)	suggestion
die Zweitplatzierung	second positioning
der Endverbraucher (-)	end user
der Umsatz (¨e)	turnover
die Rahmenkondition (-en)	general conditions
die Zulassung	authorisation
der Hersteller (-)	manufacturer
die Nachlieferung (-en)	follow-up delivery
die Mindestauftragshöhe	minimum-order size
die Anleitung (-en)	instructions
Some specialist words:	
die Rinne (-n)	gutter
der Sicherheitsschalter	safety switch
die Veralgung	build-up of algae

Practising listening and understanding
Hörverständnisübungen

You will find a workplan to help you in Sequence 1, page 11.

Information
Exercise A
What are they saying?

Vorstellung bei Herrn Schwarz

1. Wie soll die neue Rinne zum bestehenden Programm stehen?
2. Für welchen Markt ist die Dachrinne vorgesehen?
3. Die Rinne ist symmetrisch gebaut. Welchen Vorteil hat das?

Answers

Vorstellung bei Herrn Schwarz

1. Die neue Rinne soll das bestehende Programm *ergänzen.*
2. Die Dachrinne ist *für* kleine *Gartenhäuser, Garagen* und *Carports* vorgesehen.
3. Die Rinne ist symmetrisch gebaut, und deswegen dient *die gleiche Ecke als Innen- und Außenecke.*

die Reaktion von Herrn Schwarz

4. Welche Probleme könnte Knauber mit einem dritten Dachrinnenprogramm haben?
5. Welche Möglichkeit sieht Mike Evans?

die Lösung

6. Was schlägt Mike Evans vor?
7. Wofür entscheidet sich Herr Schwarz?

die Vorstellung der Pumpe

8. Wie lange läuft die Garantie?
9. Wie steht es mit Nachlieferungen?

die Vorstellung der Teichbecken

10. Wer klebt den Text ein?

11. Was wird Bernhard Grünhäus mit der Garantie liefern?

die Reaktion von Herrn Schwarz

4. Knauber könnte *Präsentationsprobleme* mit einem dritten Dachrinnenprogramm haben.
5. Mike Evans sieht die Möglichkeit *einer Zweitplatzierung im Gartencenter*.

die Lösung

6. Mike Evans schlägt *einen Test* vor.
7. Herr Schwarz entscheidet sich, *einen Testverkauf* zu machen.

die Vorstellung der Pumpe

8. Die Garantie läuft *ein Jahr*.
9. Nachlieferungen *sind unproblematisch*, weil die Firma ein *Lager in Mannheim* hat.

die Vorstellung der Teichbecken

10. *Bernhard Grünhäuser* sorgt dafür, daß der deutsche Text fest eingeklebt wird.
11. Bernhard Grünhäuser wird *eine zusätzliche Einbauanleitung* mit der Garantie liefern.

Summary

Exercise B

What are they saying?

1. Die erste Reaktion von Herrn Schwarz auf die Rinne ist ablehnend. Warum eigentlich?

2. Bei der Vorstellung der Pumpe gibt Herr Kaiser einen kurzen Bericht ab. Was berichtet er?

3. Warum geht es bei der Diskussion um die Farbe der Teichbecken?

Possible answers

1. Firma Knauber legt großen Wert auf eine gute Präsentation für ihre Waren. Sie ist der Meinung, daß diese einen guten Abverkauf bedeutet. Knauber hat schon zwei Dachrinnenprogramme. Ein drittes Programm kann Platzprobleme bedeuten. Die neue Dachrinne kommt vielleicht als Austausch in Frage.

2. Bei einer früheren Vorstellung der Pumpe hat es Probleme gegeben. Sie war ohne Stecker und hatte den VDE-Test noch nicht durchlaufen. Die Pumpe hat jetzt deutsche Kondensatoren, einen Sicherheitsschalter und ist auf zweihundertzwanzig Volt ausgelegt.

3. In England ziehen die Kunden grau vor, in Deutschland aber nicht. In Deutschland meint man, daß bei schwarz die Veralgung nicht so schnell stattfindet. Frau Troscheit findet weder die eine noch die andere Farbe richtig. Ihrer Meinung nach wäre dunkelgrün viel besser.

Close listening

We recommend that you only attempt this exercise if you need, or are keen, to understand the precise details of a discussion. Instead of doing the exercise as a listening comprehension exercise, you may like to try it as an exercise in reading comprehension. You are looking for what the words in italics refer to:

Exercise C	Answers
What are they referring to?	
Vorstellung bei Herrn Schwarz	*Vorstellung bei Herrn Schwarz*
1. *fünf Millionen*	1. . . . für die kleinen *Gartenhäuser* und für *Garagen* und *Carports* und so weiter, das sind *insgesamt* in der Bundesrepublik *um die fünf Millionen* . . .
2. *zwei Farben*	2. *Wir haben die Rinne in zwei Farben:* in braun und auch in grau.
die Reaktion von Herrn Schwarz	*die Reaktion von Herrn Schwarz*
3. *ein drittes* dazunehmen	3. . . . wenn wir jetzt ein *drittes*, kleines *Dachrinnenprogramm* dazunehmen, werden wir sicherlich *Präsentationsprobleme* bekommen.
4. *Zweitplatzierung*	4. Es gibt auch die Möglichkeit einer *Zweitplatzierung im Gartencenter.*
die Lösung	*die Lösung*
5. *drei* Prozent	5. . . . *Rahmenkonditionen.* Das heißt, einmal *drei Prozent* mit Bonus kommt oben drauf.
6. *zwei* Märkte	6. . . . ein oder *zwei Märkte*, die wir nach *Umsatz bemessen* wollen . . .
7. *vier* Monate	7. . . . daß wir uns vielleicht in einem Vierteljahr oder *vier Monaten* nochmal *zusammensetzen* . . .
die Vorstellung der Pumpe	*die Vorstellung der Pumpe*
8. *zweihundertzwanzig*	8. Dann war die ganze *Pumpe* auf den englischen *Strom* und zwar zweihundertvierzig Volt ausgelegt. Das ist jetzt geändert worden, das ist *zweihundertzwanzig Volt.*
9. *ein* Jahr	9. Auf jeden Fall *ein Jahr Garantie* geben wir.
die Vorstellung der Teichbecken	*die Vorstellung der Teichbecken*
10. *das* wäre wahrscheinlich das Beste	10. . . . wir werden eine *zusätzliche Einbauanleitung* liefern . . . mit dem Zertifikat oder mit der Garantie . . . *das* wäre wahrscheinlich das Beste.
11. *das* wäre noch schöner	11. Meiner Meinung (nach) müßte das ganze *dunkelgrün* sein . . . *das* wäre noch schöner . . .

Consolidation
Konsolidierung

In this sequence, the language points for consolidation are:
- likes
- dislikes
- adjectival endings 3.

We see how much trouble Marley and Bernhard Grünhaus have taken to get their products to meet the requirements of the German market. How admirable Herr Kaiser's patience is at the end when he is told that the ponds, which his company has specially changed from grey to black, to please the customer, would have been better in dark green anyway!

This raises the question of how to say clearly and accurately what it is you **like**. There are many ways of doing this; let us, though, concentrate on three ways, two of which are simple, one less so.

Likes

You want to know what the person you are talking to thinks of your company, product or services. Probably the easiest way is to ask:

Wie finden Sie das Produkt?

This will give your partner plenty of opportunity to give his/her opinion.

Here are some exercises to help you consolidate this ability.

Practice A

Use these words taken from the meetings at Knauber to find out what your partner thinks of products and conditions. Start each question with *Wie finden Sie . . .*

1. die Anleitungen	1. Wie finden Sie die Anleitungen?
2. die Mindestauftragshöhe	2. Wie finden Sie die Mindestauftragshöhe?
3. der Sicherheitschalter	3. Wie finden Sie den Sicherheitsschalter?
4. das Eckstück	4. Wie finden Sie das Eckstück?
5. der Hersteller	5. Wie finden Sie den Hersteller?
6. die Rinne	6. Wie finden Sie die Rinne?
7. das Programm	7. Wie finden Sie das Programm?
8. die Konditionen	8. Wie finden Sie die Konditionen?

Saying what you like

When you are asked for your opinion, probably the simplest way to reply is to use the same word *finden* and say:

Ich finde das Produkt preiswert.

Practise this by working through the next exercise.

Practice B

You have been asked *Wie finden Sie . . . ?*. Reply by using the words below. Start each answer with *Ich finde . . .* What about adding an appropriate adverb of your own choice?

1. die Verstärkung	klein	1.	Ich finde die Verstärkung (ziemlich) klein.
2. die Vorbereitung	einfach	2.	Ich finde die Vorbereitung (etwas) einfach.
3. die Geräte (plural)	unproblematisch	3.	Ich finde die Geräte (wirklich) unproblematisch.
4. die Zahlen (plural)	unterschiedlich	4.	Ich finde die Zahlen (recht) unterschiedlich.
5. der Testverkauf	normal	5.	Ich finde den Testverkauf (ganz) normal.
6. der Rand	groß	6.	Ich finde den Rand (schön) groß.
7. das Material	fest	7.	Ich finde das Material (angenehm) fest.
8. der Prospekt	klar	8.	Ich finde den Prospekt (sehr) klar.

Dislikes
Saying what **you do not like**

In discussing what you like, you will almost inevitably need to express your reservations or dislikes. The simplest and clearest way to do this is to say:

*Das ist **mir zu** lang/kurz/hoch/niedrig.*

It is too long/short/high/low for me.

Practice C

Here are some adjectives taken from the video sequence. Say what **you** found was wrong as in this example: Die Verstärkung *war mir* zu klein.

1. die Präsentation	frei	1.	Die Präsentation war mir zu frei.
2. die Frage	technisch	2.	Die Frage war mir zu technisch.
3. das Center	altmodisch	3.	Das Center war mir zu altmodisch.
4. das Argument	stark	4.	Das Argument war mir zu stark.
5. der Einbau	teuer	5.	Der Einbau war mir zu teuer.
6. der Auszug	kurz	6.	Der Auszug war mir zu kurz.
7. die Modelle (plural)	verschieden	7.	Die Modelle waren mir zu verschieden.
8. die Mengen (plural)	hoch	8.	Die Mengen waren mir zu hoch.

Saying what **other people** do not like

Das ist dem Vertreter zu lang/kurz/hoch/niedrig.
Das ist meiner Chefin zu lang/kurz/hoch/niedrig.

Practice D

In the to and fro of a discussion you will probably want to save time and replace the nouns by pronouns.
Prepare yourself for this by replacing the nouns in Practice C with pronouns.
You might feel that *gefallen* is hard to handle because you instinctively want to say 'I like it', but, with the verb *gefallen*, you have to think:

it pleases me . . .

1. Sie war mir zu frei.
2. Sie war mir zu technisch.
3. Es war mir zu altmodisch.
4. Es war mir zu stark.
5. Er war mir zu teuer.
6. Er war mir zu kurz.
7. Sie waren mir zu verschieden.
8. Sie waren mir zu hoch.

Practice E

Using the nouns and adjectives from Practice C, say that the person indicated did not like what they found, for the reason given:

1. Die Präsentation	die Werbeagentur	frei	1. Die Präsentation war *der Werbeagentur* zu frei.
2. Die Frage	ihr Mitarbeiter	technisch	2. Die Frage war *ihrem Mitarbeiter* zu technisch.
3. Das Center	unsere Kunden	altmodisch	3. Das Center war *unseren Kunden* zu altmodisch.
4. Das Argument	das Meeting	stark	4. Das Argument war *dem Meeting* zu stark.
5. Der Einbau	der Spezialist	teuer	5. Der Einbau war *dem Spezialisten* zu teuer.
6. Der Auszug	sein Techniker	kurz	6. Der Auszug war *seinem Techniker* zu kurz.
7. Die Modelle (plural)	der Händler	verschieden	7. Die Modelle waren *dem Händler* zu verschieden.
8. Die Mengen (plural)	der Vertreter	hoch	8. Die Mengen waren *dem Vertreter* zu hoch.

If you have already looked at the trade fair sequence, you will probably remember the comment made by the prospective purchaser at the Wedgwood stand:

Wedgwood. Doch ein sehr hübsches Dekor.
Mir *gefällt* es eigentlich.

In fact, you will mainly use this verb in the third person, and probably only in two tenses:

	singular	plural
present	es *gefällt* mir	sie *gefallen* mir
past	es *hat* mir *gefallen*	sie *haben* mir *gefallen*
	es *gefiel* mir	sie *gefielen* mir

The problems may arise with the associated words, so let's look at them now.

Practice F

Use the appropriate form of *gefallen* and of the personal pronoun to say that these people like it (whatever it is!):

	ich	1. es gefällt *mir*
	Sie	2. es gefällt *Ihnen*
es *gefallen*	er	3. es gefällt *ihm*
	sie (singular)	4. es gefällt *ihr*
	wir	5. es gefällt *uns*
	sie (plural)	6. es gefällt *ihnen*

Practice G

Now say what it is they like:

1. die Messe – ich
2. der Rechner – Sie
3. die Firma – er
4. die Bilder – sie (singular)
5. die Arbeitsabläufe – wir
6. das Lager – sie (plural)

1. Die Messe gefällt *mir*.
2. Der Rechner gefällt *Ihnen*.
3. Die Firma gefällt *ihm*.
4. Die Bilder gefallen *ihr*.
5. Die Arbeitsabläufe gefallen *uns*.
6. Das Lager gefällt *ihnen*.

Practice H

Let's end by giving the people in Practice G an identity. Say these are the people who like what they see:

1. die Messe — der Vertreter
2. der Rechner — der Kunde
3. die Firma — der Vorabinteressent
4. die Bilder — die Arbeiterinnen
5. die Arbeitsabläufe — die Bediener
6. das Lager — der Lieferant

1. Die Messe gefällt dem Vertreter.
2. Der Rechner gefällt dem Kunden.
3. Die Firma gefällt dem Vorabinteressenten.
4. Die Bilder gefallen den Arbeiterinnen.
5. Die Arbeitsabläufe gefallen den Bedienern.
6. Das Lager gefällt dem Lieferanten.

It may feel as if you will have to spend too much time thinking all this out and then preparing a statement. Yes, you will feel this at first. Think, though, of how impressive the end result will be!

Adjectival endings 3

Here we shall be revising the endings which adjectives take after the **definite article**, i.e. in sentences such as:

The German text is on the carton.

or
We have brought *the new gutter* with us.

or
We can deliver from *the new warehouse*.

In German, this is what happens:

Der deutsche Text steht auf dem Karton.
Wir haben *die neue Rinne* mitgebracht.
Wir können von *dem neuen Lager* liefern.

If you already feel confident about using adjectival endings after *der/die/das*, go straight on to the exercises. If you need to remind yourself of the pattern they follow, consult the Grammar Guide on page 167.

Practice A

You have brought a new product to show to one of your existing customers and want to highlight some of the main features. You have made notes to remind yourself what you want to draw attention to. Using adjectives and nouns drawn from the list below state the features in a full sentence. Start each sentence with:

Das ist der/die/das . . .

Examples:

Item	*Feature*
der Karton	stark
die Garantie	neu
das System	preiswert

Das ist der starke Karton.
Das ist die neue Garantie.
Das ist das preiswerte System.

Your notes

Item	*Feature*
1. der Aufkleber	klar
2. der Kondensator	groß
3. der Stecker	zugelassen
4. die Pumpe	stark
5. die Rinne	flexibel
6. die Lieferung	schnell
7. das Programm	englisch
8. das Gerät	preiswert
9. das Zertifikat	deutsch

Answers

1. Das ist der klare Aufkleber.
2. Das ist der große Kondensator.
3. Das ist der zugelassene Stecker.
4. Das ist die starke Pumpe.
5. Das ist die flexible Rinne.
6. Das ist die schnelle Lieferung.
7. Das ist das englische Programm.
8. Das ist das preiswerte Gerät.
9. Das ist das deutsche Zertifikat.

Practice B

It is a few weeks later and you can now tell your customer of some further improvements to the product. Using the list of adjectives and nouns above, form new sentences, changing the ending where necessary. Start each sentence with:

Wir haben jetzt den/die/das . . .

And finish it with *verbessert.*

Examples:

Wir haben jetzt den starken Karton verbessert.
Wir haben jetzt die neue Garantie verbessert.
Wir haben jetzt das preiswerte System verbessert.

Answers

1. Wir haben den klaren Aufkleber verbessert.
2. Wir haben den großen Kondensator verbessert.
3. Wir haben den zugelassenen Stecker verbessert.
4. Wir haben die starke Pumpe verbessert.
5. Wir haben die flexible Rinne verbessert.
6. Wir haben die schnelle Lieferung verbessert.
7. Wir haben das englische Programm verbessert.
8. Wir haben das preiswerte Gerät verbessert.
9. Wir haben das deutsche Zertifikat verbessert.

Practice C

This time you are telling your customer about another element in the package and how it can be combined. Using the above list of adjectives and nouns, form new sentences, changing the endings where necessary. Start each sentence with:

Es kann mit dem/der

End your sentence with . . . *kombiniert werden*

Examples:

Es kann mit dem deutschen Stecker kombiniert werden.

Es kann mit der kleinen Rinne kombiniert werden.

Es kann mit dem gleichen Programm kombiniert werden.

1. Es kann mit dem klaren Aufkleber kombiniert werden.
2. Es kann mit dem großen Kondensator kombiniert werden.
3. Es kann mit dem zugelassenen Stecker kombiniert werden.
4. Es kann mit der starken Pumpe kombiniert werden.
5. Es kann mit der flexiblen Rinne kombiniert werden.
6. Es kann mit der schnellen Lieferung kombiniert werden.
7. Es kann mit dem englischen Programm kombiniert werden.
8. Es kann mit dem preiswerten Gerät kombiniert werden.
9. Es kann mit dem deutschen Zertifikat kombiniert werden.

Finally, this is the pattern for the plural. It can be used with all plural nouns.

Examples:

Das sind die neuen Stecker.
Wir haben jetzt die deutschen Pumpen.
Es kann mit den üblichen Geräten kombiniert werden.

Development
Erweiterung

In this sequence on taking action, the development exercises concentrate on
● getting things done
● saying when things will be done.

Getting things done

In most of the filmed sequences we see British nationals operating in Germany. When they get back to their companies there will be innumerable items to deal with as a result of the business transacted in Germany. Clearly they will not be able to do everything themselves. They will have to get a lot of things done for them. There are examples in the video sequences of how to talk about getting things done in German.

At the THV stand at the trade fair in Frankfurt the prospective purchaser who runs a *Geschenkartikelgeschäft* wants to know from Sally Taylor whether he can have a sample sent. He asks:

Kann ich mir denn auch ein Muster schicken lassen?

Peter Rehberger tells Peter Cobbett that he had his computer print out the sales figures in preparation for their meeting. He says:

Ich hatte mir mal vor Ihrer Ankunft von unserem Computer die Verkaufszahlen ausdrucken lassen.

How is this put together? Quite simply, you take the verb *lassen* (to leave) and a second verb e.g. *schicken*. Leave the second verb alone, it does not change in this construction.

Sally Taylor's answer to her prospective customer could have been:

Ja, natürlich. Ich lasse Ihnen sofort ein Muster schicken.

Yes, of course, I'll have (get) a sample sent (to you) immediately.

Exercise A

Practise reassuring your business partner that you will get the things he/she wants done, by saying in German:

1. I will get the programme translated.
2. I will have the delivery company informed.
3. I will have the adjustability checked.
4. I will get the contract copied.
5. I will have the delivery date extended.

1. Ich lasse das Programm übersetzen.
2. Ich lasse die Zulieferfirma informieren.
3. Ich lasse die Verstellbarkeit prüfen.
4. Ich lasse den Vertrag kopieren.
5. Ich lasse die Lieferzeit verlängern.

Every training course on business communication will advise you to be as personal as you can in your business dealings. If Sally Taylor had wanted to let her customer know who she would be asking to send the sample, she would almost certainly have said:

Ich lasse unser Verkaufsbüro direkt nach der Messe ein Muster an Sie schicken.

Exercise B

Using the sentences in Exercise A add details of the person or office who(m) you will have carry out the corresponding tasks:

1. das Programm übersetzen   unser Importeur   1. Ich lasse unseren Importeur das Programm übersetzen.

2. die Zulieferfirma informieren   mein Kollege   2. Ich lasse meinen Kollegen die Zulieferfirma informieren.

3. die Verstellbarkeit prüfen   Ihr Techniker   3. Ich lasse Ihren Techniker die Verstellbarkeit prüfen.

4. den Vertrag kopieren   der Empfang   4. Ich lasse den Empfang den Vertrag kopieren.

5. die Lieferzeit verlängern   mein Partner   5. Ich lasse meinen Partner die Lieferzeit verlängern.

With a modal auxiliary verb

In the original question at the trade fair:

Kann ich mir denn auch ein Muster schicken lassen?

there is a modal auxiliary verb, *können*, which gives the expression an added dimension.

Exercise C

Supposing you wanted to know whether you and your company could have the following things done, how would you phrase the question? Start each question with:
Könnten wir
and finish it with . . . *lassen.*

1. das Lager   vergrößern
2. das Problem   beseitigen
3. die Form   ändern
4. das Gerät   abschließen
5. die Farbe   verbessern

Answers

1. Könnten wir das Lager vergrößern lassen?
2. Könnten wir das Problem beseitigen lassen?
3. Könnten wir die Form ändern lassen?
4. Könnten wir das Gerät abschließen lassen?
5. Könnten wir die Farbe verbessern lassen?

In case you need to check, here is what you have just said:

1. Could we get the warehouse enlarged?
2. Could we get the problem settled?
3. Could we get the shape changed?
4. Could we get the implement locked?
5. Could we get the colour improved?

I do not know whether . . .

Now that you are this far, it is only a small step to add an introductory phrase to the above sentence which will enable you to hedge and say that you do not know whether you could get the jobs done.

Exercise D

Say that you do not know whether you can get the things referred to in Exercise C done, by putting:

Ich weiß nicht, ob . . .

in front of the sentence. Remember that you will have to change the word order accordingly:

Answers

1. Ich weiß nicht, ob wir das Lager vergrößern lassen könnten.
2. Ich weiß nicht, ob wir das Problem beseitigen lassen könnten.
3. Ich weiß nicht, ob wir die Form ändern lassen könnten.
4. Ich weiß nicht, ob wir das Gerät abschließen lassen könnten.
5. Ich weiß nicht, ob wir die Farbe verbessern lassen könnten.

In the past

So far, so good. We have had you do some examples (*Wir haben Sie einige Beispiele bilden lassen!*), but they did not refer to the past. What if you need to talk about something which you had done for yourself or for someone else in the past? Have another look at Peter Rehberger's statement:

Ich hatte mir mal vor Ihrer Ankunft von unserem Computer die Verkaufszahlen ausdrucken lassen.

You know how to form past tenses. You are probably wondering, though, why there is no *ge-*. After all, it does say *lassen gelassen* in every verb list. The explanation is quite simple. When *lassen* is used in this way, you do not say *gelassen* in the past, but *lassen*.

Exercise E

How do you say the following sentences in the other language? This is an exercise which you can approach from the English, or from the German.

If you approach it from the German, ask yourself what you would probably have said in the same situation.

1. Wir haben die Kartons sehr hoch stapeln lassen.
2. Sie haben die Frage erklären lassen.
3. Er hat das Eckstück liefern lassen.
4. Sie haben den Sicherheitsschalter mitbringen lassen.
5. Sie haben das Büro schließen lassen, nicht wahr?
6. Sie haben die Ergebnisse vergleichen lassen.
7. Wir haben die Reparatur machen lassen.
8. Ich habe die Garantie noch einmal verlängern lassen.
9. Er hat die Preisliste neu drucken lassen.
10. Sie hat den Spezialteil einbauen lassen.
11. Ich habe ein Sonderprodukt anfertigen lassen.
12. Wir haben die Vorteile erklären lassen.

If you approach it from the English, ask yourself what your German counterpart would probably have said.

1. We had the cardboard boxes stacked very high.
2. They had the problem explained.
3. He had the cornerpiece delivered.
4. I had the safety switch brought along.
5. You had the office closed, didn't you?
6. They had the results compared.
7. We had the repair done.
8. I had the guarantee extended once again.
9. He had the price-list reprinted.
10. She had the special part built in.
11. I had a special product manufactured.
12. We had the advantages explained.

To conclude this section on *lassen* we should let one of the German speakers have the last word. It is Dr Gründer, the agent for BYG, talking at the trade fair. He uses the word *lassen*, but you might like to aim for something *slightly* simpler:

Darüber hinaus geben wir unseren englischen Partnern Anregungen, wie sie ihre Produkte auch für unseren Markt weiterentwickeln und verbessern können, so daß wir insgesamt über den normalen Vertreterstatus hinaus eine Reihe von Aufgaben erfüllen, die uns – und das wollen wir schließlich auch – bei unseren Kunden verankern und uns nicht so schnell austauschbar werden lassen.

Ladies and gentlemen:

Lassen Sie sich das durch den Kopf gehen!

Think about it!

Saying when

One of the striking things about this sequence is the number of times people refer to the time when things were done or are going to be done. Here are two examples taken from the scene:

Herr Schwarz of Knauber has been persuaded to try out Marley's new gutter system and he suggests meeting at a future date to see how things have gone:

. . . daß wir uns vielleicht in einem Vierteljahr oder vier Monaten zusammensetzen . . .

When talking about guarantees, Frau Troscheit says:

. . . ein halbes Jahr ist normal . . .

Ask yourself what you would have said in English in these cases. Probably, something like:

. . . that we meet in three or four months
. . . six months is usual

You will not have any trouble making yourself understood if you express these ideas in the familiar English way but you can make your German sound more professional and authentic by copying the Germans. It is not hard to do; nearly always it is a question of learning a single word or short phrase.
  Let's start by looking at some of the expressions used to talk about the past:

Ich war *vor* ungefähr vier Wochen beim VDE.
I was at the VDE about a month *ago*.

As you can see, this expression is very similar to English but its position in the sentence is important. In German, *vor* introduces the period of time, whereas in English *ago* comes after it.

Exercise A

How do you say the following sentences in the other language? This is an exercise which you can approach from the English or from the German.

If you approach it from German ask yourself how an English speaker would say:

1. Wir sind vor drei Jahren mit diesem Produkt in den Markt gegangen.
2. Vor einer Woche war er beim VDE.
3. Ihr Prospektmaterial haben wir vor vierzehn Tagen bekommen.
4. Die Konkurrenz hatte schon vor einem halben Jahr eine Preiserhöhung.
5. Den Gartenteich habe ich Ihnen vor einem Vierteljahr gezeigt.

If you approach it from English ask yourself how you would say these sentences in German:

1. We entered the market with this product three years ago.
2. I was at the VDE a week ago.
3. We received your brochure material two weeks ago.
4. The competition already had a price increase six months ago.
5. I showed you the garden pond three months ago.

Now take a look at another expression from the sequence:

Wir haben diese Pumpe eben *erst* auf der Kölner Messe präsentiert.
We *only* presented this pump at the Cologne Trade Fair.

Again, you can see the similarity with English and again the position in the sentence is important. In German, *erst* always comes close to the subject-matter it is emphasising, noun or verb, but *only* is nearly always used with a verb in English.

Exercise B

How do you say the following sentences in the other language? This is an exercise which you can approach from the English or from the German.

If you approach it from the German ask yourself how an English speaker would say:

1. Die Kölner Messe findet erst im November statt.
2. Wir sind erst im August mit diesem Produkt in den Markt gegangen.
3. Erst letzte Woche haben wir die neuen Kondensatoren bekommen.
4. Erst nach dem Testverkauf können wir entscheiden.
5. Die Lieferung wurde erst gestern abgeschickt.

If you approach it from English ask yourself how you would say these sentences in German:

1. The Cologne Trade Fair only takes place in November. (not until)
2. We only entered the market with this product in August.
3. We only received the new condensers last week.
4. We can only decide after the sales trial. (not until)
5. The delivery was only dispatched yesterday.

Finally, look at these sentences taken from the scene:

Seit Oktober ist die Pumpe beim VDE.

Da läuft sie im Gartencenter *seit* der Kölner Messe.

In Sequence 3 we practised using *seitdem* so *seit* on its own will not seem unfamiliar. It is very useful for expressing the idea that something is still continuing. It is used with a noun – *seitdem* introduces a clause with a verb in it – and the important thing to remember is that, in German, the article that goes with that noun will change, depending on the gender of the noun.
For example:

Da läuft sie im Gartencenter *seit dem Frühling*.
Da läuft sie im Gartencenter *seit der Kölner Messe*.
Da läuft sie im Gartencenter *seit dem Frühjahr*.
Da läuft sie im Gartencenter *seit den Herbstferien*.

What do you notice about the tense of the verb in these examples? How would you say the same thing in English?

Probably something like:

It *has been* in the garden centre since the spring.

It *has been* in the garden centre since the Cologne Trade Fair.

You can also use *seit* followed by a number, such as in this example:

Da läuft sie im Gartencenter seit vier Wochen.

In English, this would be:

It has been (running) in the garden centre *for* four weeks.

Exercise C

How do you say the following sentences in the other language? This is an exercise which you can approach from the English or from the German.

If you approach it from the English, ask yourself how a German speaker would say:

1. We have been testing the product for three months.

2. My company has had an agent in Germany for ten years.

3. The factory has been developing this gutter since the summer.

4. The manufacturer has been using German condensers since October.

5. We have been selling this model in Germany for one year.

If you decide to start with German, ask yourself how you would express these sentences in English.

1. Wir testen das Produkt seit einem Vierteljahr.

2. Meine Firma hat seit zehn Jahren einen Vertreter in Deutschland.

3. Die Fabrik entwickelt diese Rinne seit dem Sommer.

4. Seit Oktober verwendet der Hersteller deutsche Kondensatoren.

5. Dieses Modell verkaufen wir in Deutschland seit einem Jahr.

Practising speaking
Sprachpraktische Übungen

This section will help you to prepare for explaining and questioning in a features/benefits situation.
You will find ● a scripted dialogue
● a dialogue chain
● dialogue practice.

How do you put over information about your product quickly and clearly? How do you receive and ask about such information?

Scripted dialogue

Stage 1: *Listen* to the scripted dialogue on the study cassette. It is a simple discussion between a seller and a buyer.

Dialogue chain

Stage 2: *Study* the plan below. It is a diagram of the dialogue, showing you the various stages of the conversation. You will see that the script follows this plan closely.

VERKÄUFER: Guten Morgen, Frau Witt! Wie geht es?

KÄUFERIN: Grüß Gott, Herr Schneider. Nett, daß Sie gekommen sind. Wir haben uns seit der Herbstmesse nicht mehr gesehen. Haben Sie etwas Schönes für uns?

VERKÄUFER: Selbstverständlich! Unsere Abteilung Forschung und Entwicklung sucht schon lange nach einem einfacheren System für die Außenseite. Bitte schön. Darf ich Ihnen das Ergebnis zeigen?

KÄUFERIN: Was ist das Besondere an dem Produkt?

VERKÄUFER: Weil die einzelnen Teile symmetrisch sind, kann man Innenseite und Außenseite nicht mehr verwechseln.

KÄUFERIN: Und welchen Vorteil bringt das dem Kunden?

VERKÄUFER: Das Produkt ist, wie Sie wissen, für den Hobby-Segler gedacht. Er möchte segeln können und nicht dauernd bauen oder umbauen müssen.

KÄUFERIN: Das sehe ich ein. Allerdings muß ich sagen, daß wir keinen Platz mehr im Laden für so etwas haben. Wir können kein neues System vernünftig präsentieren.

VERKÄUFER: Wir sind der Meinung, daß das neue Produkt Ihre Kunden sehr schnell interessieren wird. Ich schlage vor, daß wir es als Austausch in zwei oder drei Ihrer Läden einführen.

KÄUFERIN: Ich bin gern bereit, daß wir einen kurzen Testverkauf vornehmen, damit wir feststellen können, ob das neue Produkt die Kunden wirklich anspricht.

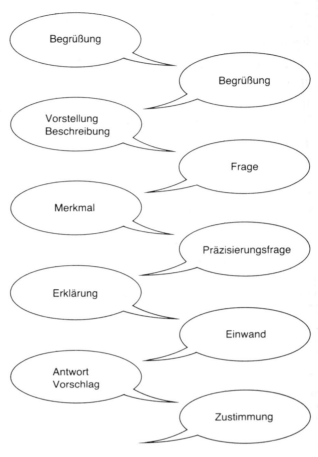

Stage 3: Now *listen* to the dialogue while following the chain.

Stage 4: *Take* the role of the missing person on the study cassette. It will help you to practise speaking German in a sales situation.

Read the text of the dialogue chain to check what is actually being said.

Dialogue practice

Stage 5: Finally, *use* it as a guide to make sure that you can explain, question and object quickly and politely.

Use the headings below to prepare what you might say if you were visiting a client:

greeting	Begrüßung
presentation	Vorstellung
description	Beschreibung
feature	Merkmal
explanation	Erklärung
answer	Antwort
suggestion	Vorschlag

Use the headings below to prepare what you might say if you had to deal with a visitor who wanted to show you something new:

greeting	Begrüßung
question	Frage
request for precision	Präzisionsfrage
objection	Einwand
agreement	Zustimmung

Review
Überblick

Language comment

Listening to a normal German conversation, such as the one between Herr Schwarz and Mike Evans, can have one of two effects. On the one hand, it is very encouraging to hear someone like Mike Evans. He really does seem to have German taped, right down to the last detail and it is very reassuring to know that this is possible, that German is an accessible language and not a closed book to foreigners. On the other hand, it is not really very easy to identify with that standard. Mike Evans makes it all seem so effortless that it is hard to imagine that he ever had to struggle with *der/die/das*, or the complexities of German word order, not to mention the actual words themselves.

Well, if it is any consolation, every foreign language learner, however advanced, has the occasional 'off' day – Mike Evans will be no exception. Likewise, when you are trying hard to improve your standard of German, there will always be times when you think you have set yourself an impossible task.

And that's the time to take stock of your progress in a positive way. Do not think about what lies ahead, yet to be mastered. Make a checklist of the ground you have already covered and feel confident about. If possible, find a speaker of German to measure yourself against. Listen to him or her and identify the words and constructions that you could handle successfully, too. However limited your German may be at the moment, there will still be areas which you have totally under control.

No handy German speaker to call upon? Well, look no further than Ulrich Kayser. First, try to remember the impression he made upon you when you watched the video sequence. Possibly not a particularly striking one. Although the sense of what he is saying is straightforward, his delivery is not as clear as it might be. His is a very even style. But now try to stand back from what he says in conversation with Frau Troscheit. Have a look at the transcript or replay the video sequence and ask yourself if you could have said the same thing. The chances are that you could. Take this sentence as an example:

Ja, seit Oktober ist also diese Pumpe jetzt beim VDE, und ich war vor ungefähr vier Wochen noch mal beim VDE, um noch einiges abzuklären.

If you look at it, you will see that it consists of three very simple ideas which Ulrich Kayser has joined together in an equally simple way. This is his technique all the way through. Here is another example: Frau Troscheit wants to make sure that the guarantee is for one year and Ulrich Kayser replies:

. . . steht jetzt da nicht, seh' ich grad, aber auf dem Prospekt, der im Moment in Vorbereitung ist, steht es drauf, und ich meine, es steht irgendwo auf der anderen Seite . . .

What can you learn from Ulrich Kayser's approach? Well, first and foremost, that German does not have to be difficult to be effective. Of course, it is going to take time for you to be as relaxed and unconstrained in conversation as someone like Ulrich Kayser. All the same, it is worth remembering that everyone brings their own personal stamp to the language they are speaking. Whatever you say in a foreign language will reflect something of you and the trick is really to focus on the areas of German where you feel confident, master them and then go on to something else.

Make the language work for you; do not make yourself work unnecessarily for the language.

Pocket phrasebook

Some of the key phrases that will be useful to you when presenting a new product to an established customer have been recorded on to the study cassette. You can practise your pronunciation by repeating them in the pause provided or you can use the pause to supply your own version in English and then compare it with our suggestion.

These are the phrases selected from this video sequence for you to learn:

– Wir haben 'was Schönes für Sie.
– Dieser Markt ist für uns und auch für Sie zu erschließen.
– Seh' ich nicht ganz so.
– Wir haben das Produkt auf der Kölner Messe präsentiert.
– Das werden wir wahrscheinlich machen, nach Ihrer Anregung.

Sequence summary

In this sequence showing two British companies extending their markets in Germany, you have covered the following language points:

● how to express likes and dislikes
● how to use adjectival endings with definite articles
● how to get things done
● how to say when things were/will be done
● how to present a new product.

Business guide – Retailing in Germany

Selling into a large retail chain would appear to offer many small UK manufacturers the ideal way into the German market. But how easy is it?: What are the pitfalls? In this next sequence, John Herbert M.D. of Knauber GmbH, offers his own ideas about German retailing, and advises would-be UK exporters, about the best way in to the market.

Generally speaking, the German people are very *fleißig* (hard working). They expect everything to be in working order and, as a nation, they are very disciplined; they like to keep to a timetable. They tend to take life more seriously than the British and are less flexible. They definitely do not share the same sense of humour. With these characteristics, it is no wonder that German manufacturers produce such excellent quality products: Mercedes, Siemens and Nixdorf, to name but three. All are at the top of their chosen fields.

However, Germans are often not good retailers. *Einzelhandel* (retailing) requires emotion and flexibility and these are not the strengths of the German people. German retailing lacks flair and imagination, has *wenig Erlebnis* (little excitement) and is *preisfixiert* (price dominated). The German consumer is more quality and price conscious than the British counterpart and there is less impulse buying. Again, everything is planned.

In England, many people enjoy shopping. It is seen as a pleasurable experience to browse around the shops and to spend one's hard-earned money. In Germany, the attitude is not quite the same: 'I must go shopping. I must go and buy some food'. Whereas the British tend to take time shopping, the German people seem to be in a rush. There may be several reasons for this:

● **Shopping hours.** Shopping hours are very restricted in Germany. It is *verboten* (forbidden) to open your store after 18.30 hrs. There is no late night shopping allowed. On Saturdays, the shops have to close at 14.00 hrs except on the first Saturday of the month and the last four Saturdays before Christmas. The shops may then remain open until 18.00 hrs. On public holidays, the shops must remain closed.

Consequently, *Einkaufen* (shopping) has to be done in a rush and the stores tend to be overcrowded in the late afternoons between 17.00 and 18.30 hrs and on Saturdays, as this is the only opportunity for working people to shop. There are plans to open one evening in the week and this could come into force within the next two years.

- **Target marketing – shop design.** Target marketing, or what the Germans call *Zielgruppen-Marketing* is much more widely practised in the United Kingdom than in Germany. It means knowing who your customers are. They could be young, middle-aged or older people, with a high or low income. The shops in Britain have much more flair and imagination and have a clearer *Erscheinungsbild* (corporate identity) than their German counterparts.

- **Price**. There is a great emphasis on *Preis* (price). Price is, of course, only one motivating factor for customers to buy. Nearly all advertisements and leaflets have the word *billig* (cheap).

  It is possible to show that *Preis-Leistungs-Verhaltnis* (value for money) is more important than price and that customers are willing to pay more if the presentation and services are better than the competitors'. So, it is not surprising that the financial results of even the largest, most successful, German retailers show a net profit margin of only one per cent of sales. In the United Kingdom, it is rarely less than 3%

on food and more than 6% on non-food companies.

- **Staff attitudes.** *Man dient nicht gern in Deutschland* (there is little love to serve in Germany) although there are many excellent training programmes. The *Auszubildende* (trainees) train for two years and have to pass an examination to qualify as a *Verkäufer* (sales assistant), but the status of shop assistants in the community is no higher than in the United Kingdom and therefore the retail trade does not attract the best people.

  The German managers are super-efficient when it comes to computer statements showing statistics such as sales, good or bad selling lines, rate of stock turnover, costs, etc., but, occasionally, the customer is forgotten.

- **Future trends.** Since the war, retailing has gone through two stages and has now entered the third.
  — Immediately after the war, it was a producer's market. Whatever was produced sold. The demand was there.
  — Then came the retailer's market. The shops were full of goods and of customers who needed to buy.
  — Today we have a consumer-dominated market. The consumer has the money, has already purchased most items and now has a wide choice of where to buy from.

With the emergence of modern technology, BTX (video text) for example, retailing is becoming more competitive. Only those retailers offering the consumer more than the competitor will survive. Service and customer care are becoming important ingredients of successful retailing. So we are now seeing the emergence of new *Fachmärkte* (specialist shops), where the retailer is offering a range and depth of specialist merchandise far greater than ever before.

The organisation of retailing in Germany

The continued growth of large retailing companies at the expense of the smaller independent groups is a notable feature in *Einzelhandel*. Germany has the following types of retail outlet:

- *Verbrauchermärkte* (hypermarkets)
- *Kaufhäuser* (department stores)
- *Fachmärkte* (specialist stores)
- *Tante-Emma-Läden* (small, all-purpose-stores, corner shops)
- *Versandhandel* (mail order)

- *Verbrauchermärkte* (**hypermarkets/ superstores**). Similar to hypermarkets and superstores in the United Kingdom. These stores are generally on 'green field sites'. They are large retail units, normally over 2,500 square metres in sales area. The characteristics of these stores are: free parking, everything under one roof and a central checkout.

   The problem of car parking in the inner cities means that this type of store is very successful. However, the number is not likely to increase because of government restrictions on building.
- *Kaufhäuser* (**departmental stores**). Situated in the high street, four groups dominate market share: 'Karstadt', 'Kaufhof', 'Horten' and 'Hertie'. There are also private department stores that tend to be linked to a buying group such as 'Kaufring' in Düsseldorf.

   The department stores grew very rapidly in the 1950–1960s, but with the upsurge of *Verbrauchermarkte* they have lost a lot of ground. Total market share of the *Kaufhäuser* has dropped from over 10% in 1975 to approximately 7% today.

   Many such stores failed to move with the times and became less attractive to the consumer. However, they have now woken up and there has been a massive investment over the past two or three years. The *'alles unter einem Dach'* (everything under one roof) concept with its many departments is dead. There is now greater specialisation.

   Despite the enormous potential of these stores, the net profit margins are barely over 1%.
- *Fachmärkte* (**specialist shops**) There are many large specialist stores such as D.I.Y., furniture, clothing warehouses and, more recently, toys. These stores carry a very wide range of products in their chosen fields.

   As in the UK, there are thriving shopping centres in the inner cities. Shops selling items such as specialised clothing, jewellery, cosmetics and books flourish in these locations.

   Rather regrettably some excellent specialist retail shops are being driven out of the High Street because of high rents. In their place you are likely to find fast food restaurants and amusement arcades.
- *Tante-Emma-Läden* (**corner shops**) As in the United Kingdom (but less so) you will find the much loved 'Tante Emma Läden'. These general, all-purpose but very small stores are used as a 'filler' between visits to larger hypermarkets or department stores.
- *Versandhandel* (**mail order**) One of the areas with the highest growth rate in retailing and expected to continue due to the increasing use of home shopping by video text. The central buying power of these organisations makes them an attractive target for UK exporters.

The opportunities for British exporters in Germany

The German people and, in particular, younger Germans, do not differentiate between foreign and home products. Three of the most successful retailers are foreigners: IKEA of Sweden, Benetton of Italy and Laura Ashley.

The British have a very good image in Germany and are not seen as *Ausländer* (foreigners) as the Turks or Yugoslavs are.

Good British products, such as jam and biscuits, and drinks such as tea (exported from Britain),

whisky, sherry and gin, are very popular. However, British foods are not regarded as 'gourmet delights' in Germany.

Traditional British clothing and footwear enjoy an excellent reputation. The clothing firm Burberry is considered one of the best.

However, the industrial chaos in the car industry in the 1960s had disastrous effects and has almost totally destroyed our reputation for quality cars delivered on time. We are still considered to be a nation of strikers and, when it comes to delivery, not too reliable.

One ray of light is that Jaguar, considered unreliable some years ago, has had excellent press coverage and the image has improved dramatically so sales are on the increase.

How can a UK producer sell into German retailing?

Before selling in Germany, or anywhere in the world, you must first examine the market. The following questions must be answered:

- Is there a market for my products?
- Are there similar products on the market?
- If so, where are they sold?
- At what price? Research the market to ascertain the prices at which similar products are being sold to the retailer.

Distribution

The biggest problem of all, compared with the United Kingdom, is that of distribution. Distribution of goods into retail outlets is much more streamlined in Germany. Manufacturers, large retailing companies and buying groups tend to have regional depots situated up and down the country. It is not at all rare to deliver goods at two days' notice or certainly, in most cases, no longer than a week. Because retailers do not like to carry a lot of stock at any one time it is essential for a UK producer who wants to export to Germany to set up regional depots or find an agent. There may, of course, be the possibility of delivering directly from England to major retailers on a regular basis, but that could be unreliable. If, for example, there is a strike anywhere along the line, your reputation as the supplier will suffer. Should you decide to set up your own distribution service, you could always start by opening up one depot, to 'test market' before investing heavily in a national market.

Purchasing groups

Central and group purchasing in Germany is more developed than in the UK. These groups consist of independent traders who join together on a voluntary basis for the purpose of bulk buying. The total market share of these groups is a mighty 25% of the market. For information about group purchasing, contact the German Chamber of Commerce in London.

Approach to the buyers – tips for the producer

Whenever you are dealing with German buyers, remember that you must do so professionally. It is easier to win on the German lottery than to find a British producer who knows the German market, understands the German buying mentality and speaks fluent German! Part of any investment a British producer must make when entering the German market is to ensure that the company has employees who speak *gutes Deutsch*.

Here is a recent illustration. The Export Director from a UK producer of disposable overalls came into the office of a company in Bonn. Unfortunately he could not speak German but the German company just happened to have someone who spoke English. They thought he had an excellent product. When they enquired about the wholesale price he said that if the company bought 200 or more the price would be DM 9. (At least he had worked out the price 'frei Haus' [free delivery] and in DM.) Then they asked him what price they would have to pay if they bought 1,000 or 10,000. He said the price would be the same, DM 9. For the German buyer this is unbelievable.

He expects the price to be cheaper if the quantities are greater. Also remember that German buyers (and maybe buyers all over the world) must feel that they have 'won' at the end of the *Gespräch* (talk) and they must feel that they have squeezed out more than the seller was prepared to sell for. Therefore, always ensure that you have some *Luft* (room for manœuvre) when you state the conditions of purchase.

Price lists, product information

Always have a price list *frei Haus* (free delivery). The list should contain all relevant information giving an accurate description of the products. All product information accompanying the price list must be in German. Nothing annoys buyers more than when they have the necessary interest in a product and there is no product information available in German.

Depending upon the importance of the company, buyers expect a *Rabatt* (discount) from the price list. So ensure that your price list is priced for your smallest customers. You may then offer a larger customer, for example, price list minus 10% *Rabatt*.

Skonto – terms of payment

The next question is 'How many days can I have the goods before I pay?'. The British producer will no doubt have thought this out. Let us say 21 days. The good buyer will try and extend this. 'How much *Skonto* (discount on payment) do I get?', will be the next question. '3 or 5%?' Be prepared.

Jahresbonus (annual bonus)

The next question may be „Wieviel Jahresbonus?". It is fairly normal that you agree to purchase a certain amount from a producer and couple this with an annual bonus. For example, buy up to DM 200,000 and you get 2% *zurück* (back), over DM 200,000 and you get 3% *zurück*, over DM 300,000 and you get 4% *zurück*.

WKZ Werbekostenzuschuß (contribution to advertising costs)

WKZ is a payment some retailing companies require for promoting your products, although the exact nature or cost of the promotion may not be precisely specified. Try to avoid WKZ. If you have to make a payment, treat the money as written off. Then you will not be disappointed later if your product is not promoted or not promoted enough.

Conclusion

Germany is an exciting country to live in. There is a very high standard of living and the market is tremendous and, above all, open.

Bearing in mind the differences between German and British retailing, the opportunities for British exports are excellent. It needs only a bit of grit and determination, some knowledge of German, and, of course, a very professional approach.

John Herbert M.D.,   *Viel Spaß!*
Knauber GmbH

Business Magazine

For a nation that doesn't like shopping, the average German is induced to part with a lot of cash through retail outlets. What are the best channels for UK suppliers to target and how do you convince a German buyer? Listen to Business Magazine 5 and find out.

The board meeting

„Wer möchte das Wort ergreifen?"

The video sequence
Der Video-Abschnitt

In this sequence, we eavesdrop on a board meeting. PCM Fischbach is a joint German/Dutch company manufacturing plastic containers. Its UK subsidiary is in Runcorn. The company holds its board meetings in all three countries; this one is being hosted by the German parent company at Ründeroth, near Cologne.

There are two particular features of this meeting which are of interest. One is its modern, international outlook. More and more companies are experiencing a situation where they are reporting to an overseas board or, indeed, where a company based abroad is reporting to the UK. As a result, senior management is becoming conversant with market conditions, government legislation and company structure in foreign countries. This is evident in the video sequence where the conversation hinges upon the relative strengths of the mark and the pound against the dollar, the manufacturing capacity of the Canadian subsidiary and the company's performance in the UK market.

At the same time, there are glimpses into traditional aspects of Germany company organisation. For example, Herr Schröder, the Group Chairman, lays particular emphasis on his company's total independence. Listening to him describe the company's various departments, makes it clear that PCM Fischbach likes to be responsible for almost every stage of the process, even to building its own machinery. That way the company can guarantee the quality of its end-product.

The twin strands running through this meeting, the international and the German, are also reflected

HORST SCHRÖDER
Geschäftsführer
der Fischbach Beteiligungsgesellschaft mbH

5250 ENGELSKIRCHEN
RÜNDEROTH

Telefon 02263 / 5057·
Telex 884745
Telefax 02263 / 60358

in the language of the board meeting. Though conducted in German, the occasional English expression creeps in – like the term 'board meeting' itself. And the meeting is conducted in a way that is entirely familiar to a British participant – orderly but not always formal.

For Chelvin Hibbert, the only British participant at the meeting, this familiarity, both with the structure of the meeting and the items under discussion, is a real help. The main item on the agenda is a matter of direct and crucial importance to the UK company. Chelvin has to defend his company's interests with only limited German at his disposal. But this is a clear example of how a little goes a long way. Everyone is willing to help him out because he is making the effort.

Working with German companies is a good incentive for British business people to get down to learning German. Many have already found that it pays dividends in terms of better relationships. In the early stages, everyone finds operating in a foreign language a strain – and that goes for Germans having to speak English, too. So, if you make the effort to speak German, it is likely to be appreciated. There is, however, one risk and that is that your German colleagues will assume that your German is better than it is. Chelvin Hibbert handles that situation by asking his German colleagues to speak more slowly. You will have your own way of dealing with the same situation; whatever you choose to say, provided you make the effort, it will get easier all the time.

Key words

Here is a list of the key words in German used at the board meeting. Study the list and the meaning in this context, so that you can follow the video more easily. The words are listed in the order in which they occur.

das Produktionswerk (-e)	production plant
der Jahresverlauf (-e)	year's progress
die Zulieferung (-en)	supply
die Erweiterung (-en)	expansion
die Berücksichtigung (en)	consideration
die Erfahrung (-en)	experience
das Hauptwerk (-e)	main plant
das Hauptprodukt (-e)	main product
die Stückzahl (-en)	number of units
der Tagespunkt (-e)	item on the agenda
das Ergebnis (-sse)	result
der Verkaufsumsatz (¨e)	sales turnover
der Lieferant (-en, -en)	supplier
die Entwicklung (en)	development
der Hersteller (-)	manufacturer
die Einkäufe (plural)	purchases
der Gewinn (-e)	profit
die Kostenrechnung	costing
die Frachtkosten (plural)	freight costs
die Anlage (-n)	plant
die Marktprognose (-n)	market forecast
die Fertigungskosten (plural)	production costs
der Beschluß (¨sse)	decision
die Entscheidung (-en)	decision

Practising listening and understanding
Hörverständnisübungen

You will find a workplan to help you in Sequence 1, page 11.

Information

Exercise A

What are they saying?

die Eröffnung

1. Worüber sprechen sie heute?

bei dem Rundgang

2. Welche Industriezweige nennt Herr Schröder?

3. Wie steht es mit Patenten?

4. Wieviele Teile produziert CPM-Fischbach pro Tag aus diesem Werk?

5. Wie unabhängig ist die Firma?

Punkt 4

6. Was ist Punkt 4?

7. Was möchte Werner Brüning von Chelvin Hibbert wissen?

8. Beim letzten Board Meeting wurde schon darauf hingewiesen, daß Herr Brüning Untersuchungen durchführt. Mit wem führt er sie durch?

Deutschland–Kanada–England

9. Warum denkt Herr Brüning daran, auf Lieferungen aus dem kanadischen Werk überzugehen?

10. Wie steht es mit den Einkäufen aus Deutschland?

11. Welche Bedeutung hat das Verhältnis des kanadischen Dollars zum Pfund?

12. Wie steht es mit den Frachtkosten von Kanada nach England? Was hat man festgestellt?

13. Was zeigen die Marktprognosen Herrn Hibbert?

Answers

die Eröffnung

1. Sie sprechen über *den bisherigen Jahresverlauf* der Produktion des englischen Werkes.

bei dem Rundgang

2. Wir (stellen) Kunststoffteile für *die medizinische und die pharmazeutische Industrie* her.

3. Wir haben *eine große Anzahl von Patenten* für diese Teile.

4. Wir fabrizieren sie in großen Stückzahlen, *zirka dreihunderttausend Stück* pro Tag aus diesem Werk.

5. Wir sind *völlig unabhängig*.

Punkt 4

6. Das sind *die finanziellen Ergebnisse*.

7. Er möchte wissen, *ob es möglich wäre*, bei den Kunden *mehr Kartuschen zu verkaufen*.

8. Herr Brüning (führt) Untersuchungen *mit Maschinenlieferanten* (durch) (und) *auch mit unseren eigenen Technikern*.

Deutschland–Kanada–England

9. *Die Untersuchungen haben . . . positive Ergebnisse gezeigt*.

10. Die Einkäufe aus Deutschland *werden immer teurer*.

11. Das Verhältnis des kanadischen Dollars zum Pfund (hat gezeigt, *daß man*) *von Kanada aus günstig nach England liefern kann*.

12. . . ., *daß die Frachtkosten von Kanada nach England geringer* (sind) *als die Kosten von Deutschland nach England*.

13. Die Marktprognosen, die uns vorliegen, . . . zeigen, *daß er im nächsten Jahr mit steigenden Verkäufen rechnen kann*.

Summary

Exercise B

What are they saying?

	Possible answers
1. Warum ist es nicht möglich, neue Maschinen sofort zu kaufen?	1. Die Maschinen werden speziell für CPM-Fischbach hergestellt. Dies dauert zwischen neun Monaten und einem Jahr nach der Bestellung.
2. Wieso entscheidet das Board Meeting, Teile aus Kanada nach Runcorn zu importieren?	2. Das Werk in Runcorn hat nicht genug Produktionskapazität für den jetzigen Markt, deswegen muß es importieren, und zwar entweder aus Kanada oder aus Deutschland. Trotz der Frachtkosten ist es möglich, aus Kanada nach Runcorn zu importieren und mit Gewinn zu arbeiten. Diese Lösung ist aber nur eine Brückenlösung.
3. Warum braucht Chelvin Hibbert neue Maschinen und neue Technologie?	3. Das Werk Runcorn braucht sie, um seine Produktion zu erweitern und um seine Fertigungskosten zu senken.

Close listening

Exercise C

We recommend that you only attempt this exercise if you need, or are keen, to understand the precise details of a discussion. Instead of doing the exercise as a listening comprehension exercise, you may like to try it as an exercise in reading comprehension. You are looking for what the words in italics refer to:

1. *dreihunderttausend Stück*	1. . . . ein Kunststoff-Spritzgußwerk, in dem wir . . . technische Teile herstellen . . . *Wir fabrizieren sie in großen Stückzahlen, zirka dreihunderttausend Stück* pro Tag aus diesem Werk.
2. *über sechzig Prozent*	2. . . . und *(wir) exportieren über sechzig Prozent* in den europäischen und den außereuropäischen Raum.
3. *Punkt vier*	3. . . . dann kommen wir zu *Punkt vier. Das sind die finanziellen Ergebnisse* . . .
4. *von einem Jahr*	4. . . . Es kann nur eine Notlösung sein für *die Zeitdauer von einem Jahr.*
5. für *wenigstens ein Jahr*	5. . . . Das heißt also, daß Sie für *wenigstens ein Jahr Liefersicherheit aus Kanada* (bekommen können)?
6. *das* wir nicht nachvollziehen können	6. . . . *das Marktgeschehen im Container-Bereich, das* wir nicht nachvollziehen können . . .

7. *das* müssen wir einfach ausnützen

8. *sie* ergeben ihm die richtigen Stückzahlen

9. *die* uns vorliegen
10. das wir *damit* Klarheit geschaffen haben

7. . . . *das Marktgeschehen im Container-Bereich, . . . das eben für uns heute günstig ist.* Das müssen wir einfach ausnützen.
8. (Herr Hibbert legt Wert darauf), *die nächsten Anlagen modernster Technologie* zu bekommen, weil *sie* ihm die richtigen Stückzahlen ergeben.
9. . . . *die Marktprognosen, die* uns vorliegen . . .
10. . . . *wir lasten die Kapazität in Kanada bis ganz zum Ende aus . . .* dann bin ich der Meinung, daß wir *damit* Klarheit geschaffen haben.

Consolidation
Konsolidierung

In this sequence, the language points for consolidation are:

● *werden* – the versatile verb
● possessive adjectives.

Werden – the versatile verb

You probably know *werden* as the German for *to become*. That is one of its main uses, as in this sentence taken from the video:

Wir können feststellen, daß die Einkäufe aus Deutschland immer teurer *werden*.
We can see that buying from Germany *is becoming* more and more expensive.

But *werden* is a very versatile verb which has at least two other uses, both of which are much in evidence in the board meeting sequence

The first use is a fairly straightforward one. Start by looking at these sentences taken from the video:

Herr Dr. Meyer wird nachher Näheres sagen . . .
Afterwards Herr Dr. Meyer will say more . . .

Herr Brüning wird etwas über die geplanten neuen Technologien sagen . . .
Herr Brüning will say something about the new technologies planned . . .

In these examples, *werden* combines with an infinitive to express something that will happen – in other words, the **future tense**. It is possible that you have not really worked on the future before because, like English, German often uses the present tense to convey the same idea:

I am having a meeting with the supplier next week.
Ich habe nächste Woche ein Gespräch mit dem Lieferanten.

Practice A

Using *werden* and the appropriate verb, put these sentences into German:

1. We shall discuss the financial report.
2. Sales to the Dutch market will increase.

Answers

1. Wir werden den Finanzreport besprechen.
2. Die Verkäufe an den holländischen Markt werden steigen.

3. The Canadian company will supply the British company.
4. We shall take the decision today.
5. We shall place the order next week.

3. Das kanadische Werk wird das britische Werk beliefern.
4. Wir werden heute den Beschluß fassen.
5. Wir werden nächste Woche den Auftrag geben.

The second use of *werden* occurs in sentences like these ones taken from the board meeting:

. . . als Hauptprodukt Kartuschen, die von uns *erfunden wurden*.
. . . daß in England . . . kein großer Gewinn *erzielt werden* kann.

If you translate these sentences into English, you will see that here *werden* has changed its meaning,

. . . containers which *were invented* by us
. . . that a large profit cannot *be made* in England

In these examples, *werden* combines with a **past participle** to express the idea that something is being done or was done – in other words, the **passive voice**.

The passive voice

The passive is used in German in the same way as in English; all you need to know is the way the other verb changes in the past tense. Take *kaufen* as an example:

How do you say *I have bought* in German?

The answer is:
Ich habe gekauft

and *gekauft* is the part you are looking for when you want to form the passive.

Practice A

Now practise forming the passive with these verbs. First, work out the past tense form and then start each answer with *es wird* . . .

1. produzieren	produziert	1. Es wird produziert.
2. nehmen	genommen	2. Es wird genommen.
3. her/stellen	hergestellt	3. Es wird hergestellt.
4. vergessen	vergessen	4. Es wird vergessen.
5. zu/machen	zugemacht	5. Es wird zugemacht.

Practice B

Look through the transcript and note all the examples of the passive that you can find. Take your time on this – there are some traps and you could easily mix up a true passive with something else. . . . (More about that later.) When you have finished, study the list of all the passives used in this sequence carefully, then go on to Practice C.

Practice C

How do you say the following sentences in the other language?
   You are reporting to your MD who wants to know the state of play of a number of different company activities. Say that they are all in hand. Again, you can tackle this exercise either from English or from German.

If you prefer to begin from the English ask yourself how a German would have said this:

1. The financial report is being sent to the Canadian company.
2. The capacity in Holland is being increased.
3. The freight costs are being studied.
4. The tools are being manufactured.
5. The machine is being ordered.

If you decide to begin from the German, ask yourself how you would say this in English:

1. Der Finanzreport wird an das kanadische Werk geschickt.
2. Die Kapazität in Holland wird erweitert.
3. Die Frachtkosten werden untersucht.
4. Die Werkzeuge werden produziert.
5. Die Maschine wird in Auftrag gegeben.

How did you get on? Simple really, nicht wahr? And saying that things were done, or have been done – that is, referring to them in the past – is also straightforward. Hold on to the past participle because you still need that, but in the past *es wird* becomes *es wurde*.

Try it out with the verbs in Practice A:

1. produzieren	produziert	1. Es wurde produziert.
2. nehmen	genommen	2. Es wurde genommen.
3. her/stellen	hergestellt	3. Es wurde hergestellt.
4. vergessen	vergessen	4. Es wurde vergessen.
5. zu/machen	zugemacht	5. Es wurde zugemacht.

Practice D

You are now able to confirm to your MD that you have acted on all instructions. Start either from English or from German, as you prefer.

If you prefer to begin from the English, ask yourself how a German would have said this.

1. The financial report was sent to the Canadian company.
2. The capacity in Holland was increased.
3. The freight costs were studied.
4. The tools were manufactured.
5. The machine was ordered.

If you decide to begin from the German, ask yourself how you would say this in English.

1. Der Finanzreport wurde an das kanadische Werk geschickt.
2. Die Kapazität in Holland wurde erweitert.
3. Die Frachtkosten wurden untersucht.
4. Die Werkzeuge wurden produziert.
5. Die Maschine wurde in Auftrag gegeben.

Here is a list of all the passives used in this sequence:

Passive

. . . weil mit dem Pfund sehr schlecht eingekauft werden kann
. . . daß also in England kein großer Gewinn erzielt werden kann
. . . daß die Kapazitäten dort erweitert werden müssen
. . . die . . . Maschine, die im Werk Runcorn aufgestellt wird

. . . dann kann alles beschleunigt werden
. . . daß diese Maschine . . . sofort in Auftrag gegeben wird
. . . daß die notwendigen Werkzeuge dazu disponiert werden
. . . daß diese ganzen Dinge beschleunigt werden

Well done, if your notes match this list exactly. They may not, which leaves you with the question of how to categorise the non-passives. Well, they could be futures, so here is the list of all the futures used in this sequence.

Future
. . . *Herr Dr. Meyer wird nachher Näheres sagen können*
. . . *Herr Brüning wird im Verlauf des Board Meetings etwas über die geplanten neuen Technologien*
. . . *sagen*
. . . *und das wird Herrn Hibbert besonders interessieren*
. . . *und die Marktsituation in England wird sich . . . verschärfen*
. . . *daß es noch im Verlauf des Tages sein wird*
. . . *wir werden für Runcorn diese Anlage fest in Auftrag geben*

Still some examples left which do not fit in? Did you fall into the trap hinted at earlier. Check carefully. They must include:

● *werden* + past participle as a passive
 or
● *werden* + infinitive as a future

Do they meet these criteria?

What you might have is a description of a situation or object which uses a past participle but uses *sein* instead of *werden*. There are several examples in this sequence. It is very easy for English speakers to confuse these because they are so close to the way an English passive is formed.
Here is the list of examples of this construction taken from the scene.

Descriptions with a past participle
. . . *ein Jahr früher als ursprünglich geplant war.*
. . . *eine Maschine, die sehr spezifisch auf unsere Belange zugeschnitten ist.*
. . . *daß die Kapazitäten . . . durch die Lieferungen nach England ausgelastet sind.*
. . . *so daß Herr Hibbert darauf angewiesen ist.*

Remember, you can use this construction to describe a situation, so it is useful as a way of extending your language range.

Possessive adjectives

In the semi-formal atmosphere of a board meeting it is hardly surprising that there are few occasions when speakers use a possessive adjective. Here, in fact, it is only Herr Schröder who uses them, and he only uses two different ones:

– **unser** *Rechtsvertreter*
– mit . . . einem angeschlossenen Maschinenbau, in dem wir **unsere eigenen Vorrichtungen** bauen
– Untersuchungen *mit* **unseren** *eigenen Technikern*
– wir fordern eine Maschine, die sehr spezifisch *auf* **unsere** *Belange hin* zugeschnitten ist
– die Frachtkosten . . . *bis zu* **Ihrem** *Werk*
– einer der wichtigsten Punkte **unseres** *heutigen Gesprächs*
– ich beglückwünsche Sie *zu* **Ihrem** *fortgeschrittenen Deutsch*
– wir müssen uns bemühen, **unser** *Englisch zu verbessern*

Normally you will want to use more. They enable you to personalise what you are saying by talking of **my** company, **your** order, **his** opinion, **her** objective, **its** advantage, **our** aim, **their** needs. As you would expect with an adjective in German, the ending of the possessive adjective changes depending on the function of the word in the sentence.
Also, adjectives following the possessive adjective and preceding the noun will change their endings.
Although you will nearly always be understood even if you do not get the endings of possessive adjectives strictly correct, you must make a real effort to get them right. You will not be criticised for getting them wrong, but you will certainly be awarded lots of 'brownie points' when you get them right! These are the points that go towards the overall rating of you, your company, your product – your chances!
If you feel that possessive adjectives are an area of the German language where you do not have too

much of a problem, try the exercises below. If, on the other hand, you feel you need to revise possessive adjectives, have a look at the Grammar Guide on page 167 first, before you attempt the exercises.

Possessive adjectives checklist

- What is the **gender** of the thing I am talking about?
- What is the **case**?
- Does the **adjectival ending** change?

Practice A

What is the correct ending for the possessive adjective in the following sentences? In this exercise you are shown which possessive adjective you should work with and whether the appropriate noun is *der*, *die*, or *das*.

1. Das Hauptwerk ist in Ründeroth – wie finden Sie *sein--* Kapazität?   die
2. *Mein--* Techniker konnte kein Deutsch.   der
3. Ich möchte *Ihr--* Rechtsvertreter sprechen.   der
4. Ich habe ihm zu *sein--* Patent beglückwünscht.   das
5. Wann beginnen Sie mit *Ihr--* Kapazitätserweiterung?   die
6. Hoffentlich ist dann Schluß mit *Ihr--* Problemen.   das
7. Das ist der Vorteil *Ihr--* Kunststoffs.   der
8. Hier ist das Hauptprodukt – *sein--* Möglichkeiten sind enorm!   die
9. Was hat die Firma mit *ihr--* Finanzreport gemacht?   der
10. *Sein--* Produktionswerk war in Runcorn.   das
11. Kennen Sie die Organisation *ihr--* Konstruktionsabteilung?   die
12. Das war der wichtigste Punkt *mein--* Gesprächs.   das
13. *Ihr--* Entwicklungsabteilung ist sehr modern.   die
14. Kennen Sie *unser--* Verfahren?   das
15. Was halten Sie von *ihr--* Maschinen?   die
16. Wir wollen *unser--* Ergebnisse zeigen.   das

1. Das Hauptwerk ist in Ründeroth – wie finden Sie *seine* Kapazität?
2. *Mein* Techniker konnte kein Deutsch.
3. Ich möchte *Ihren* Rechtsvertreter sprechen.
4. Ich habe ihm zu *seinem* Patent beglückwünscht.
5. Wann beginnen Sie mit *Ihrer* Kapazitätserweiterung?
6. Hoffentlich ist dann Schluß mit *Ihren* Problemen.
7. Das ist der Vorteil *Ihres* Kunststoffs.
8. Hier ist das Hauptprodukt – *seine* Möglichkeiten sind enorm!
9. Was hat die Firma mit *ihrem* Finanzreport gemacht?
10. *Sein* Produktionswerk war in Runcorn.
11. Kennen Sie die Organisation *ihrer* Konstruktionsabteilung?
12. Das war der wichtigste Punkt *meines* Gesprächs.
13. *Ihre* Entwicklungsabteilung ist sehr modern.
14. Kennen Sie *unser* Verfahren?
15. Was halten Sie von *ihren* Maschinen?
16. Wir wollen *unsere* Ergebnisse zeigen.

Practice B

What do I do with the adjectives which follow possessive adjectives? Put the adjectives numbered below into the corresponding sentence in Practice A:

1. heutig	1. Das Hauptwerk ist in Ründeroth – wie finden Sie *seine heutige Kapazität?*
2. bisherig	2. *Mein bisheriger Techniker* konnte kein Deutsch.
3. jetzig	3. Ich möchte *Ihren jetzigen Rechtsvertreter* sprechen.
4. zusätzlich	4. Ich habe ihm zu *seinem zusätzlichen Patent* beglückwünscht.
5. nächst	5. Wann beginnen Sie mit *Ihrer nächsten Kapazitätserweiterung?*
6. bekannt	6. Hoffentlich ist dann Schluß mit *Ihren bekannten Problemen.*
7. eigen	7. Das ist der Vorteil *Ihres eigenen Kunststoffs.*
8. technisch	8. Hier ist das Hauptprodukt – *seine technischen Möglichkeiten* sind enorm!
9. groß	9. Was hat die Firma mit *ihrem großen Finanzreport* gemacht?
10. ursprünglich	10. *Sein ursprüngliches Produktionswerk* war in Runcorn.
11. europäisch	11. Kennen Sie die Organisation *ihrer europäischen Konstruktionsabteilung?*
12. geplant	12. Das war der wichtigste Punkt *meines geplanten Gesprächs.*
13. kanadisch	13. *Ihre kanadische Entwicklungsabteilung* ist sehr modern.
14. spezifisch	14. Kennen Sie *unser spezifisches Verfahren?*
15. deutsch	15. Was halten Sie von *ihren deutschen Maschinen?*
16. finanziell	16. Wir wollen *unsere finanziellen Ergebnisse* zeigen.

Practice C

Finally to help you consolidate possessive adjectives, you should be able to express other ideas in a personal way. As you listen and re-listen to the various encounters on the video, you will notice that it is particularly necessary for you to be able to handle statements about **our** and **your**.

This is an exercise which you may approach from either German or English, depending on your level of confidence and/or your actual needs in German.

How can you express the following ideas in German?	How can you express the following ideas in English?
1. We give our German partners ideas on how they can improve their products for our market.	1. Wir geben unseren deutschen Partnern Ideen, wie sie ihre Produkte für unseren Markt verbessern können.
2. These tasks anchor us to our customers.	2. Diese Aufgaben verankern uns bei unseren Kunden.
3. Here are some of our machines.	3. Hier sind einige unserer Maschinen.

4. The special feature about our machine is . . .
5. That is guaranteed by our sales conditions.

6. I have been to your parent company.
7. In the case of our machines . . .
8. Can I talk to you about our articles?

9. I would like to hear about your advertising.
10. Our advertising agency wants this theme.
11. What about your delivery times?
12. Our sales figures are very good at the moment.

13. My name is . . .
14. Before your visit I had the sales figures printed out.
15. You were speaking about your new development.
16. I assume that our prices will not rise?

17. Let us begin with your articles.
18. We will remain your customer.
19. That is a big advantage for your future customer.
20. That is our aim too.

4. Das Besondere an unserer Maschine ist . . .
5. Das wird durch unsere Verkaufsbedingungen gewährleistet.

6. Ich war bei Ihrer Muttergesellschaft.
7. In dem Fall von unseren Maschinen . . .
8. Darf ich mit Ihnen über unsere Artikel sprechen?

9. Ich möchte von Ihrer Werbung hören.
10. Unsere Werbeagentur möchte dieses Thema.
11. Wie steht es mit Ihren Lieferzeiten?
12. Unsere Verkaufszahlen sind sehr gut im Moment.

13. Mein Name ist . . .
14. Vor Ihrem Besuch habe ich die Verkaufszahlen ausdrucken lassen.
15. Sie sprachen über Ihre neue Entwicklung.

16. Ich nehme an, daß unsere Preise nicht steigen werden?

17. Fangen wir bei Ihren Artikeln an.
18. Wir bleiben Ihr Kunde.
19. Das ist ein großer Vorteil für Ihren zukünftigen Kunden.
20. Das ist auch unser Ziel.

Development
Erweiterung

In this sequence on participating in a formal meeting, the development exercises concentrate on:

- stating reasons and causes
- the language of meetings.

Stating reasons and causes

Stating your position in a meeting also means explaining it. This meeting is no exception. The company is faced with a situation which requires decisions to be made and reasons to be stated. Let's look at three different ways the people attending this meeting state their reasons.

They are:

weil	because
so daß	so that
um . . . zu	in order to

Exercise A

Look through the transcript and note all the sentences containing *weil*, and *so daß*.

Now check against this list:

. . . weil es sich vor Monaten abzeichnete, daß . . .

. . . weil das Pfund sich vom Kurs her sehr stabil erweist . . .

. . . weil der Wechselkurs . . . so viel niedriger ist . . .

. . . weil sie ihm auch die richtigen Stückzahlen ergeben . . .

. . . weil sie von der Kostensituation her nicht so günstig sind . . .

. . . so daß also auch das englische Werk noch Profit machen kann

. . . so daß Herr Hibbert darauf angewiesen ist, . . .

What do these two constructions have in common? Well, a quick glance will tell you that it is the position of the verb:

. . . weil es sich vor Monaten abzeichnete, . . .

. . . so daß auch das englische Werk . . . noch Profit machen kann

So the first thing to remember when using these two constructions is that the verb goes to the **end** of the clause.

Exercise B

How do you say the following sentences in the other language?

The following exercise can be approached from English or German, depending on your needs and ability.

If you take English as your starting point, imagine that you are presenting a report to a company meeting. Give your explanations for the following activities in German. Start each explanation with

We are importing from Canada because . . .

1. — the British company needs new technology.

2. — the Canadian company can deliver more cheaply.
3. — the exchange rate is so favourable.
4. — the freight costs are much lower.
5. — buying from Germany is getting more and more expensive.

If you prefer to approach this exercise from the German, ask yourself how you would give the following information in English. Start each explanation with

Wir importieren aus Kanada,

1. — weil das britische Werk neue Technologie braucht.
2. — weil das kanadische Werk billiger liefern kann.
3. — weil der Wechselkurs so günstig ist.
4. — weil die Frachtkosten viel niedriger sind.
5. — weil die Einkäufe aus Deutschland immer teurer werden.

Exercise C

Again, this exercise can be tackled from English or German.

If you start with English, imagine you are reporting on a course of action to a company meeting. Explain the effects of this course of action in German.

The company is buying new machinery so that . . .

1. — production will increase.
2. — the British company can make a profit.

3. — we do not depend on imports from Germany.

4. — we do not put a strain on the capacity in Canada.
5. — we can exploit the market situation.

If you prefer to approach this exercise from German, ask yourself how you would describe this course of action in English.

Die Firma kauft neue Maschinen ein,

1. — so daß die Produktion steigt.
2. — so daß das britische Werk Profit machen kann.
3. — so daß wir nicht auf Importe aus Deutschland angewiesen sind.
4. — so daß wir die Kapazität in Kanada nicht auslasten.
5. — so daß wir die Marktsituation ausnützen können.

Exercise D

Look at this sentence taken from the transcript:

In Kanada haben wir die Kapazität, *um das zu machen*.

um . . . zu is a useful way of expressing something that you, your company or someone else wants to do – provided that consistency is maintained right through the sentence. In other words, you can use it to say something like:

We have the capacity *to do* that

but you cannot use it to say something like:

We have the capacity for the company to do that

There are two more points to bear in mind with *um . . . zu*. First, the verb goes to the **end** of the sentence or clause. Second, the form of the verb never changes. It always remains in the **infinitive**, as you can see in these sentences based on the video sequence.

Wir importieren aus Kanada, *um unsere Kosten zu senken*.

Wir kaufen neue Maschinen, *um mehr Kartuschen zu fabrizieren*.

If the verb is **separable**, the infinitive will separate to accommodate *zu*, as in these examples:

Er lernt deutsch, *um am Board Meeting teilzunehmen*.

Wir kaufen diese Maschine, *um sie im Werk Runcorn aufzustellen*.

You can approach this exercise from English or German. If you start with English, imagine you are advising a board meeting on possible courses of action. How would you make these points in German?

We must invest in new technology in order to . . .

1. — extend the capacity.
2. — increase sales.
3. — make a profit.
4. — exploit the market situation.
5. — reduce our costs.

If you prefer to take German as your starting point, ask yourself how you would express the following ideas in English.

Wir müssen neue Technologie kaufen,

1. — um die Kapazität zu erweitern.
2. — um den Verkauf zu steigen.
3. — um ein Profit zu machen.
4. — um die Marktsituation auszunützen.
5. — um unsere Kosten zu senken.

You should now feel more confident about explaining your position, and be ready to move on to the language of meetings.

The language of meetings

As you look at the way Herr Schröder steers the discussion politely but firmly through the various items on the agenda, it is probably difficult to imagine yourself, as a non-native speaker of German, ever being able to perform at this level. Have a look, though, at the words and phrases Herr Schröder uses at different stages of the meeting. They are not difficult in themselves.

Although we meet them here in the limited and specific situation of a board meeting, they are the phrases which enable you to take the lead and keep control in most business meetings in German.

We recommend you work through this exercise as follows:

- **read** the words and phrases through, section by section,
- **ask** yourself what an English person would say in the same situation. To help you do this we have laid out the words and phrases in such a way that you can test yourself on this task,
- **check** with our suggestions whether your

version conveys the same message,

- **identify** the words and phrases which you feel you can handle confidently and accurately,
- **adapt** those words and phrases to your own situation – the dialogue chain will also help you to do this,
- **check** that you are handling them correctly and

accurately. You may need a German speaker to help you here.

The right-hand column is what could have been said in English in the same situation. Be careful not to think of this answer as right and any deviation on your part as therefore wrong. You should be asking yourself whether your version conveys the same message.

Stage 1

Introduction
Einführung

Herr Schröder sets the tone of the meeting formally:

– ich begrüße Herrn Hibbert vom Produktionswerk Runcorn
– anwesend sind
– ich eröffne heute das Juni Board Meeting

Introduction
Einführung

– I extend a welcome to Mr Hibbert from the Runcorn production plant.
– those present are . . .
– I declare today's June board meeting open.

Stage 2

The agenda
Die Tagesordnung

The main words and phrases Herr Schröder uses to work through the agenda are:
– um kurz über die ausstehenden Fragen zu sprechen
– wir kommen damit zu Punkt vier
– wir reden darüber später
– wir wollen über den rückliegenden Monat sprechen
– wir sprechen heute über den bisherigen Jahresverlauf
– wer möchte dazu das Wort ergreifen?
– wir kommen heute außerordentlich schnell durch die einzelnen Tagespunkte
– wenn wir den Finanzreport sehen
– Herr Hibbert, beginnen Sie wieder?

The agenda
Die Tagesordnung

– to talk about the questions that are outstanding

– and so we come to point four
– we'll talk about that later
– we want to talk about the previous month

– we're talking today about the year to date

– who would like to address this?
– we're getting through the individual items on the agenda exceptionally quickly
– if we look at the financial report
– Mr Hibbert, would you like to begin again this time?

Stage 3

Explanations
Erklärungen

From time to time, Herr Schröder feels he needs to explain or comment in greater detail. To do this he uses introductory phrases which announce that

Explanations
Erklärungen

important and/or more specific detail is involved:

– das heißt	– that is to say . . .
– das wird Herrn Hibbert besonders interessieren	– this will be of particular interest to Mr Hibbert
– ich habe damals schon darauf hingewiesen	– I drew your attention to this at the time
– Näheres dazu sagen	– say more about it
– wir haben diese Frage schon angeschnitten	– we have already addressed this question
– man muß berücksichtigen, daß	– one has to take into account (the fact) that . . .
– das Problem liegt darin, daß	– the problem is (in the fact) that . . .
– die gleiche Frage stellt sich auch in	– the same question arises in . . .
– unter Berücksichtigung der erschwerten Verhältnisse	– taking into account the more difficult conditions
– weil es sich vor Monaten abzeichnete	– because it stood out clearly months ago

Stage 4

Summary
Zusammenfassung

Summary
Zusammenfassung

Likewise Herr Schröder makes brief summaries of results to keep the meeting on course:

– wir können feststellen, daß	– we can see that . . .
– kein großer Gewinn kann erzielt werden	– no big profit can be targeted
– die Untersuchungen haben positive Ergebnisse gezeigt	– investigations have shown positive results

Stage 5

Closing
Abschluß

Closing
Abschluß

Finally, Herr Schröder uses these words and phrases to bring the meeting to a positive close:

– wir haben dann beschlossen,	– we have therefore decided . . .
– die Entscheidung ist eigentlich gefallen	– the decision has been taken
– ich danke den Anwesenden	– I thank those of you present
– ich schließe hiermit das Board Meeting	– with this I declare the board meeting closed

Practising speaking
Sprachpraktische Übungen

Before any meeting you need to think through what you are going to say. Before a meeting in German, you need to think through what to say, and how to say it.

This section will help you to prepare for taking part in a formal business meeting.

You will find
- a scripted dialogue
- a dialogue chain
- dialogue practice

Scripted dialogue

Stage 1: *Listen* to the scripted dialogue on the study cassette. It is a simple formal meeting.

VORSITZENDER: Guten Morgen, meine Damen und Herren. Ich begrüße Sie zu diesem Meeting. Wir sprechen heute über die Produktion in Deutschland. Wer möchte dazu etwas sagen?

TEILNEHMER: Als Erstes möchte ich wissen, wie es mit den neuen Maschinen steht?

VORSITZENDER: Wir haben diese Frage letztes Mal angeschnitten. Wir müssen berücksichtigen, daß der Hersteller diese Maschinen speziell für uns entwickelt hat. Das hat neun Monate gedauert. Sie sind für nächsten Monat geplant.

TEILNEHMER: Ich möchte darauf hinweisen, daß unser Werk in England einen eigenen Maschinenbau und eigene Techniker hat. Ich bin der Meinung, daß wir einen gemeinsamen Entschluß fassen müssen, immer unsere eigenen Vorrichtungen zu bauen.

VORSITZENDER: Das Problem liegt darin, daß der Wechselkurs und also die Frachtkosten im Moment ungünstig sind.

TEILNEHMER: Ich möchte zum nächsten Punkt kommen, und zwar . . .

VORSITZENDER: Gibt es noch andere ausstehende Fragen? Nein? Damit haben wir alle Punkte abgehandelt. Ich schließe hiermit das Meeting und danke den Anwesenden.

Dialogue chain

Stage 2: *Study* the plan below.

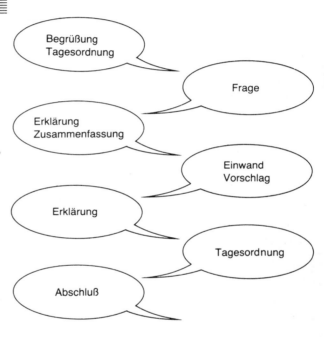

Stage 3: *Listen* to the dialogue while following the chain.

Stage 4: *Take* the role of the missing person on the study cassette. It will help you to practise speaking German in a formal business meeting.

Well done! You are now at the end of the language exercises. Familiarisation is all-important, so do get into the habit of listening repeatedly to material which you have worked through. The next part of this section will help you to put what you have seen, heard and worked at, into perspective.

Dialogue practice

Stage 5: Finally *use* the chain as a guide to make sure that you can operate in a formal meeting, either as chairperson or as participant.

Use the headings below to prepare what you might say if you were the chairperson:

greeting	Begrüßung
agenda	Tagesordnung
explanation	Erklärung
summary	Zusammenfassung
closing	Abschluß

Use the headings below to prepare what you might say if you were a participant:

question	Frage
objection	Einwand
suggestion	Vorschlag
agenda	Tagesordnung

Review
Überblick

Language comment

The American author Mark Twain once said this about German:

> A verb has a hard time enough of it in this world when it is all together. It's downright inhuman to split it up. But that's just what those Germans do. They take part of a verb and put it down here, like a stake, and they take the other part of it and put it away over yonder like another stake and between those two limits they just shovel in German.

Well, if you have made it through to this stage of the course, you will know exactly what Mark Twain meant! In this video sequence, the features which stand out are the length of sentences and the formality of the language used. But it would be unfair to describe the main speaker, Herr Schröder, as using a shovel. He is naturally a fluent and elegant speaker and it is a pleasure to listen to him handling German so correctly and effortlessly. His sentences are long and sometimes involved but he is easy to listen to and understand. He does not pause to clear his throat, he does not stumble over words, interrupt or repeat himself but simply maintains the flow and the clarity, observing all the rules of grammar and word order as he goes.

We cannot all be lucky enough to have a model like Herr Schröder in our everyday dealings with German-speaking colleagues. But he is not unique: there are many like him who will rise to the formality of the occasion. There are two ways in which you can benefit from observing Herr Schröder. First, it will help you to distinguish between formal and less formal occasions; recognising the signs will help you to respond in the appropriate manner. And second, it will help you improve your own German. Nobody expects you to produce such long sentences but even short sentences can be polished ones. And applying polish has got to be easier than wielding a shovel!

Pocket phrasebook

Some of the key phrases that will be useful to you when participating in a formal meeting have been recorded on to the study cassette. You can practise your pronunciation by repeating them in the pause provided or you can use the pause to supply your own version in English and then compare it with our suggestion.

These are the phrases selected from this video sequence for you to learn:

- Wer möchte das Wort ergreifen?
- Wir haben diese Frage schon angeschnitten.
- Das ist doch einfach zu teuer.
- Ich bin der Meinung, daß wir damit Klarheit geschaffen haben.
- Damit haben wir alle Punkte abgehandelt.

Sequence summary

In this sequence showing a company board meeting you have covered these language points:

- how to use *werden*
- how to handle possessive adjectives
- how to give reasons and causes
- how to participate in formal meetings
- how to chair a formal business meeting.

Business guide — Company environment

Understanding how German companies function, and how Germans approach their working day, can benefit would-be exporters who wish to create a good impression on customers and clients. In the following business guide, Andrew Castley sheds some light on the German business environment.

The popular conception of Germans at work is one of unremitting dedication, thoroughness, discipline and long hours of toil. Nothing (well, little) could be further from the truth. The fact is that Germans enjoy on average more holidays per year than employed people in the UK and the working week is about the same length. With the wholesale adoption of flexitime, working hours are put on a footing where the individual can decide his or her preferred working routine within limits. Add to that the co-determination laws, which we shall look at later, and we begin to see that the working situation in the FRG is fairly enlightened.

Here are some of the key words which express aspects of German business life:

das Wirtschaftswunder	economic miracle
die Arbeitsgesellschaft	society based on the work ethic
die Leistungsgesellschaft	society based on performance/efficiency
die Rationalisierung	rationalisation
die Arbeitszeit-verkürzung	reduction in working hours
die 35-Stunden-Woche	35 hour week
die Humanisierung der Arbeit	humanisation of work
die flexible Arbeitszeit	flexitime
die Machindustrielle Gesellschaft	post-industrial society
die Freizeitgesellschaft	leisure society

These are concepts which over the past three decades have had great currency in Germany and which, in the above order, trace the development

"There's no-one here!"

of the the FRG to a post-industrial society with the problems this brings.

A turning point was reached in the bitter dispute between 'IG Metall', the metal workers' union, and the employers over the issue of the *35 Stunden-Woche*. 'IG Metall' gives the lead for other pay and conditions agreements and in 1985/6 pursued the aim of reducing the average working week to 35 hours. The union argued that this would create jobs for the 2,000,000 unemployed. Increased productivity would justify the same wage levels as for the traditional 40-hour week. In the end, agreement was reached at 38.5 hours per week 'with flexibility'.

- **The importance of training.** The FRG has traditionally set greater store by education and training than England (n.b. not Scotland!). *Schulpflicht* – the requirement to attend school – was first adopted in Saxony in 1662. For a long time, secondary education has continued to the age of 18. For those who leave school at 15, there is a statutory right, taken up by 90% of 15-year-old school leavers, to be released from work for between 8 and 12 hours per week for off-the-job training at the *Berufsschule*. Education and training in a high technology economy is crucial, both for vocational and personal development reasons. Firms, the 4,000 *Volkshochschulen* (adult education) centres, the unions, and employers' organisations all contribute to provision for both vocational and non-vocational continuing education. The FRG spends over 2% of turnover on vocational training, the UK less than 0.3%.

- **Functional specialist or manager?** Ask a fairly senior person in a UK company what his or her profession is and we are not surprised to hear 'manager', 'company director' or 'company executive'. In Germany, one's profession is the discipline in which one is trained. So the same question asked of a German might elicit the answer *Chemiker* (chemist) or *Ingenieur* (engineer). Even though performing a similar managerial function to the UK respondant, the German's professional identity is seen more in terms of the functional discipline.

  Not unrelated to this is the fact that there is a much lower incidence of accountants in senior management positions in the FRG than in the UK. One is much more likely to find a technically qualified person in the top managerial position there. We shall see later that banks play a major part at supervisory board level, so this phenomenon is perhaps a good counterbalance!

- **The working routine, remuneration.** The German working day starts earlier than in the UK, generally speaking. Office staff may begin at 8.00 or even 7.30! Flexitime is widely adopted, with a core time of a few hours in the middle of the day. The manual worker works an average of 38.5 hours per week.

  The average annual holiday entitlement is 5 weeks, plus religious holidays.

  In the mid- and late-80s, blue collar male workers earned $1,000 per month gross and white collar male workers $1,500, on average. Stoppages and prices are broadly on a par with the UK.

  Normal practice is for a company to pay a thirteenth month bonus depending on its performance; some automatically pay this plus part of a fourteenth month, depending on performance. In addition, a holiday bonus (*Urlaubsgeld*) is often paid. Given higher wages than in the UK, more investment in training, high productivity, a shorter working week, and less pressure to pay a high dividend, the turnover/profit ratio of German firms is generally smaller than that in the UK.

- **Mobility of labour and company loyalty.** Generally speaking, the German workforce is not as mobile as in the UK. In other sequences we have discussed the strong regionalism of the FRG, which means that a *Bundesbürger* (= West German) sees him or herself quite strongly as a *Bayer*, *Pfälzer*, or *Schwabe*, and will often want to stay in the home *Land*. It is difficult to say if the same degree of loyalty is applied to the employing company; probably it is little different than in the UK. But it is interesting to observe the employees' car park at 'Daimler Benz', Untertürkheim, where without exception, Mercedes stand bumper to bumper with Mercedes, and it might not only be because the company gives discounts to its employees!

- **Foreign workers.** At the time of the *Wirtschaftswunder*, many foreign workers from the Mediterranean countries came to the FRG in search of work. In 1973, a halt was put on recruitment, and the number dropped from 2.6 million at that time to around 200,000 in the early '80s. Today, 4.5 million foreigners live in the Federal Republic, the largest group, at 1.5 million, being Turks. Despite concerted attempts by the authorities to ensure harmonious relations, there are difficulties, particularly in cities where the foreign people form a large proportion of the population. At their place of work, the *Gastarbeiter*, or *ausländische Arbeitnehmer* have exactly the same rights as their German counterparts.

- **Economic trends.** Throughout the 1980s economic growth has slowed down, with investment in industry giving way to investment in securities. Germany's strength today lies in the application of new technologies, rather than at the leading edge of research and development.

  As a strong export-oriented country, the FRG is very much anti-protectionist as far as trade in

manufactured goods is concerned. However, non tariff barriers such as the need to comply with standards, and a certain amount of national consumer loyalty, could make the anti-protectionist claim ring a little hollow.

The current trend in industry is for the concentration of economic and industrial power in fewer and fewer companies. Automation and rationalisation have led to unemployment and reduced spending power. Inflation is still the great enemy, with the horrific experiences of the 1923 soaring inflation, still very much alive in folk memory.

Organisation

The phrase 'the two sides of industry' translates usually as *die Sozialpartner*, or tariff partner, which perhaps indicates a striving for consensus and identity of interest to a greater extent than in the UK. The same approach can be found in the political system, which is based on proportional representation; in vocational training, which private companies see as an investment rather than a cost; or indeed in the whole concept of the 'social market economy' within the framework of which it seeks to reconcile different social economic interests in ways other than confrontation.

As usual, theory and practice are distinct, and a dispute in the FRG is just as bitter as its UK equivalent. Yet until recently the number of working days lost through industrial action in the FRG was one-tenth of the UK figure. On the other hand, do not forget that the UK has the lowest absenteeism rate in Europe!

Factors such as this make it an attractive proposition to invest in the FRG, of course.

- **The unions.** The unions are organised by industry (*Industriegewerkschaft*) rather than by trade, which means there are far fewer of them than in the UK; the *Deutscher Gewerkschaftsbund* (DGB) is the equivalent of the TUC and comprises 17 unions. The largest is 'IG Metall', with around 2.5 million members. 'Bergbau und Energie' and 'Handel, Banken und Versicherungen' stand at the median point of around 325,000 members. There are also four unions which look after the interests of mainly public sector employees. Around 35% of German employees are unionised, whereas in the UK the figure is over 60%.

- **The employers.** There are around 800 employers' organisations, of which most belong to the BDA ('Bundesvereinigung der Deutschen Arbeitgeberverbände'), which more or less equates with the CBI.

- **Disputes.** If the dispute remains unresolved after negotiation and arbitration, industrial action can only be taken after union committees and 75% of the membership of the union have taken that decision by ballot.

  The employer has the right to lock out (*das Aussperrungsrecht*) as a countermeasure. This is specifically stated in law, and is particularly effective where unions undertake selective strike action. Since strikers and locked-out workers cease to receive unemployment benefit, this situation can be very expensive for a union. Not surprisingly, the *Aussperrungsrecht* is highly controversial.

- **Free collective bargaining** (*Tarifautonomie*). Collective bargaining is a matter for *die Sozialpartner*; the government does not interfere. There are two kinds of agreement: the *Manteltarifvertrag*, governing issues such as holidays, notice, working hours and so on, which will run for several years and the *Tarifvertrag*, usually running for one year, which governs wages and salary levels. Both forms of agreement have the force of law.

- **Co-determination** (*Mitbestimmung*). Co-determination exists and functions effectively in the FRG.

  Under the 1976 Co-determination Law, in all companies of more than 2,000 employees having the legal form of an AG or GmbH, one half of the supervisory board must be elected by the employees. The shareholders, however, elect the chairperson, who has the casting vote. Furthermore, the unions have only 2 of the 6 employee seats, and a third seat is reserved for a member of the senior management (*leitender Angestellter*), who will tend towards the interests of the shareholders in any closely-fought issue.

  Under the company constitution law (*Betriebsverfassungsgesetz*) of 1952/1972, which applies to most other AGs and all GmbHs with more than 500 employees, a milder form of co-determination applies, by which one third of the membership of the supervisory board is elected by employees. The law also provides for the establishment of works councils in all companies of more than five employees. The works council has the right to participate in social and personnel matters and the right of access to certain information.

- **The role of the banks.** Banks play a major role in German industry; bank loans far outstrip joint stock financing as a source of capital in the Federal Republic. The commercial banking sector is dominated by the Big Three – the 'Deutsche Bank', the 'Dresdner Bank' and the 'Commerzbank'.

Traditionally, banks are willing to place a company's longer-term interests above the need for short-term profits and further, to be restrained in their dividend demands. This philosophy was crucial to the success of the post-war economic rebuilding programme.

When a bank lends significant sums, it will be represented on the board of the borrowing company. Not surprisingly, therefore, banks' influence in the boardroom is very strong: in the top 100 AGs, around 33% of the supervisory board seats reserved for the shareholders are occupied by bank representatives, and bank personnel occupy the chair in almost 50% of them.

A further source of influence is the proxy vote (*Depotstimmrecht*) exercised by the banks. Slightly under 50% of all security deposits (1981 = 3.5 million of 8.1 million) are in the custody of private banks. Provided the bank has the written consent of the depositor, it may exercise a proxy voting right at shareholders' meetings. Consequently banks currently have voting control over 60% of the total capital of stock exchange quoted companies.

This degree of control may explain the tendency of German banks to make long-term loans to finance industrial expansion – a tendency much envied by UK businesses.

The legal forms of company

You will note after many German companies' names, letters which denote their legal structure (like plc in the UK):

OHG KG AG GmbH GmbH & Co KG KGaA

- **Partnerships.** *Offene Handelsgesellschaft* (OHG): this is a general partnership in which all partners have an unlimited liability. *Kommanditgesellschaft* (KG): in this form of partnership, the *Kommanditist* (limited partner) has limited liability and limited managerial responsibilities, whilst the *Komplementär*, the general partner(s), has unlimited liability and is responsible for running the firm.

- **Incorporated organisations.** *Aktiengesellschaft* (AG): this is a joint stock company with limited liability and quoted shares. The minimum share capital of the AG is DM100,000; the largest companies take this form, for example, 'Siemens AG', 'Volkswagenwerk AG', 'Bauer AG', 'Thyssen AG', 'Deutsche Shell AG'. Unlike UK companies, the AG consists of two boards of directors, the supervisory board, which decides broad, long-term strategy, and the managing board which deals with shorter-term policy. *Gesellschaft mit beschränkter Haftung* (GmbH) is a private, unquoted company with limited liability; the minimum share capital of this type of company is DM50,000. There are many sizeable companies of this type. One of them is 'Bosch GmbH', Stuttgart.

Kommanditgesellschaft auf Aktien (KGaA) is similar to the KG above, but has quoted shares.

Conducting business with a German firm

For a document issued by a German company to be binding on that company, it must carry the signature of an official empowered to speak on behalf of the company – a *Prokurist*. You may have noticed at the foot of correspondence the initials i.A. (*im Auftrag*) and i.V. (*im Vertrag*), each followed by a signature. The signature under i.V. is that of the *Prokurist*, that under i.A. that of the officer dealing with the transaction.

As noted above, the working day begins and ends earlier than in the UK. If the proceedings threaten to go into the late afternoon, you might think of concentrating on getting the business out of the way in a fairly intensive manner, having a break, and meeting socially in the evening to celebrate the deal.

In negotiations involving German partners of different rank, you should be sensitive to the relationship between them. Relationships differ widely from company to company, just as in the UK, so it is difficult to generalise on how you might approach this situation; but sensitivity in this direction is always to be advised.

You might notice some words which suggest partnership, like *Sozialpartner*, *Mitarbeiter* (where we might say worker), *Entgegenkommen* (co-operation in the sense of making concessions), *Kollege* (used much more widely than colleague in English).

Senior management (if not the directors) of a German company will eat in the same dining-room as the workforce and will be less likely to drive a company car.

If flexitime is in operation, everyone is subject to it.

In short, you might find there are fewer status symbols, or outward signs of a 'pecking order' in workday life in the Federal Republic than in the UK, but this does not mean these do not exist.

Setting up or managing a company in the Federal Republic

Contact the DTI (Export Europe Services), 1–9 Victoria Street, London, SW1H 0ET for their background information on setting up a company in the FRG.

As an employer, you would not be bound to promote the formation of a works council (*Betriebsrat*), but where one exists or is formed, a continuous dialogue should be maintained on workforce level – actual and potential – to smooth the way for hiring. The *Betriebsrat* must be informed of intended dismissals at least 7 days before notice is given, otherwise the termination of contract will be invalid.

If you have a German subsidiary, remember that the turnover/profit ratio is not as high as in the UK, mainly because German salaries are higher in absolute and relative terms than UK salaries and because investment/profit ratios are higher than in the UK.

Your German subsidiary should be allowed considerable autonomy to manage its own affairs (British parent companies apparently are quite good in this way!). The German market will have different demands which the management of the parent company might not always appreciate. Of course, if there are questions to be answered, answered they must be.

The parent and subsidiary should constantly 'sell' themselves to each other; for example, the German manager of the subsidiary might have access to the board or general manager when this is necessary – but the hand must not be overplayed.

Conclusion

Working with German companies will in general be similar to dealing with UK organisations, except in matters of detail – but it is often attention to detail which wins or loses orders. Being flexible and prepared to learn will win you the support of German colleagues, as we saw demonstrated in the video sequence with Chelvin Hibbert. Because Chelvin is learning German and attending board meetings, he is safeguarding the interests of his company and cementing working relationships.

Business Magazine
So you're big – you want to establish a base in Germany, or perhaps take over a German company. Chris Serle finds out how in Business Magazine 6.

Supporting the market

„Wir unterstützen unsere Handelspartner sehr aktiv."

The video sequence
Der Video-Abschnitt

the task of improving its tarnished image in Germany and succeeded. We are given valuable insights into the company's marketing strategy and approach. The key elements are a quality product, excellent customer care, reliable parts delivery, sophisticated advertising and an efficient, needs-related training programme.

The company concerned is Austin Rover Deutschland – the German national sales company of Austin Rover. In its previous existence as British Leyland, it would be hard to imagine a British company more in need of a positive change of image – as Austin Rover Deutschland is the first to admit.

In March 1987, Austin Rover launched the new Rover 800 series on to the German market. We hear about the merits of this model range, during a meeting between a prospective new dealer in the Cologne area and Herr Hermann, Austin Rover's German sales director. We also go for a test drive

Corporate image is an important aspect of any company's activities; a positive image abroad is essential for a company operating in foreign markets. In a foreign land, companies play the role of ambassador for their country to some degree. Some German companies operating in Britain regard themselves also as shop windows for other German products and have a policy of buying German for company cars, office equipment and so on. There may be a lesson here for British companies operating abroad!

This video sequence tells something of a success story. We hear how one British company set about

and hear the language of advertising in snippets from the promotional video and the welcome cassette.

The main speaker in the video sequence is Herr Hermann. As you would expect, he is very enthusiastic about the new model. Herr Hermann clearly has a routine worked out and its main feature is a very personal style of address – he is careful to involve Herr Idelberger, the prospective dealer, in every step of his presentation. Listen out for the little phrases he uses for this purpose.

The main message that comes across is one we have heard before, that success in Germany is possible for British exporters. But success depends on getting a number of factors right and working at keeping it that way. One of those factors is an ability to operate in German. So, with that in mind, study the list of key words and watch and enjoy the video sequence.

Key words

Here is a list of the key words in German used in a discussion between a principal and a prospective dealer. Study the list and the meanings in this context, so that you can follow the video more easily. The words are listed in the order in which they occur.

die Gelegenheit (-en)	opportunity
die Verbesserung (-en)	improvement
die Vergangenheit	past
die Tagesordnung	agenda
der Musterbetrieb (-e)	showroom
der Vertragspartner (-)	concessionnaire
die Ausbildung	training
der Teilnehmer (-)	participant
die Teilversorgung	delivery of spare parts
der Lagerbestand ("e)	stock level
der Vorteil (-e)	advantage
die Reparatur (-en)	repair
der Bestandteil (-e)	component
das Verkaufsförderungs-programm	sales drive
die Anzeige (-n)	advertisement
die Geldmittel (plural)	funds
die Unterlage (-n)	support material (documentation)
das Händlernetz (-e)	dealer network
der Konkurrenzvergleich (-e)	comparison with the competition
die Zielgruppe (-n)	target group

Practising listening and understanding
Hörverständnisübungen

You will find a workplan to help you in Sequence 1, page 11.

Information

Exercise A

What are they saying?

Einführung

1. Worüber möchte Herr Hermann sprechen?

Answers

Einführung

1. Herr Hermann möchte *über die Aktivitäten im Rahmen der Image-Verbesserung* sprechen.

---

2. Wie war das bisherige Image von Austin Rover in Deutschland?

2. *Das bisherige Image* von Austin Rover in Deutschland *war schlecht*.

Dienstleistung

3. Warum will die Firma Austin Rover möglichen Vertragspartnern viele Aktivitäten anbieten?

3. Die Firma Austin Rover will möglichen Vertragspartnern viele Aktivitäten anbieten, *damit der Erfolg gemeinsam sichergestellt werden kann*.

4. Was passiert im Musterbetrieb?

4. Im Musterbetrieb werden Vertragspartner in das *Kundendienstprogramm* eingewiesen.

5. Wie ist die Ausbildung für die Mechaniker?

5. Die Ausbildung für die Mechaniker ist sehr *praxisnah*.

Teile

6. Warum ist die Teilversorgung nun kein Problem?

6. Austin Rover Deutschland hat ein *Teillager*, das alle Teile lagert, die benötigt werden.

7. Wie schnell erfolgt die Teillieferung?

7. Die Teillieferung erfolgt *innerhalb von vierundzwanzig Stunden*, wenn man sie vor zwölf Uhr bestellt.

Werbung

8. Wer führt die bundesweite Werbung durch?

8. *Austin Rover Deutschland* führt die bundesweite Werbung durch.

9. Was erzielt die bundesweite Werbung?

9. Die bundesweite Werbung erzielt einfach einen *besseren Bekanntheitsgrad*.

10. Wie steht es mit der Unterstützung durch Austin Rover Deutschland?

10. Austin Rover Deutschland *unterstützt* seine Handelspartner *sehr aktiv*.

im Musterbetrieb

11. In welcher Wagenklasse steht der Austin Rover Achthundertfünfundzwanzig?

11. Der Austin Rover Achthundertfünfundzwanzig ist ein Fahrzeug der gehobenen Klasse. Er steht *in der oberen Mittelklasse*.

12. Welche Zielgruppe spricht Austin Rover mit dem Austin Rover Achthundertfünfundzwanzig an?

12. Mit dem Austin Rover Achthundertfünfundzwanzig spricht Austin Rover *die Leute* an, *die ein hohes monatliches Einkommen haben*.

Summary

Exercise B

What are they saying?

1. Warum legt Austin Rover jetzt so viel Wert auf Kundendienst?

Possible answers

1. Austin Rover legt jetzt großen Wert auf den Kundendienst, weil das Image bisher ausgesprochen schlecht war. Früher hat man in

Deutschland nicht von „British Leyland" sondern von „Britisch Elend" gesprochen. Um die früheren Probleme der Qualität und der Teillieferungen zu beseitigen, muß Austin Rover den Kundendienst verbessern.

2. Wie geht die Werbung vor sich?	2. Austin Rover Deutschland führt die Werbung auf bundesweiter Ebene durch, um einen besseren Bekanntheitsgrad zu erzielen. Die verschiedenen Vertragspartner erhalten Geldmittel, Anzeigevorlagen und andere Unterlagen, die sie für die Werbung auf lokaler Ebene verwenden sollen.
3. Was meint Herr Idelberger zu der Frage der Konkurrenz?	3. Herr Idelberger möchte die Frage der Konkurrenz nicht diskutieren. Er ist aber der Ansicht, daß der Austin Rover Achthundertfünfundzwanzig die gleiche Zielgruppe wie Mercedes und BMW anspricht.

Close listening

We recommend that you only attempt this exercise if you need, or are keen, to understand the precise details of a discussion. Instead of doing the exercise as a listening comprehension exercise, you may like to try it as an exercise in reading comprehension. You are looking for what the words in italics refer to:

Exercise C	Answers
What are they referring to?	
Teile	
1. *Null*	1. Sollte ein Teil überaus gefragt sein, so daß der *Lagerbestand* sich auf *Null* gesenkt hat . . .
2. *vierundzwanzig Stunden*	2. . . . sind wir in der Lage, innerhalb von *vierundzwanzig* Stunden . . . *ein neues Teil* zu *beschaffen.*
3. *zwölf Uhr*	3. Alle Teile, die Sie *bestellen bis zwölf Uhr . . .*
im Musterbetrieb	*im Musterbetrieb*
4. *zweihundert*	4. Das ist der *Rover Zweihundert, . . .*
5. *am siebenundzwanzigsten März*	5. . . . *vorgestellt am siebenundzwanzigsten März* in diesem Jahr . . .
6. *bei hundert Händlern*	6. . . . *vorgestellt* . . . in diesem Jahr *bei insgesamt hundert Händlern.*
7. *Honda*	7. Ich hörte, daß dieses Fahrzeug *in Zusammenarbeit mit Honda* gebaut wird, . . .
8. *für den europäischen Markt*	8. . . . die Rover Achthundert Serie wird *in England gebaut für den europäischen Markt . . .*
9. *die asiatischen Märkte*	9. . . . *in Japan wird bei Honda* der Rover *für die asiatischen Märkte gebaut, . . .*
10. *sechs Lautsprecher*	10. *Das Radio,* ein Vollstereo-Radio mit *sechs integrierten Lautsprechern, . . .*

Consolidation
Konsolidierung

In this sequence, the language points selected for consolidation are:
- verbs which take the dative
- recognising the genitive case.

Verbs which take the dative

Austin Rover and Austin Rover Deutschland are taking great trouble to counter the negative image previously associated with their name. As a prospective dealer, Herr Idelberger is introduced to the way Austin Rover Deutschland now wants to present itself to the market.

As part of this introduction, Herr Hermann shows Herr Idelberger the key features of the dealer network and of the product:

Er zeigt ihm die Bilder.
He shows him the pictures.

Er bietet ihm Hilfe an.
He offers him help.

Er stellt ihm den Rover 825 vor.
He demonstrates the Rover 825 to him.

English does not make any distinction between **what** is shown/offered/demonstrated, the **direct object**:

the pictures – *die Bilder*
help – *Hilfe*
the Rover 825 – *den Rover 825*

and **whom** it is shown/offered/demonstrated to, the **indirect object**:

(to) him – *ihm*

You will have met this distinction in German early on in your learning – but, even so, it is an area which requires a great deal of consolidation work. The theory may be easy, the practice is less so!

If you look back through the meetings and discussions you will find the speakers saying the following:

Stellen Sie dem Handel auch Leaflets zur Verfügung?
Darf ich Ihnen meine Karte geben?
Das kann ich mir nicht vorstellen.
Wir geben unseren englischen Partnern Anregungen.

The verbs you will need most frequently are:

an'bieten	to offer
bringen	to bring
erzählen	to tell
geben	to give
hin'weisen (auf)	to indicate
holen	to fetch
sagen	to say
schicken	to send
senden	to send
vor'führen	to demonstrate
vor'schlagen	to suggest
sich (etwas) vor'stellen	to imagine
zeigen	to show

The two potential difficulties for the English-speaking person using German are the **form** and the **order** of the words.

To be sure of getting the **form** right, you have to know what happens to any articles, adjectives, nouns, pronouns and possessive adjectives involved. If you are not sure and would like to revise these, look at the Grammar Guide and the tables on pages 172–175.

The right word **order** is far less of a problem, because it is essentially the same as in English.

Practice A

Here there are two nouns. Look at the following sentence adapted from the trade fair sequence:

Stellen Sie *dem Handel Ihre Prospekte* zur Verfügung?
Do you make your prospectuses available to the trade?

Put the words from the two lists below into the same question form:

(to) who(m)   what
wem   *was*

1. der Handel	die Prospekte (plural)	1. Stellen Sie *dem Handel Ihre Prospekte* zur Verfügung?
2. die Konkurrenz	die Literatur	2. Stellen Sie *der Konkurrenz Ihre Literatur* zur Verfügung?
3. die Kunden (plural)	die Software	3. Stellen Sie *den Kunden Ihre Software* zur Verfügung?
4. die Firmen (plural)	die Handbücher (plural)	4. Stellen Sie *den Firmen Ihre Handbücher* zur Verfügung?
5. der Markt	das Programm	5. Stellen Sie *dem Markt Ihr Programm* zur Verfügung?
6. die Niederlassung	die Zeichnungen (plural)	6. Stellen Sie *der Niederlassung Ihre Zeichnungen* zur Verfügung?
7. das Lager	das System	7. Stellen Sie *dem Lager Ihr System* zur Verfügung?
8. die Industrie	die Maschinen (plural)	8. Stellen Sie *der Industrie Ihre Maschinen* zur Verfügung?
9. der Industriezweig	das Material	9. Stellen Sie *dem Industriezweig Ihr Material* zur Verfügung?
10. der Bediener	der Roboter	10. Stellen Sie *dem Bediener Ihren Roboter* zur Verfügung?

Practice B

And here there is one noun and a pronoun. Using the same structure and the same content, express the direct object (*Ihre Prospekte . . .*) as a pronoun. Remember that, here, the pronoun comes **before** the noun:

Answers

1. Stellen Sie *sie dem Handel* zur Verfügung?
2. Stellen Sie *sie der Konkurrenz* zur Verfügung?
3. Stellen Sie *sie den Kunden* zur Verfügung?
4. Stellen Sie *sie den Firmen* zur Verfügung?
5. Stellen Sie *es dem Markt* zur Verfügung?
6. Stellen Sie *sie der Niederlassung* zur Verfügung?
7. Stellen Sie *es dem Lager* zur Verfügung?
8. Stellen Sie *sie der Industrie* zur Verfügung?
9. Stellen Sie *es dem Industriezweig* zur Verfügung?
10. Stellen Sie *ihn dem Bediener* zur Verfügung?

Practice C

Now, one noun and a pronoun: using the same structure and content, express the indirect object (*dem Handel . . .*) as a pronoun. Remember that, now, the pronoun comes **before** the noun:

Answers

1. Stellen Sie *ihm Ihre Prospekte* zur Verfügung?
2. Stellen Sie *ihr Ihre Literatur* zur Verfügung?
3. Stellen Sie *ihnen Ihre Software* zur Verfügung?
4. Stellen Sie *ihnen Ihre Handbücher* zur Verfügung?

5. Stellen Sie *ihm Ihr Programm* zur Verfügung?

6. Stellen Sie *ihr Ihre Zeichnungen* zur Verfügung?

7. Stellen Sie *ihm Ihr System* zur Verfügung?

8. Stellen Sie *ihr Ihre Maschinen* zur Verfügung?

9. Stellen Sie *ihm Ihr Material* zur Verfügung?

10. Stellen Sie *ihm Ihren Roboter* zur Verfügung?

Practice D

Finally, working with two pronouns and using the same structure and content, express the indirect object (*dem Handel . . .*) and the direct object (*die Prospekte . . .*) as pronouns. Remember that, this time, the direct object comes **before** the indirect object (as in English):

Answers

1. Stellen Sie *sie ihm* zur Verfügung?

2. Stellen Sie *sie ihr* zur Verfügung?

3. Stellen Sie *sie ihnen* zur Verfügung?

4. Stellen Sie *sie ihnen* zur Verfügung?

5. Stellen Sie *es ihm* zur Verfügung?

6. Stellen Sie *sie ihr* zur Verfügung?

7. Stellen Sie *es ihm* zur Verfügung?

8. Stellen Sie *sie ihr* zur Verfügung?

9. Stellen Sie *es ihm* zur Verfügung?

10. Stellen Sie *ihn ihm* zur Verfügung?

Any other problems?

Some German verbs put their object automatically into the **dative case**:

begegnen	to meet
bei'treten	to join
danken	to thank
folgen	to follow
gefallen	to please
gehören	to belong
an'gehören	to belong to (a larger unit – club, group, etc.)
helfen	to help

Let's look at some examples from the various meetings and discussions:

Kann ich *Ihnen helfen?*
Ich *danke Ihnen.*
Glücklicherweise muß ich so *einem* nicht jeden Tag *begegnen!*
Wenn Sie *unserer Organisation beitreten . . .*
Doch ein sehr hübsches Dekor – *mir gefällt* es eigentlich.

Practice E

Practise using these very useful verbs in the following sentences. You can approach the exercise either from English or from German. If you decide to start with English, ask yourself how you would say the following sentences in German. Or you could start with the German and express them in English.

1. Please, thank your colleague.

2. We will willingly help your subsidiary.

3. They will follow your advice.

1. Danken Sie Ihrem Kollegen, bitte.

2. Wir helfen Ihrer Tochtergesellschaft gern.

3. Sie werden Ihrem Rat folgen.

---

4. This order will please our sales office.

5. I met their agent at the trade fair.
6. We belong to the Sparex group.
7. Does she want to join the trade delegation?

4. Dieser Auftrag wird unserem Verkaufsbüro gefallen.

5. Ich bin ihrem Vertreter auf der Messe begegnet.
6. Wir gehören der Sparex-Gruppe an.
7. Möchte sie der Handelsdelegation beitreten?

Practice F

Practise using these verbs with pronouns by changing the **object** from a noun to a pronoun. You can approach the exercise either from English or from German. If you decide to start with English, ask yourself how you would say the following sentences in German. Or you could start with the German and express them in English.

1. Please, thank him/her. (your colleague)
2. We will willingly help it. (your subsidiary)
3. They will follow it. (your advice)
4. This order will please it/them. (our sales office)
5. I met him/her (their agent) at the trade fair.
6. We belong to it. (the Sparex group)
7. Does she want to join it? (the trade delegation)

1. Danken Sie *ihm/ihr*, bitte.
2. Wir helfen *ihr* gern.
3. Sie werden *ihm* folgen.
4. Dieser Auftrag wird *ihm/ihnen* gefallen.
5. Ich bin *ihm/ihr* auf der Messe begegnet.
6. Wir gehören *ihr* an.
7. Möchte sie *ihr* beitreten?

Recognising the genitive

As you know, there are four **cases** in German. So far we have been concentrating on the three cases most commonly used, but we are now going to take a closer look at the **genitive** case.

First, a simple definition. The genitive case is used to convey the idea of **possession** or **belonging**. Everybody knows this French phrase:

La plume de ma tante.

Well, *de ma tante* expresses the genitive:

The pen *of my aunt*.

English and French are very similar here; they both use a single word – *de* in French, *of* in English – to put across the idea. German can often do the same thing with *von* but it also has the genitive case.

Here are examples of the genitive case which occur in this video sequence:

Die perfekte Verwirklichung *eines ganz individuellen Autofahrertraums*
im Rahmen *unserer Image-Verbesserung*
einer *der wichtigsten Punkte*
die Ausbildung *der Mechaniker*
die bisher etwas unbekannteren Fahrzeuge *englischer Hersteller*
auf dieser Basis *der nationalen Werbung*
ein Fahrzeug *der oberen Mittelklasse*
ein Fahrzeug *der gehobenen Klasse*
in die Kundengruppe *der Steuerberater, der Rechtsanwälte . . .*
alle Vorzüge *modernster Technik . . .*

If you need more information about forming the genitive consult the Grammar Guide on page 167.

Understanding the genitive when you come across it is not usually a problem. English would use an almost identical construction for many of these phrases.

Practice A

Answers

Here are some expressions containing the genitive in German. How would you say them in English?

1. einer der wichtigsten Punkte	1. one of the most important points
2. die Ausbildung der Mechaniker	2. the training of the mechanics
3. auf der Basis der nationalen Werbung	3. on the basis of national advertising
4. die Kundengruppe der Steuerberater und der Rechtsanwälte	4. the client group of accountants and lawyers
5. alle Vorzüge moderner Technik	5. all the benefits of modern technology

What if you **have** to use the genitive? If you are using certain constructions, you will not be able to avoid it. This is the case after some prepositions:

außerhalb	outside	außerhalb der Stadt
innerhalb	inside/within	innerhalb einer Woche
einschließlich	including	einschließlich aller Frachtkosten
mittels	by means of	mittels eines neuen Programms
statt	instead of	statt des alten Produktes
während	during	während des Gesprächs
wegen	because of	wegen der Preiserhöhung
zuzüglich	in addition/plus	zuzüglich deutscher Mehrwertsteuer

Practice B

Now practise using these prepositions. You can approach this exercise either from English or from German.

If you start with English, ask yourself how a German speaker would express these sentences:

1. We cannot export to the United States because of the strength of the mark.
2. Our Head Office is in Exeter, outside the city centre.
3. The company will deliver within a month.
4. We have received the material, including the price list.
5. You have sent us the price list instead of the publicity material.
6. The price is DM 995.00, plus German VAT.

7. We first got to know your company during the Stuttgart trade fair.
8. We are improving our image by means of first class advertising.

If you prefer to start with German, how would an English speaker express these sentences?

1. Wegen der Stärke der Mark können wir nicht nach den Vereinigten Staaten exportieren.
2. Unser Hauptsitz ist in Exeter, außerhalb des Stadtzentrums.
3. Die Firma wird innerhalb eines Monats liefern.
4. Das Material, einschließlich der Preisliste, haben wir bekommen.
5. Statt des Werbematerials haben Sie uns die Preisliste geschickt.
6. Der Preis ist DM 995.00, zuzüglich deutscher Mehrwertsteuer.
7. Ihre Firma haben wir erst während der Stuttgarter Messe kennengelernt.
8. Wir verbessern unser Image mittels erstklassiger Werbung.

Using the genitive in this way is only a matter of practice but make sure you are really confident about using the other three cases before you tackle it. It is not difficult but it is used less frequently than the other three cases. In fact, surveys of German language use have sometimes predicted that it will fall into disuse in spoken German. That may be the case in general conversation but certainly the German spoken in these video sequences shows plenty of examples of the genitive in practice.

What are the alternatives to the genitive? The main one is *von* but, of course, that is followed by a different case. This exercise will help you move from one case to the other.

Practice C

Here is a list of phrases using the genitive case. Replace the genitive with *von* . . ., making the appropriate changes to the endings:

1. der Vorteil dieses neuen Modells
2. ein wichtiger Aspekt des deutschen Marktes
3. das Thema der nationalen Werbung
4. die Unterstützung der amerikanischen Partner
5. das Hauptziel unserer Marketing-Strategie
6. der Status des Vertreters
7. die Frage der Garantie
8. die Nachlieferung der Ersatzteile
9. der Preis des elektrischen Wasserkochers
10. das Produkt der holländischen Konkurrenz

1. der Vorteil von dem [vom] neuen Modell
2. ein wichtiger Aspekt von dem deutschen Markt
3. das Thema von der nationalen Werbung
4. die Unterstützung von den amerikanischen Partnern
5. das Hauptziel von unserer Marketing-Strategie
6. der Status von dem Vertreter
7. die Frage von der Garantie
8. die Nachlieferung von den Ersatzteilen
9. der Preis von dem elektrischen Wasserkocher
10. das Produkt von der holländischen Konkurrenz

Development
Erweiterung

In this sequence on stating your case, the development exercises concentrate on
- being more specific
- saying why.

Being more specific

Look at the following sentences taken from earlier meetings:

Ich habe einen Termin, und *zwar* um 10 Uhr.
Wir bauen Maschinen für die Einzelkornsaat, *und zwar* sind wir in der Lage, den kleinsten Samen, den es gibt, exakt einzeln zu säen.
Es gibt nur eine Bezahlungsmodalität bei uns, *und zwar* 30 Tage netto per Scheck.
Wir haben heute etwas Schönes für Sie mitgebracht, *und zwar* die neue Rinne.

You can see what the speakers are doing here, can't you? Having made a general introductory statement, they use two very simple words *und zwar* to be both more explicit and more dramatic.

Can you identify the tone of what they are saying?

I've an appointment, and it is for 10 o'clock.
We build machines for single-seed sowing, and in particular we are able to sow exactly and individually the smallest seed there is.
We only have one method of payment, and that is 30 days net by cheque.
We have brought you something very nice today, namely the new guttering.

We want you to raise your impact by making a
determined effort to use this phrase. Here is an
exercise to help you practise it.

Exercise A

Here are some straightforward statements. Give them more impact. Where there are two sentences, do
this by joining them with *und zwar*. Where there is a single sentence, insert *und zwar* at the appropriate
point to highlight what is special:

1. Unser Hauptsitz ist im Südwesten Englands. Er
ist nicht weit von Southampton.

1. Unser Hauptsitz ist im Südwesten Englands,
und zwar nicht weit von Southampton.

2. Wir spezialisieren uns auf die Zulieferung von
Erstausrüstung. Sie ist für die Automobilindustrie.

2. Wir spezialisieren uns auf die Zulieferung von
Erstausrüstung, *und zwar* für die
Automobilindustrie.

3. Meine Verantwortung erstreckt sich auf die
gesamte Produktion. Sie erstreckt sich
hauptsächlich auf den Export.

3. Meine Verantwortung erstreckt sich auf die
gesamte Produktion, *und zwar* hauptsächlich auf
den Export.

4. Ihr Programm interessiert mich auf Grund der
Qualität.

4. Ihr Programm interessiert mich, *und zwar* auf
Grund der Qualität.

5. Das hätten wir lieber in zwei Farben. Wir
hätten gern grau und rosa.

5. Das hätten wir lieber in zwei Farben, *und zwar*
grau und rosa.

6. Das neue Produkt muß auf die DIN-Norm
geprüft werden.

6. Das neue Produkt muß geprüft werden, *und
zwar* auf die DIN-Norm.

7. Wir haben die zusätzlichen Teile letzte Woche
abgeschickt. Es war am Montag.

7. Wir haben die zusätzlichen Teile letzte Woche
abgeschickt, *und zwar* am Montag.

8. Ich bin das nächste Mal im August in Ihrer
Nähe. Ich bin am dreißigsten da.

8. Ich bin das nächste Mal im August in Ihrer
Nähe, *und zwar* am dreißigsten.

9. Wir müssen leider eine Preiserhöhung
ankündigen. Sie wird 4,5 Prozent betragen.

9. Wir müssen leider eine Preiserhöhung
ankündigen, *und zwar* 4,5 Prozent.

10. Unsere Produkte haben zwei große Vorteile.
Das sind Raumersparnis und Stabilität.

10. Unsere Produkte haben zwei große Vorteile,
und zwar Raumersparnis und Stabilität.

Changing the emphasis politely

While we are looking at what *zwar* can do, let's
look at another service it can perform.

Mike Taylor wants to stress the quality of the
product he is selling and Michael Hassenkamp
would prefer to talk about delivery. To change the
subject without upsetting the quality of the
established communication, Michael Hassenkamp
says:

Also, was ich gesehen habe, ist *zwar* interessant,
aber . . .

Can you identify the tone it gives to his words? He
is in fact saying:

It is all very interesting, but . . .

But he is saying it gently. He accepts Mike
Taylor's legitimate interest, but says it is not what
really interests him.

Exercise B

You will find two statements below. Admit that the first statement is correct, but stress your real area of concern by emphasising the second part. Do this by using *zwar* in the first part of the statement and linking the two statements with *aber*:

1. Southampton liegt günstig. Wir möchten nicht so weit von Dover sein.

2. Erstausrüstung ist interessant. Standardprodukte sind für uns dringender.

3. Produktion ist wesentlich. Marketing ist wichtiger.

4. Die Qualität ist gut und schön. Sind die Lieferzeiten garantiert?

5. Zweifarbig ist hübsch. Der Preis ist entschieden höher.

6. Die Prüfung ist wichtig. Ist der neue Teil so viel besser?

7. Ihre Bemühungen sind hilfreich. Die Waren sind immer noch nicht angekommen.

8. Ein weiterer Besuch ist willkommen. Wir sind an dem Tage gerade geschlossen.

9. 4,5 Prozent ist nicht extrem. Die Konkurrenz ist in der Lage, ihre Preise zu halten.

10. Raumersparnis und Stabilitat sind nötig. Konkurrenzfähigkeit ist noch nötiger.

---

1. Southampton liegt *zwar* günstig, *aber* wir möchten nicht so weit von Dover sein.

2. Erstausrüstung ist *zwar* interessant, *aber* Standardprodukte sind für uns dringender.

3. Produktion ist *zwar* wesentlich, *aber* Marketing ist wichtiger.

4. Die Qualität ist *zwar* gut und schön, *aber* sind die Lieferzeiten garantiert?

5. Zweifarbig ist *zwar* hübsch, *aber* der Preis ist entschieden höher.

6. Die Prüfung ist *zwar* wichtig, *aber* ist der neue Teil so viel besser?

7. Ihre Bemühungen sind *zwar* hilfreich, *aber* die Waren sind immer nocht nicht angekommen.

8. Ein weiterer Besuch ist *zwar* willkommen, *aber* wir sind an dem Tage gerade geschlossen.

9. 4,5 Prozent ist *zwar* nicht extrem, *aber* die Konkurrenz ist in der Lage, ihre Preise zu halten.

10. Raumersparnis und Stabilität sind *zwar* nötig, *aber* Konkurrenzfähigkeit ist noch nötiger.

Saying why

In conversation there are many occasions when you want to explain a course of action. German is very helpful here because it has a handy little phrase *und deswegen* (and therefore, because of that, and that is why), which you can use to link two sentences or phrases. Getting into the habit of using *und deswegen* will improve the quality of your German in two ways: you will be able to get your message across clearly and, by producing longer sentences, you will convey a more confident impression.

Let's see how to make *und deswegen* work for you. First, take these two sentences:

In der Vergangenheit war unser Image schlecht.
Wir sind bemüht, unser Image zu verbessern.

We can join them together like this:

In der Vergangenheit war unser Image schlecht, und deswegen sind wir bemüht, es zu verbessern.

Here are some examples of sentences for you to join together with *und deswegen*:

1. Ein wichtiger Punkt ist der Bereich Kundendienst.
Wir bieten unseren Partnern viele Aktiväten an.

Ein wichtiger Punkt ist der Bereich Kundendienst und deswegen bieten wir unseren Partnern viele Aktivitäten an.

2. Wir haben hier ein Teillager.
Alle Teile, die Sie bestellen, sind innerhalb von 24 Stunden bei Ihnen.

Wir haben hier ein Teillager, und deswegen sind alle

Teile, die Sie bestellen, innerhalb von 24 Stunden bei Ihnen.

You will have noticed that joining these sentences together involves minor changes to word order and sometimes, for the sake of style, it is better to change a noun to a pronoun. In general though, the effort it takes to get all the elements right is far outweighed by the effect you can achieve.

Exercise A

How would you say these sentences in the other language? You can approach this exercise from English or German.

If you start from English, ask yourself how a German would offer these explanations:

If you prefer to approach this exercise from German, ask how an English speaker would offer these explanations:

1. My company wants to enter the German market and that is why we are developing our product.

1. Meine Firma will in den deutschen Markt gehen, und deswegen entwickeln wir unser Produkt.

2. The manual is in German and therefore the technical draughtsmen can read it.

2. Das Handbuch ist auf Deutsch, und deswegen können die technischen Zeichner es lesen.

3. We have a warehouse near Coblenz and therefore we can deliver within a week.

3. Wir haben ein Lager in der Nähe von Koblenz, und deswegen können wir innerhalb einer Woche liefern.

4. The product is new to the German market and that is why we are reckoning on a market share of 40%.

4. Das Produkt ist neu auf dem deutschen Markt, und deswegen rechnen wir mit einem Marktanteil von 40%.

5. The price of raw materials has gone up and therefore we have to have a price increase as well.

5. Der Preis des Rohstoffes ist gestiegen, und deswegen müssen wir auch eine Preiserhöhung haben.

6. The packaging is simply not strong enough and therefore we cannot sell the goods.

6. Die Verpackung ist einfach nicht stark genug, und deswegen können wir die Waren nicht verkaufen.

7. We are the German importer and therefore we are responsible for national advertising.

7. Wir sind der deutsche Importeur, und deswegen sind wir für die bundesweite Werbung zuständig.

8. My company wants to improve its image in Germany and that is why we are all learning German.

8. Meine Firma will ihr Image in Deutschland verbessern, und deswegen lernen wir alle Deutsch.

9. We can sell more in Britain and therefore we must extend the capacity of the plant.

9. Wir können in England mehr verkaufen, und deswegen müssen wir die Kapazität des Werkes erweitern.

10. This is a luxury car and therefore it appeals to a client group which has a high monthly income.

10. Das ist ein Luxuswagen, und deswegen spricht er eine Kundengruppe an, die ein hohes monatliches Einkommen hat.

Practising speaking
Sprachpraktische Übungen

This section will help you to anticipate and prepare for your role as principal or prospective dealer.

You will find
● a scripted dialogue
● a dialogue chain
● dialogue practice.

Scripted dialogue

Stage 1: *Listen* to the scripted dialogue on the study cassette. It is a simple discussion between a principal and an agent.

AUFTRAGGEBER: Unsere Boote haben eine dicke Schaumschicht zwischen zwei Glasfiberlaminaten.
HÄNDLER: Und welchen Vorteil bringt das?
AUFTRAGGEBER: Das bedeutet Sicherheit, weil die Boote dadurch unsinkbar sind. Außerdem haben alle drei Ausführungen diese sehr flache Form, wie Sie selber feststellen können.
HÄNDLER: Wozu eigentlich?
AUFTRAGGEBER: Diese Form bedeutet Stabilität. Das ist für Familienboote besonders wichtig. Außerdem ist dieser Teil hier flach.
HÄNDLER: Was ist das Besondere daran?
AUFTRAGGEBER: Das bedeutet Universalität. Alle geläufigen Motoren lassen sich hier drauf montieren.
HÄNDLER: Donnerwetter! Einmalig!

Dialogue chain

Stage 2: *Study* the plan below. It represents in diagrammatic form how a simple discussion between a principal and a prospective dealer might proceed.

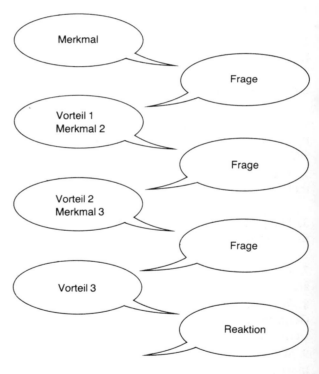

Stage 3: *Listen* to the dialogue while following the chain.
Stage 4: *Take* the role of the missing person on the study cassette. It will help you to practise speaking German in an agency situation.

Dialogue practice

Stage 5: You can use the dialogue chain as a guide to make sure that you can control the information you need to be able to handle this kind of encounter.

Use the headings below to prepare what you might say if you were the principal:

Feature 1	Merkmal 1
Benefit 1	Vorteil 1
Feature 2	Merkmal 2
Benefit 2	Vorteil 2
Feature 3	Merkmal 3
Benefit 3	Vorteil 3

Use these headings to prepare what you might say if you were the prospective dealer. All you can really predict is that you will have to ask **why** in different ways. Try to ensure you can ask more than just *warum*.

Question 1	Frage 1
Question 2	Frage 2
Question 3	Frage 3
Reaction	Reaktion

Review
Überblick

Language comment

This sequence has been about supporting the market and we have seen how this British company supports its German dealer network in a variety of ways – including thorough product training. It is unusual to look at a foreign language in these terms, that is, as a product, but that is what it is. It is the product of the people who speak it and shape it, it is the product of the society they live in, that society's history, its culture and its relationship with other countries. Taking a long-distance view of a language will tell you a lot about the people who have made it.

One of the striking characteristics about German as a language is its combination of orderliness and flexibility. Maybe this applies to the Germans too? There is a well-structured grammatical system at the heart of German but at the same time German is very receptive to new ideas and new words. In the nineteenth century when the industrial revolution finally came to Germany, it brought with it many words of French origin, such as *produzieren*, *die Fabrik*. Think back to the language used in the CAD/CAM trade fair: what strikes you about words such as *das Paket*, *die Software*? Is this an effect of the twentieth century computer revolution on the German language?

Of course, it is impossible to tell which came first: the ideas or the words. Do people make a language or does the language make the people? In our view, it does not really matter which came first. For us, and for you too, they go hand in hand. Knowing something of the language will help you to understand the people and knowing the people will support your knowledge of the language.

This brings us back to product training. By this stage, you have gone well beyond the basics of the German language; you will have a thorough grounding in grammar, an extensive range of business vocabulary and also a number of useful expressions and phrases to bring into play in your business dealings in Germany. By using the audio-cassettes you can also create for yourself opportunities to practise your listening and speaking skills between visits to Germany. The video sequences and the transcripts offer valuable revision practice. Will all this make you 'fully conversant' with the product? Not exactly. But what it does give you is the tools you need to become more and more conversant.

Language learning is a continuous process. If you ignore your language skills, they go away. That can happen all too easily but it need not, provided you are prepared to invest a little time and effort on a regular basis. Take the opportunities there are, at home and in Germany, to develop your existing skills. Some German language radio stations can be received without too much difficulty in Britain – listen to them now and again. Buy a German magazine or newspaper, especially one of interest to you in your job, and read it for pleasure. Create some new opportunities. Insist that your German business partners send their telexes and correspondence to you in German. Maybe you will pick up some new business that way too. When you are in Germany, try to absorb something of the language environment. Look at the advertisements, watch German TV, pick up brochures and leaflets and read them. Even if the main substance of your meeting is not in German, everything else can be: your conversations with the hotel staff, the company reception staff, the pleasantries exchanged with colleagues before and after the meeting. The opportunities for listening and speaking practice are endless; they are only limited by the extent of your willingness to make them or to take them.

Communication is fundamental to all aspects of business activity and there is nothing like effective communication in a foreign language for giving a personal boost. We all admire foreigners who speak good English but although that makes it easier for us, there is no reason why they or their companies should be the only ones to boost their image in this way. Language skills, however far from perfect they may be, are just as important as the quality of the product, the reliability of the delivery, the availability of spare parts and the efficiency of the after-sales service for any British exporter wanting to make his or her mark in Germany.

Pocket phrasebook

Some of the key phrases that will be useful to you when describing the way your company supports its market have been recorded on to the study cassette. You can practise your pronunciation by repeating them in the pause provided or you can use the pause to supply your own version in English and then compare it with our suggestion.

These are the phrases selected from this video sequence for you to learn:

- Darf ich vielleicht die Gelegenheit nutzen?
- Einer der wichtigsten Punkte ist der Bereich Kundendienst.
- Alle Teile, die Sie bis zwölf Uhr bestellen, sind innerhalb von 24 Stunden bei Ihnen.
- Wir unterstützen unsere Handelspartner sehr aktiv.
- Ich hätte noch eine Frage dazu.

Sequence summary

In this sequence showing how a British company supports its German market, you have covered the following language points:

- how to handle verbs which take the dative
- how to recognise and use the genitive
- how to explain how something has been done
- how to explain why something has been done
- how to promote a product.

Right: Equipped with all this you should now be able to go out into the marketplace and really let them have it!

Also, worauf warten Sie?

Auf die Plätze! – fertig! – los!

Business guide – Supporting the product

So far in the course, we have dealt mostly with getting into the German market and obtaining initial orders. But once you have a foothold you'll need to support and develop your operation in Germany through promotion both of the product and the product image. The following section is compiled with the help of Ted Jarrold, an English advertising consultant based in Düsseldorf.

There are a number of different ways in which support can be achieved. Advertising is one important area. It is essential to obtain specialist advice to understand the channels through which advertising in Germany works, and to obtain the best value for money. Also there are some cultural differences which may affect your advertising plans. For example, in the accompanying video

For many British companies 'niche marketing', i.e. developing a particular small segment of the market, can prove an effective way of creating a strong presence. Given the importance of quality to German consumers, selling a better quality product than the competition can create such a niche. Yardmaster sheds of Northern Ireland enjoy a successful export trade with their product galvanised sheds. Their unique selling point is a ten-year no rust guarantee. None of the competitors offers guarantees of this duration and as a result the company is able to sell at a premium price. Another example is Penrhyn quarries from North Wales. The company cannot compete with the influx of cheap slate tiles into Germany from Spain, but it does compete in terms of quality and design. The tiles are specially cut to suit the German taste for decorative roofing tiles and thus attention to detail has won the company a significant share of the market, again at a premium price.

Many companies leave the development of their market in the hands of their German agents. This will often work well. German agents can be highly professional and effective, but often they are dealing with a wide range of products, and may not be able to provide the attention to detail that you require.

It is therefore useful to have a knowledge yourself of the channels through which products can be promoted in Germany, and how the image of your product and your company can be tailored for the German market.

sequence, Herr Idelberger, the potential new agent for Austin Rover, asks about the number of components in the Rover 800 series which are made in Japan. This is because Japanese products are not automatically associated with luxury and status in Germany.

Establishing a base for your company in Germany could also be a way of creating more market potential. First, it demonstrates a commitment to the market, and is therefore likely to impress buyers and others with whom your company deals. Employing some German nationals will also help develop effective business relationships with other Germans. A number of companies we have already seen in the video have adopted this course of action. ICL have set up a base in Nuremburg to spearhead their European operation, and Marley Tiles have both an administrative and manufacturing base in North Germany. However, smaller companies may not have the resources to do this. In this case, the model used by Bernhard Grünhaus could be useful. This is the company which sold garden ponds to the Knauber store in Bonn, but it was done through a partnership arrangement with a German garden centre so in this case it was Herr Kayser who represented Bernhard, and conducted negotiations with the Knauber buyer, using his knowledge of business procedure in Germany to good effect. Such partnership arrangements are often informal but can prove very effective. Ideas about potential partners can be obtained from the British Chamber of Commerce in Germany.

Advertising and promotion in Germany

The usual reaction of British business people on being told what advertising budget will be needed to break into the German market, is to retire rapidly to the bar while they have still got the money. It is therefore all the more important to seek professional advice from an advertising agency experienced in the German market.

Advertising agencies in Germany are many and varied, so finding the right one for your company can be difficult. Many British advertising agencies have branches or affiliates in FRG and a good first step would be to consult your UK agency for advice. Some German advertising agencies have special links with the UK, either because of historical connections, or sometimes because they are run by or employ British nationals. These agencies can be better placed to help the needs of a small business entering the German market.

Lists of agencies can be obtained from British consulates or the British Chamber of Commerce in Germany, or the directory *Leitfaden Durch Presse und Werbung*, published annually by Stamm Verlag GmbH, Guldammerweg 16, 4300 Essen 1.

Advertising media

In Germany, the main advertising media are similar to those in the UK but follow different procedures about the presentation of copy. Newspapers, for example, in true 'Germanic' tradition, have firm rules about where copy should be placed, sometimes thwarting the more creative use of advertising space we commonly encounter in the UK. The main advertising channels are mentioned below.

Newspapers and journals

There is a well-established and well-developed regional press in the FRG. National dailies, as we know them in Britain, are uncommon, in fact.

There are really only three national daily papers, that is serious papers with distributions throughout the FRG. The biggest of these has a circulation of about 400 000 and a full page B/W ad costs in the region of DM 40 000 – (£13 500 at today's 1988 exchange rate, about DM 100.00 per thousand readers). This compares with £17 500 – (DM 52 500) for a full page in *The Daily Telegraph*, which has a circulation of about 1 250 000. It works out at less than half the cost of the German paper.

German papers regularly have 50 pages, with double that extent on Saturdays. About 25% of the pages carry ads for products and services. Some of the best-known daily papers are:
Die Welt (Bonn)
Frankfurter Allgemeine Zeitung (*FAZ*) (Frankfurt)
Süddeutsche Zeitung (*SZ*) (Munich)

Well-established regional newspapers worth considering include:
Westdeutsche Allgemeine Zeitung (Essen)

Hamburger Abendblatt (Hamburg)
Kölner Stadt-Anzeiger (Cologne)
Tagesspiegel (Berlin)
Rheinische Post (Düsseldorf)
Stuttgarter Zeitung (Stuttgart)
Handelsblatt (Düsseldorf) (5 times weekly)
Hannoversche Allgemeine Zeitung (Hannover)
Frankfurter Rundschau (Frankfurt)

German daily newspapers give very full coverage of economic developments but those which pay most attention to economic affairs, business and commerce are the *FAZ*, the *SZ* and *Handelsblatt*. The Frankfurt edition of the *Financial Times* has a small but influential circulation.

There are a number of quality weekly news magazines of which the chief is *Der Spiegel*, good for prestige advertising. Other quality magazines such as *Wirtschaftswoche*, *Capital* and *Impulse* place more emphasis on business news. The weekly newspaper, *Die Zeit*, is also prominent.

There are several weekly glossy magazines with a circulation of over one million. Most prominent are: *Stern* (Hamburg), *Bunte Illustrierte* (Munich), *Quick* (Munich). There are also a number of women's journals with circulations of over one million including *Für Sie*, *Freundin*, *Burda Moden*, *Brigitte*. Specialised trade publications are numerous; many have a wide circulation within their own sphere.

These magazines carry a predominance of product services advertisements. Colour ads account for about 75%. An A4 colour page costs typically DM 70 000 and B/W about DM 36 000. These costs do not include design, photography or any process work, just the pure insertion costs.

While these rates are high, and possibly beyond

the reach of many small companies, there are ways in which the use of skill and imagination can make effective use of limited resources. Remember in the video sequence accompanying this section how Jeff Johnson of Austin Rover Deutschland described his company's attempts to reduce the cost of advertising. Unable to compete with the regular glossy colour displays of competitors, the company launched a black and white advertising campaign which halved costs and enabled the company to double its number of insertions. Far from reducing the appeal of the advertising campaign, the black and white adverts skilfully blended images and dialogue to create an award winning series of adverts.

Local free papers

There are literally thousands of local papers distributed free in Germany. More than 1400 of them are *Lokale Anzeigen* – und *Informationsblätter* pushed free through any available letter box, as well as broadsheets produced by local supermarkets and large chain stores. Right at the opposite end of the scale are the specialist magazines. Germany is a land of specialists and every speciality has an association, some have several. Every association has its official journal. Every trade and product grouping also has at least one professionally produced magazine. This means that an advertising agency can direct its advertising to any section of the public or trade that it wants to.

Radio and television

Advertising is at present carried by the broadcasting and television companies. These are: Norddeutscher Rundfunk (Hamburg), Bayerischer Rundfunk (Munich), Süddeutscher Rundfunk (Stuttgart), Südwestfunk (Baden-Baden), Hessischer Rundfunk (Frankfurt), Radio Bremen (Bremen), Sender Freies Berlin, Saarländischer Rundfunk, Saarbrucken and Westdeutscher Rundfunk (Cologne) and Zweites Deutsches Fernsehen at Mainz. Fees for a 30-second radio transmission may cost DM 1500 and advertising on television costs DM 25 000 or more per 15-second spot on either of the two commercial programmes, depending on whether coverage is national or regional, the time of day and the season of the year. It is estimated that 75% of all households watch TV advertising.

For the manufacturer, TV advertising is both expensive and difficult to get into as time is restricted and has often to be booked many months in advance. Time is also limited to specific bands, normally early evening, where the ads come all together, separated by some nice comic animated sequences. These are judged by most people to be the highlight of the programme as the ads tend to be uninspiring. It is hard to see how anything other than supermarket shelf-fillers can get any sales benefit out of TV advertising in Germany. Cable TV has come to selected areas and a horde of local advertising magazine programmes is being produced, often of dubious quality. More useful are the many magazines built around the TV schedules, *Hör zu*, Germany's TV Times prints $3\frac{1}{2}$ million copies and commands DM 115 000 for a 4-colour page.

While TV advertising is difficult to obtain and expensive, radio advertising is much more freely available and worth exploiting, especially where products enjoy regional popularity.

Mail

The delivery of advertising circulars through the mail service has become very popular in Germany in recent years, and the Federal Post Office operates a system under which it is possible for publicity material and small samples to be sent through the post to all householders and holders of post box numbers (full details obtainable from: Zentralauskunftsstelle für Postwurfsendungen beim Postamt 1, Zeil 10, 6000, Frankfurt am Main 2). However, this is not recommended for use by British companies who are attempting to introduce their products into the Federal Republic of Germany for the first time. No matter how good a presentation is sent to companies in West Germany, experience shows that the response rate obtained by foreign companies is extremely low.

There are companies which operate similar services to the Post Office under which they will undertake to supply lists of addresses of members of various professions (e.g. all doctors, cafés, architects or wholesale dealers). Alternatively some will undertake the mailing if the material is sent to them.

Local consulates will supply the names and addresses of such companies, and the information department of the British Embassy in Bonn can offer valuable advice about the range of advertising services available. Alternatively the following two UK organisations are useful sources of advice about marketing generally.

Overseas Press and Media Association,
122 Shaftesbury Avenue
LONDON W1V 8HA
Tel: 01–734 3052
The Institute of Practitioners in Advertising,
44 Belgrave Square
LONDON SW1X 8QS
Tel: 01–235 7020

Trade fairs and promotions

Much has already been said about these in Sequence 1, so just a few reminders. Use trade fairs not only to promote your own products, but also to examine competitors' products. Look at their advertising literature, examine the quality, see who it is aimed at, and talk to prospective buyers and to competitors. Effective marketing and promotion will depend, to a large extent, on your knowledge of the market.

British promotions in major German stores are another good marketing exercise for a wide range of consumer goods. Some German store buyers will visit the UK to select goods. The DTI will advise on the scheduling of store promotions.

Further sources of advice

When deciding on your marketing strategy in Germany, do make the most of the many sources of advice available to exporters. The German Chamber of Industry and Commerce in the UK at 12/13 Suffolk Street, St James, London SW1Y 4HQ (Tel. 01–930 7231) can provide useful marketing advice. The Economics and Marketing Department provides information on the German market and advises on marketing in Germany. It maintains up-to-date statistics on industrial production, exports and imports, wages and salaries, industrial and consumer prices. It files and prepares market reports including relevant data such as market size, profile of main competitors and potential customers, distribution channels, price structures, advertising, trade fairs etc. The Department can also assist British companies considering investment in Germany.

The British Chamber of Commerce in Germany (BCCG) at Heumarkt 14, 5000 Cologne 1, West Germany (Tel: 0221 234284), is an excellent source of marketing advice. The Chamber was established in 1960 to further British business interests in trade with the Federal Republic. Its membership now totals 650 companies. Many BCCG members are prepared to share their knowledge and experience freely with newcomers to the German market or with those who face specific problems in developing existing business. Additionally, the Chamber publishes a wide range of information papers available to both members and non-members.

BBC External Services

You do not have to go to a German radio station to promote your products over German airways. The BBC External Services broadcast to Germany, and regularly feature new ideas developed by British companies. Of particular interest to exporters to Germany is the 15-minute weekly programme, 'Made in Britain'. The BBC External Services welcome as much information as possible from industry. They are interested in new processes and products, export successes, contracts and exhibits at trade fairs abroad. Information should be sent to:
Export Liaison, BBC External Services,
Bush House, Strand,
LONDON WC2B 4PH. Tel: 01–257 2039/2321.

Central Office of Information

Publicity overseas for British exporters can also be obtained through the services of the Central Office of Information, which is concerned with collecting from industry items suitable for dissemination abroad, by way of government information services. The COI are interested in news items, feature articles, tape recordings for broadcasting and films for television and other screenings. Contact:
Central Office of Information, Overseas Press Office,
Hercules Road,
LONDON SE1 7EU. Tel: 01–928 2345.

Company image

In Germany, image can be an important aspect of marketing a product. This extends right through from the company itself, its location, reputation of management etc., to the product and even the packaging. 'After Eight Mints' for example, are sold in Germany with exactly the same exclusive image that they enjoy in the UK. Packaging and promotion has played an important part in the reputation of this product.

Austin Rover was faced with a massive problem of improving both the image of the company in Germany, and creating an 'up-market' image for the new Rover 800 series. In recent years the company has marketed a broad product range, from the Mini and Metro at the lower end, to the Rover at the top. Some of its cars at the lower end of the range were sold through a German hypermarket chain. Whilst this may have benefited sales of these cars, it did not create the 'up-market' company image that was needed to promote the new Rover 800. This car was aimed at the executive sector, a traditionally status-conscious segment of the market.

To improve its image, the company appointed a largely new dealer network for the 800 series, to replace the old 'back street' image some of its dealers had acquired previously. Achieving this was a costly exercise, because, as we have seen in a previous section, getting rid of agents can incur costly penalty payments. However, in the case of Austin Rover, their dealers are their public face, and changing the image meant changing the dealers.

Other aspects of improving the company's image included much better delivery of new cars and parts to dealers, as well as effective 'on site' training of dealers' own staff.

Customer care and after sales service was given a major boost. In Germany, dealers need to be confident that the products they sell can be serviced quickly and efficiently from a German base. We have seen in Sequence 3 how Mike Taylor of THV was questioned about his ability to service Swan kettles. The same will apply to all products which may require servicing.

Attention was also paid by Austin Rover Deutschland to the media. MD, Jeff Johnson held regular briefing dinners for German motoring

journalists and slowly began to win them away from the 'British Elend' (British disaster) image that hung like a noose round the neck of the old company.

To enhance the image of the car to German consumers, a great deal of attention was paid to detail. Firstly the car complied fully with German emission control standards. It also incorporated quality features associated with the UK, such as a walnut veneer fascia. Other details included the welcome cassette which you hear in the video, as well as a signed certificate for each car, guaranteeing its readiness for delivery. As we have heard before, the German market is highly quality conscious, and if you're competing in a quality sector, detail counts.

Environmental factors

For the last couple of years, a product's image has had to include a strong environmental element, soap powder that does not contaminate the drinking water of the next city down river, aerosol cans that do not blast holes in the atmosphere, packaging made from recycled packaging etc., etc. Naturally the Germans have an Association for this and the Association awards the 'Blauer Engel' (Blue Angel) symbol to indicate that the product has been recycled or is in some way 'environment friendly'. Increasingly, attention paid to environmental detail may enhance the image of a company and its product in the minds of German consumers.

Sales literature

Sales literature is very important in creating a good image and has to be translated in thought and design and not just in language. It is not the snappy humorous headline that sells in Germany, but the small print.

For this reason, it is essential that all technical and business translation is professionally undertaken and checked by your agent or representative. You have only to walk around a trade fair in this country to see how incorrect translations into English can seriously detract from the 'quality' image of a product.

If you are selling consumer products to retail outlets you will be expected to supply point-of-sale material. You will need a sales folder describing your product, giving its main selling features and depicting your point-of-sale material. You must give details of all planned advertising, including dates, so that the shop will be able to judge when stocks should be available, etc. You may be asked to pay towards your client's advertising and other expenses. All this must be taken into account when pricing your products.

Conclusion

So what does all this mean for the British exporter? It means that, increasingly, knowing your market inside out is essential. In the case of advertising and promotion, if you know where your German competitors spend their advertising budgets, it is a good guide to where your own priorities should lie. Using expert advice, whether it be an agent, advertising agency or government service, will pay high dividends. Getting into Germany can be costly, but if you are committed to the market and prepared to work at it, your company can make its mark.

Business Magazine

You've arrived, you're confident, your product is good. How do you let the Germans know? Chris Serle looks at advertising in Business Magazine 7.

Grammar guide

Introduction

In the body of the book the number of grammatical terms has been kept to a minimum. There are times, however, when avoiding a grammatical term makes for such a complicated explanation that a technical term has been used.

For this reason the grammar guide has been included as a 'working grammar'. It has been written by John Sharp M.A. for people who feel unsure about their knowledge of the 'language of language'. In it you will find definitions of the words in the box below, together with appropriate cross-references.

The entries are arranged alphabetically, but the table shows you the grammatical model used. It is a simple operational one, to enable you to see where all the technical terms fit in.

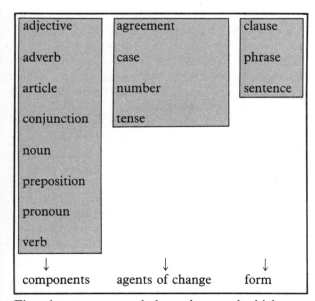

adjective	agreement	clause
adverb	case	phrase
article	number	sentence
conjunction	tense	
noun		
preposition		
pronoun		
verb		
↓	↓	↓
components	agents of change	form

First, however, a word about that word which frightens so many people, **grammar**.

What *is* grammar?

It is defined as 'a set of rules which determine correct speech'. The rules are not immutable and do in fact change gradually through the influence of common practice. (Both Shakespeare and Jane Austen wrote some things which we would today call 'ungrammatical'.)

Grammar uses a great number of technical terms (some of which make up the substance of this guide) and these are accepted by people concerned everywhere.

As a language, English uses fewer rules than most. It makes up for this (to the annoyance of foreigners) by having vast numbers of exceptions to everything and, of course, by its absurd system of spelling. But when we study German, we meet a lot of rules.

Do I need to study grammar?

No, not so long as you wish to speak only your own language and can arrange to be born of parents who speak it excellently. You can then do the same, without giving a thought to grammar.

But, if you wish to speak a foreign language – that is different. You *could* simply go to the country concerned and live there. Gradually, you would pick up the language and speak it as well or as badly as the people you mixed with. But few of us get the chance to do that.

Unless you study only on the basis of imitation – 'listen to what I say and repeat it' – you cannot avoid this sort of question: 'Why must I say *den* and not *der* in this German sentence?' (as a German might ask: 'Why is it *him* and not *he* in this English sentence?'). Most people are not content with the answer, 'Because that is how it is!' They want to understand how the machine works.

Is this easy?

No. Language is a wonderfully useful but highly complicated machine. Luckily, it can still work even if you use it badly (like crashing the gears on a car). But it is much more satisfactory for you and for the people you speak to if you can make it work properly. To do that, you have to know more. That is where this guide comes in.

What is the guide for?

It is intended to help. But it would be pointless simply for you to read it straight through. (A German might just as well try to get to know London by starting in a southern suburb, studying every street and gradually working his or her way to the centre.) As the items are arranged alphabetically, one of the most important terms – **noun** – comes in the middle, and another – **verb** – near the end. For example, if you want to confirm for yourself what a **direct object** is, look up **direct object** and you will be referred to **case**, where you will find the appropriate information. The arrow will guide you.

The grammar guide

accusative → case
adjectival endings → table 1

adjective – a word which describes or defines a **noun** e.g. a *good* deal, a *healthy* profit, *that* occasion, *every* time, *many* people.

Notes: (1) in English a **noun** can function as an adjective e.g. the *ski* slopes, a *farm* worker, our *debit* balance. Where this is done in German it gives rise to a compound noun. This is the reason for many of those seemingly endless words e.g. *Erstausrüstungsabteilung*.
  (2) grammarians distinguish between several types of adjective. We need not bother with most of these, but you should recognise **possessive adjectives**. These indicate possession and are *my, your, his, her, its, our, their* in English. See table 3 for **possessive adjectives** in German.

adverb – a word which modifies (a) a **verb** or (b) an **adjective** or (c) another **adverb**

e.g. (a) They spoke *quickly*.
       We have opened a subsidiary *there*.
       The agent *frequently* visits us.
    (b) You are a *very* good customer.
    (c) He speaks the language *quite well*.

In English many adverbs are formed from adjectives e.g. *quickly* (adverb) from *quick* (adjective). But in German the adverb generally has the same form as the corresponding **adjective**. Thus, the English footballer's comments 'It was a good game. We played *real good*.' (false adverbs: he should say *really well*) would sound in principle correct to a German who had only a little English.

agreement – this is a grammatical practice of great important to correct language. Since English has, in recent centuries, shed most of the varying endings of **nouns**, **verbs** and **adjectives** which were once used to distinguish their functions, we do not have to do a great deal about agreement. In German, however, the consequences of agreement will keep us very busy.
  Put simply, there is a rule which means that certain words, when used together, must agree in **gender**, **number** and **case**. This is best explained by examples:

(a) **gender** – The stewardess has *her* appointment at nine; *she* will be on time (not *his* or *he*, which would not agree with *the stewardess*). Because all nouns in German show gender, you have to remember to adapt all to appropriate words, 'der Kundendienst ist sehr wichtig. *Er* kostet viel Geld. Wir müssen *ihn* richtig machen.
(b) **number** – The man *is* here, the men *are* here.
(c) **case** – What about these prices? I do not like *them* – *they* are too high (they are the same prices, but the function of the **pronoun** in the two parts of the sentence is not the same).

article – it counts as an **adjective** but has a special function. You can see this by hearing what it is. We have two articles in English, the **indefinite article**: *a* or *an*, and the **definite article**: *the*. That, for us, is the end of the matter. But it is not so in German. Although the German language has *ein/eine/ein* and *der/die/das* to correspond to *a/an* and *the*, you must note:

(1) all these words change their ending to **agree** with the **noun** they are describing,

(2) they are sometimes used differently from the way in which we use them e.g. when we say 'I see you are *an* authorised signatory', the German leaves out *a/an* – *Ich sehe schon, daß Sie Prokurist sind.*

(3) *der/die/das* have other functions in which they do not mean *the* → **relative pronoun**.

auxiliary verb → **verb**

case – this is a grammatical idea for illustrating the role a **noun** or **pronoun** play in a **sentence**. We can begin the explanation by an example from English. Contrast 'I like him' with 'he likes me'. The changes in the two words in each statement occur because their function has changed. The **subject** of the first statement is *I*, of the second *he*. The **object** of the first statement is *him*, of the second *me*. Long ago our **nouns** also had different endings to show how their function in the **sentence** changed. We got rid of those endings and relied on word order to show what was subject and what was object. The Germans have kept their different endings, so case endings are still very important for them.

The **nominative** case is for the **subject**, i.e. the **noun** or **pronoun** which is responsible for the action or other verbal expression:
e.g. *The showroom* is over there!,
    Trade fairs are a source of much business.

The **accusative** case is for the **direct object**, i.e. the **noun** or **pronoun** upon which the action of the verb is exercised:
e.g. He opened *the book*.
    We discussed *the advantages*.

The **genitive** case mostly denotes **possession**. It is the only case which is easily recognised in English because of the s:
e.g. our *client's needs* – our *clients' needs*

The **dative case** (from a Latin word meaning *to give*) is used for the **indirect object** in English:
e.g. I have brought (*for*) *you* something nice.

See **table 1** for examples of **cases**.

Also, some German verbs put their object automatically into the dative case, e.g. belong – follow – help – join – meet – please – thank.

clause – this is best explained by an example:
e.g. I will give him your message if I see him.

In this statement the first half (I will give him your message) is the **main clause** because it would make sense alone, whereas the second half (if I see him) conveys no sense at all on its own. It is therefore a **subordinate** or **dependent** clause. This is not a particularly useful piece of information for English but is of enormous importance for **word order** in German, since the **finite verb** is always the second idea in the main clause. In the subordinate clause the **finite verb** always comes at the end:
e.g. ich *sage* ihm Bescheid, wenn ich ihn *sehe*.

conjunction – a word which is used to join ideas or **sentences** together:
e.g. The Chairman spoke *and* the members
        listened.
    I arrived late *because* the traffic was so heavy.
    When the meeting ended, I left quickly.
In German there are some conjunctions which do not affect the **word order**. The most frequently used are:

---

aber – but
entweder . . . oder – either . . . or
nicht nur . . . sondern auch – not only . . . but also
oder – or
sowohl . . . als auch – both . . . and
sondern – but
und – and
denn – for, because

e.g. Ich habe davon gehört, *aber* ich bin nicht von
        der Qualität überzeugt.

Some conjunctions require you to put the **verb** immediately afterwards. For practical purposes you will need:

---

also – consequently
auch – also
außerdem – in addition
dadurch – in that way
dann – then
darum – that is the reason why
dazu – in addition
deshalb – for that reason
deswegen – for that reason
trotzdem – notwithstanding that

e.g. Meiner Meinung nach müßte das ganze dunkelgrün sein, *dann* wäre es noch viel besser.

Some conjunctions require you to put the **verb** at the end of the **clause**. For practical purposes you will need:

als – when (in past)
bevor – before
bis – until
da – since, because
damit – so that
daß – that
nachdem – after
ob – whether
obgleich – although
obwohl – although
seitdem – since
so daß – so that
um . . . zu+ **infinitive** – so that
weil – because
wenn – if, whenever
wie – as

e.g. Das hat den Vorteil, *daß* der Kunde nicht lange auf Reparaturen warten *muß*.

dative → **case**
definite article → **article**
dependent clause → **clause**
direct object → **case**
finite verb → **verb**
gender → **agreement**
genitive → **case**
indefinite article → **article**
indirect object → **case**
infinitive → **verb**
main clause → **clause**
modal auxiliary → **verb**
nominative → **case**

noun – the name of (a) a person, (b) an object, (c) a quality or idea:
e.g. (a) Michael, Neuwied, Germany (these names are called **proper** nouns)
(b) book, handwriting, sample (this category, much the largest, includes everything you can see, hear or touch; these are **common** nouns),
(c) experience, price increase, needs (these are called **abstract** nouns because you cannot see, hear or touch them directly, although you can feel their effects.

In German there are a number of frequently occurring nouns which have one form for the **nominative case** and a different form for every other **case**:
e.g. Der Kunde kommt gleich.
Ich treffe den Kunden um zehn Uhr.
Wer hat die Adresse des Kunden?
Wo waren Sie mit dem Kunden?
This only happens with masculine nouns.

number – the grammatical term distinguishes between *one* and *more than one* by the names **singular** and **plural**. In English, apart from the distinction between *he* **works** and *they* **work**, number changes affect almost only **nouns**, but in German you have to ring the changes for **adjectives** and **articles** as well.

past participle → **tense**

perfect tense → **tense**

phrase – in grammatical terms we mean a set of words conveying meaning, but not capable of standing alone because they do not contain a **finite verb**:
e.g. Frankfurt, *home of the oldest trade fair*, is still very much a centre of trade today.

plural → **number**

possessive adjective → **adjective**

preposition – a word which marks the relationship (e.g. in time or place or purpose) between a **noun** or **pronoun** and another word:
e.g. They are *at* the office.
The instructions come *with* the guarantee.
The plane arrived *on* time.
What did you do that *for*?
In German, prepositions affect the **case** (and sometimes the ending) of the **noun** or **pronoun** they accompany. In grammatical jargon they are said to **put** these **into** the **accusative**, **genitive**, or **dative case**.

See **table 2** for **prepositions** and their **case(s)**.

pronoun – a word which **stands for** a **noun**
e.g. *He* (Peter Rehberger) is doing a very good job for *us* (Fibracan) in a very difficult market.

See **table 3** for **pronouns** in German.

You should note two particular categories of pronoun:

(i) **reflexive pronoun**: They reorganised *themselves*, German sometimes uses **reflexive verbs** when we do not, as in *Ich freue mich* – I am pleased, and *Wir treffen uns um zehn*. We are meeting/We meet at ten.

See **table 3** for **reflexive pronouns** in German.

(ii) **relative pronoun**: The salesman *who* came last week is here again; The guarantee (that) we give is for one year. (The bracket shows that this relative pronoun can be left out in English; it cannot be left out in German.)

See **table 4** for **relative pronouns** in German.

reflexive → pronoun

relative pronoun → pronoun

sentence – a set of words complete in itself and conveying a statement, a question or a command:
e.g. It is raining.
    Have you brought your umbrella?
    Go and get it!

Sentences can be far longer than these, constructed by joining a series of **clauses**.

singular → number

subject → case

subordinate clause → clause

tense – the word means *time* and applies only to **verbs**. Their action may take place in the **present** (I work), in the **past** (we worked), or in the **future** (we will work).

Grammar also recognises refinements of time:

e.g. **present perfect** – He *has finished*.
    past perfect – They *had arrived* by the time we left.
    future perfect – The meeting *will have started* by now.
    imperfect – She *lived/was living* there at the time.

The aspect of tenses which usually causes us most trouble is whether to use *haben* or *sein* with the **past participle** when talking about the past and using the **perfect tense**.
e.g. *Der Hersteller hat sich darauf eingestellt.*
    Sind Sie gut angekommen?

verb – a word most commonly used to indicate **action** or **state of being**:
e.g. We *buy*, they *sell* and we *are* partners.
But this, the most complex of the components of speech, has many different functions. Some can be ignored, but there are two types of verb which are important for you:

(1) **auxiliary verb** = helping other verbs
e.g. I *have* finished.
    Does she like this? No, she *does* not like the colour.

Here, *have* helps to form the past (**perfect**) **tense** and *does* helps to form questions and to say *not*. This very important use of the verb *do* in English is not found in German.

(2) **modal auxiliary verb** = there are six modal auxiliary verbs in German. It is not easy to give them an exact meaning, but as an approximate guide they mean:

---

können – to be able to
dürfen – to be allowed to
müssen – to have to
sollen – to be obliged to, to be supposed to
wollen – to want to
mögen – to like (usually used as *ich möchte* etc. – I would like)

They need a second verb to provide a complete meaning:
e.g. *Darf ich kurz über unsere Verkaufsbedingungen sprechen?*
The first verb, *darf*, is, in grammatical terms, used here in a **finite** form, i.e. it is limited to the **subject** *ich* in person and in **number**. The second verb, *sprechen*, is used here in the **infinitive** i.e. it is not limited to any number or person.

word order → clause

Table 1

(a) adjectival endings – with no definite or indefinite article

singular	masculine	feminine	neuter
nominative	*guter* Kundendienst ist wichtig	*gute* Literatur . . .	*gutes* Material . . .
accusative	wir haben . . . *guten* Kundendienst	. . . *gute* Literatur	. . . *gutes* Material
genitive	wegen . . . *guten* Kundendienstes	. . . *guter* Literatur	. . . *guten* Materials
dative	mit . . . *gutem* Kundendienst	*guter* Literatur	*gutem* Material

plural	masculine	feminine	neuter
nominative	*große* Gewinne sind wichtig	*große* Mengen . . .	*große* Geräte . . .
accusative	wir haben . . . *große* Gewinne	. . . *große* Mengen	. . . *große* Geräte
genitive	wegen . . . *großer* Gewinne	. . . *großer* Mengen	. . . *großer* Geräte
dative	mit . . . *großen* Gewinnen	. . . *großen* Mengen	. . . *großen* Geräten

(b) adjectival endings – with an indefinite article

singular	masculine	feminine	neuter
nominative	ein *klarer* Text ist wichtig	eine *klare* Basis . . .	ein *klares* Bild . . .
accusative	wir haben . . . einen *klaren* Text	. . . eine *klare* Basis	. . . ein *klares* Bild
genitive	wegen . . . eines *klaren* Textes	. . . einer *klaren Basis*	. . . eines *klaren* Bildes
dative	mit . . . einem *klaren* Text	einer *klaren* Basis	einem *klaren* Bild

plural	masculine	feminine	neuter
nominative	keine *neuen* Fälle waren da	keine neuen Fragen . . .	keine *klaren* Details . . .
accusative	wir haben . . . keine *neuen* Fälle	. . . keine *neuen* Fragen	. . . keine *neuen* Details
genitive	wegen . . . keiner *neuen* Fälle	. . . keiner *neuen Fragen*	. . . keiner *neuen* Details
dative	in keinen *neuen* Fällen	bei keinen *neuen* Fragen	von keinen *neuen* Details

(c) adjectival endings – with the definite article

singular	masculine	feminine	neuter
nominative	der *schöne* Flug war angenehm	die *schöne* Gegend . . .	das *schöne* Essen . . .
accusative	wir finden . . . angenehm den *schönen Flug*	. . . die *schöne* Gegend	. . . das *schöne* Essen
genitive	wegen . . . des *schönen* Flugs	. . . der *schönen* Gegend	. . . des *schönen* Essens
dative	mit . . . dem *schönen* Flug	. . . der *schönen* Gegend	. . . dem *schönen* Essen

plural	masculine	feminine	neuter
nominative	die *kleinen Umsätze* bereiten uns Schwierigkeiten	die *kleinen* Firmen . . .	die *kleinen* Stücke . . .
accusative	wir haben . . . diskutiert die *kleinen* Umsätze	. . . die *kleinen* Firmen	. . . die *kleinen* Stücke
genitive	wegen . . . der *kleinen* Umsätze	. . . der *kleinen* Firmen	. . . der *kleinen* Stücke
dative	wir haben mit . . . gerechnet den *kleinen* Umsätzen	. . . den *kleinen* Firmen	. . . den *kleinen* Stücken

Table 2

prepositions and cases

These are the common prepositions which always take the **accusative case**:

für – um – durch – gegen – bis – ohne

e.g. Er ist *gegen das Produkt.*	Er ist *dagegen.*
Sie kommt *für den Herrn.*	Sie kommt *für ihn.*

These are the common prepositions which always take the **dative case**:

ab – aus – außer – bei – gegenüber – mit – nach – von – zu

e.g. Ein Termin *mit dem Verkaufsleiter.*	Ein Termin *mit ihm.*
Der Vorteil *von dem Produkt*	Der Vorteil *davon.*

These are the common prepositions which always take the **genitive case**:

anläßlich – anstatt – einschließlich – hinsichtlich – laut – mittels – trotz – während – wegen – zuzüglich

e.g. Wegen *der guten Verkaufszahlen* . . .	derentwegen
Wegen *meines Chefs* . . .	seinetwegen

These are the common prepositions which can take *either* the **accusative case** OR the **dative case**, depending usually on whether movement is involved:

an – auf – hinter – in – neben – über – unter – vor – zwischen

wohin? (where to?)	*wo?* (where)
Ich fahre *in die Stadt.*	Ich wohne *in der Stadt.*
Ich lege die Zeichnung *hinter das Telefon.*	Die Zeichnung liegt *hinter dem Telefon.*
(Ich lege die Zeichnung *dahinter.*)	(Die Zeichnung liegt *dahinter.*)

Table 3

pronouns, reflexive pronouns and possessive adjectives

nominative	ich	Sie	er	sie	es	wir	Sie	sie
accusative	mich	Sie	ihn	sie	es	uns	Sie	sie
genitive (possessive adjective)	mein--	Ihr--	sein--	ihr--	sein--	unser--	Ihr--	ihr--
dative	mir	Ihnen	ihm	ihr	ihm	uns	Ihnen	ihnen
reflexive pronouns	mich	sich	sich	sich	sich	uns	sich	sich

N.B. All the possessive adjectives take the same endings as *(k)ein* – see table 1b.

Table 4

relative pronouns

	masculine	feminine	neuter
singular			
nominative	der	die	das
accusative	den	die	das
genitive	dessen	deren	dessen
dative	dem	der	dem
plural			
nominative	die	die	die
accusative	die	die	die
genitive	deren	deren	deren
dative	denen	denen	denen

Vocabulary guide

Notes

The aim of the vocabulary guide is to help you to find out the meaning of the words as they are used in the various meetings and discussions. It is not a dictionary.

If you come across a word which you are not sure of, look it up in here and you will find a guide to its meaning as used in one or more of the sequences and/or exercises.

For the sake of simplicity, we have usually limited ourselves to one meaning. In addition, we have generally only included the form and meaning which occurs first, and which appears earliest in the sequences. Sometimes, therefore, you will find a word described as an *adjective* which you meet as an *adverb*, or vice versa. Sometimes, also, you may find a meaning which does not quite fit the situation. If you are not able to work out a satisfactory meaning, we recommend that you use your own dictionary.

- Abbreviations used are: (*adj*) adjective, (*adv*) adverb, (*conj*) conjunction, (*pp*) past participle, (*phras*) phrase, (*prep*) preposition, (*pron*) pronoun, (*vb*) verb, (*vbs*) verb-separable.
- Plural forms of nouns are indicated in brackets.

(*vbs*)	ab'drucken	*to print*
	(*pp*) abgedruckt	
der	Abend (-e)	*evening*
(*vb*)	ab'fliegen	*to take off*
	(*pp*) abgeflogen	
das	Abführband ("er)	*conveyor belt*
(*vbs*)	ab'geben	*to deliver, give*
	(*pp*) abgegeben	
(*pp*)	abgeflogen	→ *ab'fliegen*
(*pp*)	abgeschlossen	→ *ab'schließen*
(*vbs*)	ab'hängen von	*to depend on*
	(*pp*) abgehangen	
(*vbs*)	ab'halten	*to hold*
	(*pp*) abgehalten	
(*vbs*)	ab'klären	*to clarify*
	(*pp*) abgeklärt	
(*vbs*)	ab'lagern	*to store*
	(*pp*) abgelagert	
der	Ablauf ("e)	*completion*
(*adj*)	ablehnend	*negative*
(*vbs*)	ab'liefern	*to deliver*
	(*pp*) abgeliefert	
der	Abruf (-e)	*call-off*
(*vbs*)	ab'runden	*to round off*
	(*pp*) abgerundet	
die	Abschaltung (-en)	*cut-out (switch)*
(*vb*)	ab'schließen	*to conclude*
	(*pp*) abgeschlossen	
der	Abschluß ("sse)	*conclusion*
der	Abschnitt (-e)	*section*
(*vb*)	ab'sehen	*to foresee*
	(*pp*) abgesehen	
(*adv*)	absolut	*absolutely*
der	Abverkauf ("e)	*sales turnover*
(*vbs*)	ab'warten	*to wait and see*
	(*pp*) abgewartet	
(*vbs*)	ab'zeichnen	*to sketch*
	(*pp*) abgezeichnet	
(*vb*)	achten	*to consider*
	(*pp*) geachtet	
(*adj*)	ähnlich	*similar*

(vb)	ändern	to change	(vbs)	an'schneiden	to cut into
(pp)	geändert		(pp)	angeschnitten	
der	Ärger	trouble	(vb)	an'siedeln	to settle
(vbs)	auf'geben	to give up	(pp)	angesiedelt	
(pp)	aufgegeben		(vbs)	an'sprechen	to address
die	Aktentasche (-n)	briefcase	(pp)	angesprochen	
(adv)	aktiv	actively	der	Anspruch ("e)	claim, demand
die	Aktivität (-en)	activity	(vb)	an'stellen	to do, get up to
(adj)	aktuell	up to date	(pp)	angestellt	
(vb)	akzeptieren	to accept	(adj)	anwesend	present
(pp)	akzeptiert		der	Anwesende (-n, -n)	person present
(adj)	allein	alone	die	Anzahl	number
(adv)	allerdings	by all means	die	Anzeigevorlage	advertisement copy
(inv)	alles	everything	der	Appetit	appetite
(adj)	allgemein	general	(vb)	arbeiten	to work
(adv)	also	so	(pp)	gearbeitet	
(adj)	altmodisch	old-fashioned	der	Arbeiter (-)	worker
die	Alufelge (-n)	aluminium hub	die	Arbeitslosigkeit	unemployment
(phras)	am Apparat	on the phone	das	Argument (-e)	argument
(adv)	am besten	best of all	die	Art (-en)	nature
(adj)	amerikanisch	American	der	Artikel (-)	article
(phras)	an Bord	on board	(adj)	asiatisch	Asian
(vbs)	an'bieten	to offer	(adv)	auch	also
(pp)	angeboten		(phras)	auf dem laufenden	up to date
(adj)	andere	other	(vb)	auf'bauen	to construct
(adv)	andererseits	on the other hand	(pp)	aufgebaut	
(adv)	anders	in another way	die	Aufgabe (-n)	task
(vbs)	an'deuten	to indicate	der	Aufgabenbereich (-e)	duties, responsibility
(pp)	augedeutet		(vbs)	auf'geben	to give up
(vbs)	an'diskutieren	to begin to discuss	(pp)	aufgegeben	→ auf'geben
(pp)	andiskutiert		(adj)	aufgeschlossen	unlocked
(adj)	anfallend	accrueing	der	Aufkleber (-)	label
der	Anfang ("e)	start	(vbs)	auf'listen	to list
(vbs)	an'fangen	to start	(pp)	aufgelistet	
(pp)	angefangen		(adj)	aufmerksam	attentive
die	Anfrage (-n)	enquiry	(vbs)	auf'schlagen	to open,
das	Angebot (-e)	quotation	(pp)	aufgeschlagen	
(adj)	angenehm	pleasant	(vbs)	auf'sparen	to save up
(pp)	angenommen	→ an'nehmen	(pp)	aufgespart	
(adj)	angeschlossen	connected	der	Auftrag ("e)	order
(vbs)	an'hängen	to add to	der	Auftragseingang ("e)	receipt of order
(pp)	anhangehangen		der	Augenblick (-e)	moment
(vbs)	an'hören	to listen to	die	Ausbildung	training
(pp)	angehört		(vbs)	aus'denken	to think out/through
(vbs)	an'kommen auf	to depend on	(pp)	ausgedacht	
(vbs)	an'kommen	to succeed, arrive	die	Ausführung (-en)	model, design
(pp)	angekommen		(adj)	ausgebildet	trained
die	Ankunft ("e)	arrival	(pp)	ausgedacht	→ aus'denken
die	Anlage (-n)	plant	(pp)	ausgegangen	→ aus'gehen
die	Anleitung (-en)	instructions	(vbs)	aus'gehen	to go out, start
der	Anmeldezettel	registration form	(pp)	ausgegangen	
(vbs)	an'nehmen	to accept	(adj)	ausgelastet	fully utilised
(pp)	angenommen		(adj)	ausgezeichnet	excellent
(vbs)	an'peilen	to take a bearing on	(vbs)	aus'handeln	to negotiate
(pp)	angepeilt		(pp)	ausgehandelt	
die	Anregung (-en)	suggestion, idea	(vbs)	aus'lasten	to put a strain on
(vbs)	an'rufen	to telephone	(pp)	ausgelastet	
(pp)	angerufen		(vbs)	aus'legen	to adapt
(adv)	anschließend	subsequently	(pp)	ausgelegt	

(vb)	aus'liefern	to deliver		der	Behälter (-)	container
	(pp) ausgeliefert			(adj)	behilflich	helpful
(vbs)	aus'nützen	to exploit		(adj)	beide	both
	(pp) ausgenützt			(adv)	beinahe	nearly
(vbs)	aus'probieren	to try out		(adv)	beiseite	aside
	(pp) ausprobiert			das	Beispiel (-e)	example
(vbs)	aus'reichen	to suffice		(vbs)	bei'treten	to join
	(pp) ausgereicht				(pp) beigetreten	
(vbs)	aus'richten	to tell, pass on		(adj)	bekannt	well-known
	(pp) ausgerichtet			der	Bekanntheitsgrad (e)	level of familiarity
(vbs)	aus'sehen	to appear, look		(vb)	bekommen	to get, receive
	(pp) aus'gesehen				(pp) bekommen	
(adv)	außen	outside		der	Belang (-e)	consequence
(adv)	außerdem	besides		(vb)	beliefern	to supply
(adj)	außereuropäisch	outside Europe			(pp) beliefert	
(prep)	außerhalb	outside		(vb)	bemessen	to measure
(adv)	außerordentlich	extraordinarily			(pp) bemessen	
die	Ausstattung (-en)	fixtures & fittings		(adj)	bemüht	concerned
(adj)	ausstehend	outstanding		(vb)	benötigen	to need
(vbs)	aus'stellen	to exhibit			(pp) benötigt	
	(pp) ausgestellt			(vb)	benutzen	to use
(vbs)	aus'strahlen	to radiate			(pp) benutzt	
	(pp) ausgestrahlt			(adj)	benützerfreundlich	user friendly
der	Austausch	exchange		die	Beobachtung (-en)	observation
(adj)	austauschbar	interchangeable		(vb)	beraten	to advise
die	Auswahl	choice, selection			(pp) beraten	
der	Auszug	extraction		(vb)	berechnen	to calculate
das	Auto (-s)	car			(pp) berechnet	
der	Autofahrertraum ("e)	car-driver's dream		der	Bereich (-e)	area
die	Automatik	automatic gear		die	Bereifung	tyres
(adj)	automatisch	automatic		(adj)	bereit	ready, willing
das	Automobil (-e)	motor car		(vb)	bereiten	to prepare, make
					(pp) bereitet	
die	Basis (-sen)	basis		(adv)	bereits	already
der	Bau (-ten)	construction		der	Bericht (-e)	report
(vb)	bauen	to construct, make		(vb)	berücksichtigen	to take into account
	(pp) gebaut				(pp) berücksichtigt	
die	Beanspruchung (-en)	stress		(vb)	beruhigen	to calm
das	Becken (-)	basin			(pp) beruhigt	
(vb)	bedauern	to regret		(vb)	beschaffen	to procure
	(pp) bedauert				(pp) beschaffen	
die	Bedeckung (-en)	cover		(vb)	beschleunigen	to speed up
(vb)	bedeuten	to mean			(pp) beschleunigt	
	(pp) bedeutet			(vbi)	beschließen	to decide
der	Bediener (-)	operative			(pp) beschlossen	
(adj)	bedingt	caused		der	Beschluß ("sse)	decision
die	Bedingung (-en)	condition		(adj)	besondere	special
der	Befehl (-e)	command		das	Besondere	the special thing
(adj)	befindlich	situated		(adj)	besonders	especially
(vb)	begegnen	to meet		(vb)	besprechen	to discuss
	(pp) begegnet				(pp) besprochen	
(vb)	begeistern	to enthuse		(adv)	besser	better
	(pp) begeistert			(vb)	bestätigen	to confirm
(vb)	beginnen	to begin			(pp) bestätigt	
	(pp) begonnen			das	Beste	the best thing
(vb)	beglückwünschen	to congratulate		(vb)	bestehen	to exist, survive
	(pp) beglückwünscht				(pp) bestanden	
der	Begriff (-e)	concept		(vb)	bestehen auf	to insist on
(vb)	begrüßen	to greet			(pp) bestanden	
	(pp) begrüßen					

(vb)	bestehen aus	to consist of
	(pp) bestanden	
(adj)	bestehend	existing
(vb)	bestellen	to order
	(pp) bestellt	
die	Bestellung (-en)	ordering
(adj)	bestimmt	certain
(adv)	bestimmt	decidedly
(der)	Besuch (-e)	visit
(vb)	besuchen	to visit
	(pp) besucht	
das	Besucherzimmer	visitor's room
(vb)	beteiligt sein	to have a share in
(vb)	betragen	to come to
	(pp) betragen	
der	Betrieb (-e)	operation
(vb)	beurteilen	to judge
	(pp) beurteilt	
(conj)	bevor	before
die	Bewegung (-en)	movement
(vb)	bewundern	to admire
	(pp) bewundert	
(vb)	bezahlen	to pay (for)
	(pp) bezahlt	
die	Bezahlung (-en)	payment
das	Bier (-e)	beer
das	Bild (-er)	picture
(adj)	bildend	forming
der	Bildschirm (-e)	screen
(adj)	billig	cheap
(adv)	billiger	more cheaply
(prep)	bis	until
(adj)	bisherig	up to the present
(adv)	bislang	up until now
(phras)	ein bißchen	a bit (of)
(vb)	bitten um	to ask for
	(pp) gebeten	
(vb)	blättern	to page through
	(pp) geblättert	
(vb)	bleiben	to remain
	(pp) geblieben	
das	Blümchen (-)	little flower
der	Boden (")	floor
die	Bohne (-n)	bean
der	Bonus (-se)	bonus
das	Boot (-e)	boat
die	Boxen (plural)	boxes
(vb)	brauchen	to need
	(pp) gebraucht	
(adj)	braun	brown
(adj)	breit	broad
(vb)	bringen	to bring
	(pp) gebracht	
die	Broschüre (-n)	brochure
die	Brückenlösung (-en)	bridging solution
die	Bundesrepublik	Federal Republic
(adj)	bundesweit	national
(adv)	bzw(beziehungsweise)	respectively
die	Campingfahrt (-en)	camping trip

das	Center (-s)	centre
der	Charakter	character
der	Chef (-s)	boss
die	Chefin (-nen)	boss
der	Computer (-)	computer
der	Containerbereich (-)	container field
(adv)	da	there
(adv)	dabei	on that
das	Dach ("er)	roof
(conj)	daher	for that reason
(adv)	damals	at the time
die	Dame (-n)	lady
(vb)	danken	to thank
	(pp) gedankt	
(vbs)	dar'stellen	to present
	(pp) dargestellt	
(adv)	darüber hinaus	over and above that
(phras)	das heißt	i.e.
(phras)	das stimmt	that's right!
(conj)	daß	that
die	Daten (plural)	data
die	Dauer	duration
(vb)	dauern	to last
	(pp) gedauert	
(adv)	dauernd	always
der	Dauertest (-s)	soak test
(vbs)	dazu'nehmen	to add to
	(pp) dazugenommen	
das	Dekor (-s)	decoration
(vb)	denken	to intend
	(pp) gedacht	
(adv)	dermaßen	to such an extent
(adj)	derselbe	the same
(conj)	deshalb	for this reason
das	Design (-s)	design
(conj)	deswegen	for this/that reason
das	Detail (-s)	detail
(adv)	deutlich	clearly
(adj)	deutsch	German
das	Deutsch	German
das	Deutschland	Germany
(adj)	deutschsprachig	German-language
(adj)	dick	thick
(vb)	dienen	to serve
	(pp) gedient	
die	Dienstleistung	customer care
(adj)	dieser	this
das	Ding (-e) ⁴	thing
(adv)	direkt	directly
die	Diskussion (-en)	discussion
(vb)	disponieren	to make arrangements
	(pp) disponiert	
die	Division (-en)	division
der	Dollar (-)	dollar
(vb)	dominieren	to dominate
	(pp) dominiert	
(adj)	doppelt	dual
(adv)	dort	there
(adv)	drauf	to that

(adj)	dritt	*third*	
(adv)	drittens	*thirdly*	
(vb)	drosseln	*to curb*	
	(pp) gedrosselt		
das	Drucken	*printing*	
(vb)	drucken	*to print*	
	(pp) gedruckt		
(vb)	dürfen	*to be allowed to*	
(vb)	dürfte	*should be*	
(adj)	dunkelgrün	*dark green*	
die	Duotonlackierung	*two-tone paintwork*	
(adv)	durchaus	*absolutely*	
(vbs)	durch'fahren	*to drive through*	
	(pp) durchgefahren		
(vbs)	durch'führen	*to carry out*	
	(pp) durchgeführt		
(vbs)	durch'gehen	*to go through*	
	(pp) durchgegangen		
(vb)	durchlaufen	*to undergo*	
	(pp) durchglaufen		
(vbs)	durch'lesen	*to read through*	
	(pp) durchgelesen		
der	Durst	*thirst*	
	(pp) entwickelt		
(adv)	eben	*a moment ago*	
die	Ebene (-n)	*level*	
die	Ecke (-n)	*corner, edge*	
die	Effizienz	*efficiency*	
das	Ei (-er)	*egg*	
die	Eigenschaft (-en)	*characteristic*	
(adv)	eigentlich	*actually*	
(phras)	ein wenig	*a little*	
der	Einbau (-ten)	*installation*	
(vbs)	ein'bauen	*to build in*	
	(pp) eingebaut		
(adv)	einerseits	*on the one hand*	
(adj)	einfach	*simple*	
(vbs)	ein'führen	*to introduce*	
	(pp) eingeführt		
die	Einführung (-en)	*introduction*	
(pp)	eingezogen	→ *ein'ziehen*	
(vbs)	ein'halten	*to keep to*	
	(pp) eingehalten		
(adj)	einige	*some*	
der	Einkauf ("e)	*purchasing*	
das	Einkaufen	*purchasing*	
(vbs)	ein'kaufen	*to buy in*	
	(pp) eingekauft		
der	Einkaufspreis (-e)	*purchase price*	
(vbs)	ein'kleben	*to stick in*	
	(pp) eingeklebt		
das	Einkommen (-)	*income*	
die	Einladung (-en)	*invitation*	
(adv)	einmal	*on the one hand*	
(adv)	einmal	*once*	
(vbs)	ein'nehmen	*to include*	
	(pp) eingenommen		
die	Einrichtung (-en)	*facility*	
(prep)	einschließlich	*including*	
(vb)	ein'setzen	*to implement*	
	(pp) eingesetzt		
(adj)	einverstanden	*in agreement*	
(vbs)	ein'weisen	*to instruct*	
	(pp) eingewiesen		
die	Einzelheit (-en)	*detail*	
die	Einzelkornsaat (-en)	*single-seed sowing*	
(adj)	einzeln	*individual*	
(adv)	einzeln	*individually*	
(vbs)	ein'ziehen	*to move in*	
	(pp) eingezogen		
die	Eleganz	*elegance*	
(adj)	elektrisch	*electrical*	
der	Empfang ("e)	*reception*	
(vb)	empfangen	*to receive*	
	(pp) empfangen		
(vb)	empfehlen	*to recommend*	
	(pp) empfohlen		
das	Ende (-n)	*end*	
der	Endverbraucher (-)	*end user*	
die	Endzahl (-en)	*bottom line*	
(adj)	eng	*narrow*	
(adv)	engagiert	*in a committed way*	
das	England	*Great Britain*	
(adj)	englisch	*English*	
das	Englisch	*English*	
(adj)	enorm	*enormous*	
(vb)	entnehmen	*to deduce from*	
	(pp) entnommen		
(vb)	entscheiden	*to decide*	
	(pp) entschieden		
die	Entscheidung (-en)	*decision*	
(adv)	entschieden	*decidedly*	
(vb)	entsprechen	*to correspond to*	
	(pp) entsprochen		
(adj)	entsprechend	*appropriate*	
(conj)	entweder . . . oder	*either . . . or*	
(vb)	entwickeln	*to develop*	
	(pp) entwickelt		
die	Entwicklung (-en)	*development*	
die	Entwicklungsabteilung	*development dept.*	
die	Erde	*soil*	
der	Erdnuß ("sse)	*peanut*	
die	Erfahrung (-en)	*experience*	
(vb)	erfassen	*to take in*	
	(pp) erfaßt		
(vb)	erfinden	*to invent*	
	(pp) erfunden		
der	Erfolg (-e)	*success*	
(vb)	erfolgen	*to take place*	
	(pp) èrfolgt		
(adj)	erfolgreich	*successful*	
(adj)	erforderlich	*necessary*	
(vb)	erfüllen	*to fulfil*	
	(pp) erfüllt		
(vb)	ergänzen	*to complete*	
	(pp) ergänzt		
die	Ergänzung (-en)	*complement*	
(vb)	ergeben	*to produce*	
	(pp) ergeben		

das	Ergebnis (-se)	result		(vb)	fabrizieren	to manufacture
(vb)	ergreifen	to take hold of		(pp)	fabriziert	
(pp)	ergriffen			die	Fachkenntnisse (plural)	specialist knowledge
(vb)	erhalten	to receive		der	Fahrcomputer (-)	on-board computer
(pp)	erhalten			(vb)	fahren	to travel, drive, ride
(vb)	erhöhen	to increase		(pp)	gefahren	
(pp)	erhöht			das	Fahrrad ("er)	bicycle
die	Erhöhung (-en)	increase		das	Fahrzeug (-e)	vehicle
(vb)	erkennen	to recognise		der	Fall ("e)	case
(pp)	erkannt			die	Familie (-n)	family
(vb)	erklären	to explain		(adj)	fantastisch	fantastic
(pp)	erklärt			die	Farbe (-n)	colour
(vb)	erlauben	to allow		(vb)	fassen	to take
(pp)	erlaubt			(pp)	gefaßt	
(vb)	eröffnen	to open		(vb)	fehlen	to be missing
(pp)	eröffnet			(pp)	gefehlt	
die	Eröffnung (-en)	opening		der	Fehler (-)	mistake
(vb)	erproben	to try out		der	Fehlquotient (en, en)	failure rate
(pp)	erprobt			der	Feiertag (-e)	public holiday
(vb)	erreichen	to reach		(adj)	fein	fine
(pp)	erreicht			die	Felge (-n)	hub
der	Ersatzteil (-e)	spare part		die	Ferien (plural)	holidays
das	Ersatzteillager (-)	spare-part warehouse		(adj)	fertig	finished, ready
(vb)	erschließen	to capture		die	Fertigung	production
(pp)	erschlossen			die	Fertigungskosten (plural)	production costs
(adj)	erschwert	aggravated		(adv)	fest	firmly
(vb)	ersetzen	to replace		(vb)	fest'legen	to lay down
(pp)	ersetzt			(pp)	festgelegt	
(adj)	erst	first		(vb)	fest'stellen	to identify
(adv)	erst	not until, only		(pp)	festgestellt	
das	Erstaunen	amazement		die	Filiale (-n)	subsidiary
(adj)	erstaunlich	amazing		(adj)	finanziell	financial
die	Erstausrüstung	original equipment		der	Finanzreport	financial report
(adv)	erstens	firstly		(vb)	finden	to find
(adv)	erstmal	first of all		(pp)	gefunden	
(vb)	erteilen	to place		die	Finish-Arbeit (-en)	finishing process
(pp)	erteilt			die	Firma (-en)	company
der	Erwachsene (-n,-n)	adult		das	Flaggschiff (-e)	flagship
(vb)	erwähnen	to mention		(adj)	flexibel	flexible
(pp)	erwähnt			(vb)	fliegen	to fly
(vb)	erwarten	to expect, wait for		(pp)	geflogen	
(pp)	erwartet			der	Flug ("e)	flight
(vbi)	erweisen	to show		das	Flugzeug (-e)	plane
(pp)	erwiesen			(vb)	fordern	to require
(vb)	erweitern	to extend		(pp)	gefordert	
(pp)	erweitert			die	Form (-en)	shape
die	Erweiterung (-en)	expansion		die	Forschung (-en)	research
(vb)	erzielen	to target		(adj)	fortgeschritten	advanced
(pp)	erzielt			der	Fortschritt (-e)	progress
(phras)	es gibt	there is/are		(adj)	frachtfrei	free of freight
das	Essen	meal		die	Frachtkosten (pl)	freight costs
(adv)	etwa	approximately		die	Frage (-n)	question
(pron)	etwas	something		(vb)	fragen	to ask
(adv)	etwas	somewhat		(pp)	gefragt	
(adj)	europäisch	European		(adj)	französisch	French
(adv)	eventuell	if possible		(adj)	frei	free
(adv)	exakt	exactly		(phra)	frei Grenze	free frontier
(adj)	exklusiv	exclusive		(phras)	frei Hafen	free port
(vb)	exportieren	to export		(phra)	frei Haus	free domicile
(pp)	exportiert			die	Freiheit (-en)	freedom

die	Freizeit (-en)	*leisure, free time*	der	Geschäftsführer	*managing director*
(*vb*)	freuen	*to please*	die	Geschäftsleute	*business people*
	(*pp*) gefreut		(*adj*)	geschaltet	*used*
(*adj*)	früher	*earlier*	das	Geschehen (-)	*happening, action*
(*adv*)	früher	*earlier (used to)*	(*vb*)	geschehen	*to happen*
(*vb*)	funktionieren	*to function*		(*pp*) geschehen	
			der	Geschenkartikel (-n)	*gift article*
der	Gärtner (-)	*gardener*	die	Geschichte (-n)	*story*
(*adv*)	ganz	*quite*	(*vb*)	geschieht	→ *geschehen*
(*adj*)	ganz	*whole*	das	Gespräch (-e)	*conversation*
die	Garantie (-n)	*guarantee*	(*vb*)	gesprochen	→ *sprechen*
die	Garantieleistung (-en)	*guarantee cover*	(*vb*)	gestalten	*to design*
(*vb*)	garantieren	*to guarantee*		(*pp*) gestaltet	
	(*pp*) garantiert		(*vb*)	gestatten	*to allow*
der	Garten (″)	*garden*		(*pp*) gestattet	
der	Gartenbereich (-e)	*garden sector*	(*adv*)	gestern	*yesterday*
(*adj*)	geändert	*changed*	(*adj*)	gewährleistet	*guaranteed*
(*vb*)	geben	*to give*	der	Gewinn (-e)	*profit*
	(*pp*) gegeben		(*adj*)	gewiß	*certain*
(*pp*)	gebeten	→ *bitten*	(*pp*)	gewußt	→ *wissen*
das	Gebiet (-e)	*area*	(*vb*)	gibt	→ *es gibt*
(*pp*)	gebracht	→ *bringen*	(*vb*)	ginge	→ *gehen*
(*pp*)	gedacht	→ *denken*	(*vb*)	glauben	*to believe*
(*adj*)	geehrt	*dear*		(*pp*) geglaubt	
(*adj*)	geeignet	*suited*	(*adv*)	gleich	*just, right*
das	Gefälle	*divide*	(*adj*)	gleich	*same*
(*vb*)	gefallen	*to please*	(*adv*)	gleichzeitig	*simultaneously*
	(*pp*) gefallen		das	Glück	*good fortune*
(*pp*)	geflogen	→ *fliegen*	(*adj*)	glücklich	*happy, lucky*
(*adj*)	gefunden	*invented*	(*adj*)	grau	*grey*
(*pp*)	gegangen	→ *gehen*	das	Griechenland	*Greece*
(*prep*)	gegen	*against*	die	Größe (-n)	*size*
die	Gegend (-en)	*area*	die	Größenordnung (-en)	*order of size*
(*vb*)	gehen	*to go*	(*adj*)	groß	*big, large*
	(*pp*) gegangen		das	Großbritannien	*Great Britain*
(*vb*)	gehören	*to belong*	(*adv*)	gründlich	*thoroughly*
	(*pp*) gehört		der	Grund (″e)	*reason*
(*vb*)	gekannt	→ *kennen*	die	Gruppe (-n)	*group*
das	Geld (-er)	*money*	das	Gruppentraining	*group training*
die	Geldmittel (plural)	*funds*	(*vb*)	gucken	*to look*
die	Gelegenheit (-en)	*opportunity*		(*pp*) geguckt	
das	Gelenk (-e)	*joint*	(*adj*)	gut	*good*
(*vb*)	gelten	*to be valid*	(*adv*)	gut	*well*
	(*pp*) gegolten				
(*adj*)	gemeinsam	*joint*	(*vb*)	haben	*to have*
(*adv*)	gemeinsam	*together*		(*pp*) gehabt	
(*adj*)	genau	*exact*	der	Händler (-)	*dealer*
(*adv*)	genau	*exactly*	das	Händlernetz (-e)	*dealer network*
(*adj*)	geplant	*planned*	(*vb*)	hängen	*to hang*
(*adj*)	geprüft	*tested*		(*pp*) gehängt	
(*adv*)	gerade	*just*	(*vb*)	hätte	*would have to*
das	Gerät (-e)	*instrument, tool*	der	Hafen (″)	*port*
(*adj*)	geräumig	*roomy*	(*adj*)	halb	*half*
(*adj*)	gerecht	*fair*	(*vb*)	halten	*to hold, keep*
(*adj*)	gering	*small*		(*pp*) gehalten	
(*adv*)	gern	*willingly*	die	Hand (″-)	*hand*
(*adj*)	gesamt	*total*	das	Handbuch (″er)	*manual*
das	Gesamtpaket (-e)	*total package*	der	Handel	*trade*
das	Geschäft (-e)	*shop, business*	die	Handhabung (-en)	*handling*
(*adv*)	geschäftlich	*in business terms*	(*adj*)	hart	*hard*

das	Hauptgericht (-e)	*main course*	*(vb)*	informieren	*to inform*
das	Hauptprodukt (-e)	*main product*		*(pp)* informiert	
(adv)	hauptsächlich	*mainly*	*(adv)*	innen	*inside*
der	Hauptsitz (-e)	*head quarters*	*(prep)*	innerhalb	*within*
das	Hauptwerk (-e)	*main plant*	die	Insel (-n)	*island*
der	Haushalt (-e)	*household*	die	Insertion	*publication*
(vb)	helfen	*to help*	*(adv)*	insgesamt	*altogether*
	(pp) geholfen		*(adv)*	insoweit	*in this respect*
(adv)	her	*from where/there*	die	Inspiration (-en)	*inspiration*
der	Herbst	*autumn*	*(vb)*	installieren	*to install*
der	Herr (-n, -en)	*gentleman*		*(pp)* installiert	
(adj)	herrlich	*wonderful*	*(adj)*	integriert	*integrated*
(vbs)	her'stellen	*manufacture*	*(adj)*	interessant	*interesting*
	(pp) hergestellt		das	Interesse (-n)	*interest*
der	Hersteller (-)	*manufacturer*	*(adj)*	interessiert	*interested*
die	Herstellung	*production*	das	Interieur (-e)	*interior*
(adv)	heute	*today*	*(adv)*	inzwischen	*meanwhile*
(adv)	heute morgen	*this morning*	*(adj)*	irgendein	*any (one)*
(adj)	heutig	*today's*	*(adv)*	irgendwo	*somewhere*
(adv)	heutzutage	*nowadays*	*(adj)*	italienisch	*Italian*
(adv)	hier	*here*			
die	Hilfe (-n)	*help*	das	Jahr (-e)	*year*
(phras)	hin und wieder	*from time to time*	der	Jahresverlauf	*progress of the year*
(adv)	hintereinander	*one after another*	*(adj)*	jeder	*every*
(vbs)	hin'weisen	*to indicate*	*(adv)*	jederzeit	*any time at all*
	(pp) hingewiesen		*(adj)*	jetzt	*now*
das	Hobby (-s)	*hobby*	*(adj)*	jetzig	*current*
(adj)	hoch	*high*	*(adv)*	jeweils	*in each case*
(adj)	höchst	*highest*			
(vb)	hören	*to hear*	der	Kaffee	*coffee*
	(pp) gehört		das	Kaffeeservice (-)	*coffee set*
(vb)	hoffen	*to hope*	*(adj)*	kanadisch	*Canadian*
	(pp) gehofft		der	Kanal ("e)	*channel*
(adj)	holländisch	*Dutch*	die	Kapazität (-en)	*capacity*
das	Holland	*the Netherlands*	die	Kapazitätserweiterung	*increase in capacity*
das	Holz ("er)	*wood*	*(adj)*	kapitalkräftig	*capital-intensive*
das	Hotel (-s)	*hotel*	*(adj)*	kaputt	*broken*
(adj)	hübsch	*pretty*	*(vbs)*	kaputt'gehen	*to break down*
(adj)	hungrig	*hungry*		*(pp)* kaputtgegangen	
			die	Karte (-n)	*card*
(adj)	ideal	*ideal*	die	Kartoffel (-n)	*potato*
die	Illustrierte (-n)	*magazine*	der	Karton (-s)	*cardboard box*
(phras)	im Argen	*undecided*	die	Kartusche (-n)	*cartridge*
(phras)	im Einkauf	*purchase price*	die	Kassette (-n)	*cassette*
(phras)	im einzelnen	*individually*	der	Katalog (-e)	*catalogue*
(phras)	im Grunde	*basically*	*(vb)*	kaufen	*to buy*
(phras)	im Hause	*in the company*		*(pp)* gekauft	
(phras)	im Moment	*at the moment*	*(adj)*	kaufmännisch	*commercial*
(phras)	im voraus	*in advance*	*(adv)*	kaum	*hardly*
das	Image (-s)	*image*	*(vb)*	kennen	*to know*
(adv)	immer	*always*		*(pp)* gekannt	
der	Importeur (-e)	*importer*	*(vbs)*	kennen'lernen	*to get to know*
(adj)	importiert	*imported*		*(pp)* kennengelernt	
(phras)	in Anspruch nehmen	*to claim*	der	Kessel (-)	*kettle*
(phras)	in Verbindung setzen	*to contact*	der	Klang ("e)	*sound, tone*
(adj)	individuell	*individual*	*(adj)*	klar	*clear*
die	Industrie (-n)	*industry*	die	Klarheit	*clarity*
der	Industriezweig (-e)	*branch of industry*	die	Klasse (-n)	*class*
die	Information (-en)	*information*	*(adj)*	klein	*small*
			die	Klinge (n)	*blade*

(vb)	kochen	to boil		(vb)	laufen	to run
	(pp) gekocht				(pp) gelaufen	
(adj)	kochend	boiling	der	Lautsprecher (-)	loudspeaker
(vb)	können	to be able	das	Leder	leather
(vb)	könnte	would be able to	(vb)	legen	to lay, place
der	Kofferraum ("e)	car boot		(pp) gelegt	
die	Kohle (-n)	coal	die	Lehrperson (-en)	instructor
(vb)	kommen	to come	(adv)	leicht	lightly
(adj)	kompatibel	compatible	(adv)	leider	unfortunately
der	Kondensator (-en)	capacitor	die	Leistung (-en)	performance
der	Konkurrent (-en, -en)	competitor	(adj)	leistungsfähig	effective
die	Konkurrenz	competition	die	Leistungsfähigkeit	efficiency
(adj)	konkurrenzfähig	competitive	(vb)	leiten	to manage, run
die	Konstruktionsabteilung	construction dept.		(pp) geleitet	
der	Konsument (-en, -en)	consumer	die	Leitung (-en)	management
der	Kontinent (-e)	continent	das	Lernprogramm (-e)	learning programme
(adv)	kontinuierlich	continuously	das	Lesen	reading
die	Kontrolle (-n)	check	(vb)	lesen	to read
(vb)	kontrollieren	to check		(pp) gelesen	
	(pp) kontrolliert		(adj)	letzt	last
(vb)	konzentrieren	to concentrate	das	Letzte	the last thing
	(pp) konzentriert		die	Leute (plural)	people
die	Konzeption (-en)	design	(adv)	lieber	rather
(vb)	konzipieren	to plan	der	Lieferant (-en, -en)	supplier
	(pp) konzipiert		(vb)	liefern	to supply
der	Kopf ("e)	head		(pp) geliefert	
das	Kopfzerbrechen	headache	die	Liefersicherheit	security of supply
(vb)	kopieren	to copy	die	Lieferung (-en)	delivery
	(pp) kopiert		die	Lieferzeit (-en)	delivery time
das	Korn ("er)	seed	(vb)	liegen an	to be due to
die	Kosten (plural)	cost, expense		(pp) gelegen an	
(vb)	kosten	to cost	(vb)	liegen	to lie
	(pp) gekostet			(pp) gelegen	
(adj)	kostengünstig	advantageous (cost)	die	Limousine (-n)	limousine
die	Kostenrechnung (-en)	costing	die	Linie (-n)	line
die	Kreativität	creativity	die	Linienführung	line
(vb)	kriegen	to get	die	Literatur	literature
	(pp) gekriegt		der	LKW (LKWs)	lorry
die	Kürze	short while	der	Löffel (-)	spoon
der	Kunde (-n, -n)	customer	die	Lösung (-en)	solution
der	Kundendienst (-e)	customer care	(adj)	lokal	local
der	Kunststoff (-e)	plastic	(vbs)	los'schicken	to send off
der	Kurs (-e)	exchange rate		(pp) losgeschickt	
(adv)	kurz	briefly	die	Lust ("e)	desire
(adv)	kurzfristig	at short notice, in the short term	(adj)	machbar	doable
			(vb)	machen	to do, make
der	Laden (")	shop		(pp) gemacht	
(adj)	länger	longer	(adv)	mal	briefly, just
die	Lage (-n)	position	das	Mal (-e)	time
das	Lager (-)	warehouse	die	Mark	German mark
der	Lagerbestand ("e)	stock level	das	Marketing	marketing
(vb)	lagern	to store	der	Markt ("e)	market
	(pp) gelagert		der	Marktanteil (-e)	market share
das	Land ("er)	country, state	das	Marktgeschehen (-)	market event
(adj)	lang	long	die	Marktprognose (-n)	market forecast
(adv)	lange	for a long time	die	Marktsituation (-en)	market situation
(adv)	langsam	slowly	die	Maschine (-n)	machine
(vb)	lassen	to cause to do	der	Maschinenhersteller	machine manufacturer
	(pp) gelassen		der	Maschinenlieferant	machinery supplier

die	Masse (-n)	*number of people*	der	Musterkarton (-s)	*sample box*
(*adv*)	massenweise	*in droves*	die	Mutterfirma (-en)	*parent company*
das	Material (-ien)	*material*	das	Mutterwerk (-e)	*parent factory*
(*adj*)	maximal	*maximum*			
der	Mechaniker (-)	*mechanic*	(*conj*)	nachdem	*after*
(*adj*)	medizinisch	*medical*	(*vbs*)	nach'denken	*to think about/over*
das	Meeting	*meeting*		(*pp*) nachgedacht	
das	Mehl	*flour*	(*adj*)	nachgeschaltet	*subsequent*
(*adv*)	mehr	*more*	(*adv*)	nachher	*afterwards*
(*adj*)	mehrsprachig	*multilingual*	die	Nachlieferung (-en)	*follow-up delivery*
die	Mehrwertsteuer	*VAT*	das	Nachschlagewerk (-e)	*reference book*
(*vb*)	meinen	*to mean*	(*vb*)	nachvollziehen	*to keep up with*
	(*pp*) gemeint			(*pp*) nachvollzogen	
die	Meinung (-en)	*opinion*	(*adj*)	nächst	*next*
das	meiste	*the greater part*	die	Nähe (-n)	*vicinity*
(*adv*)	meistens	*mostly*	(*adv*)	näher	*more closely*
die	Menge (-n)	*large amount/number*	(*adj*)	nämlich	*namely*
das	Menü (-s)	*menu*	(*adj*)	nah	*near*
(*vb*)	merken	*to notice*	der	Name (-n, -n)	*name*
	(*pp*) gemerkt		(*adj*)	national	*national*
die	Messe (-n)	*trade fair*	(*adv*)	natürlich	*of course*
das	Messer (-)	*knife*	(*vb*)	nehmen	*to take*
die	Million (-en)	*million*		(*pp*) genommen	
die	Mindestauftragshöhe	*minimum-order size*	(*adj*)	nett	*nice*
(*vb*)	mischen	*to mix*	(*adj*)	neu	*new*
	(*pp*) gemischt		die	Neuentwicklung (-en)	*new development*
die	Mischung (-en)	*mixture*	(*pron*)	nichts	*nothing*
der	Mist	*rubbish*	(*vb*)	nickeln	*to bother, niggle*
der	Mitarbeiter (-)	*colleague*		(*pp*) genickelt	
(*vbs*)	mit'berücksichtigen	*take into account*	(*adv*)	nie	*never*
	(*pp*) mitberücksichtigt		(*adj*)	niedrig	*low*
(*vbs*)	mit'bringen	*to bring along*	die	Niederlassung (-en)	*branch*
	(*pp*) mitgebracht		(*pron*)	niemand	*nobody*
(*vb*)	miteingetestet	→ *testen*	(*pron*)	nix	→ *nichts*
das	Mitglied (-er)	*member*	(*adv*)	noch	*still*
(*vbs*)	mit'nehmen	*to take with one*	(*adv*)	nochmal	*once more*
	(*pp*) mitgenommen		(*adj*)	nötig	*necessary*
(*vbs*)	mit'teilen	*tell about, announce*	der	Norden	*north*
	(*pp*) mitgeteilt		die	Norm (-en)	*norm*
die	Mittelklasse (-n)	*middle range*	(*adj*)	normal	*normal*
die	Modalität (-en)	*arrangement*	(*adv*)	normalerweise	*normally*
das	Modell (-e)	*model*	die	Notlösung (-en)	*emergency solution*
(*adj*)	modern	*modern*	(*adj*)	notwendig	*necessary*
(*vb*)	möchte	*would like (singular)*	die	Null	*nill, zero*
(*vb*)	mögen	*to like*	die	Nummer (-n)	*number*
	(*pp*) gemocht		(*adv*)	nur	*only*
(*adj*)	möglich	*possible*	(*vb*)	nutzen	*to use*
(*adv*)	möglicherweise	*if possible*		(*pp*) genutzt	
die	Möglichkeit (-en)	*possibility*			
der	Mohn (-e)	*poppy*	(*adv*)	oben drauf	*on top of that*
(*adv*)	momentan	*at the moment*	(*adv*)	oben	*up there*
der	Monat (-e)	*month*	(*adj*)	ober	*upper*
(*adv*)	monatlich	*monthly*	das	Obermenü (-s)	*main menu*
das	Monatsende (-n)	*end of the month*	das	Objekt (-e)	*object*
der	Morgen (-)	*morning*	(*conj*)	obwohl	*although*
(*adv*)	morgen	*tomorrow*	die	Öffnung (-en)	*opening*
(*vb*)	müssen	*to have to*	(*adj*)	örtlich	*local*
(*vb*)	müßte	*would have to, ought*	(*adj*)	offen	*open*
das	Muster (-)	*sample*	(*prep*)	ohne	*without*
der	Musterbetrieb (-e)	*showroom*	(*adj*)	optimal	*optimal*

(vb)	ordern	*to order*		der	Prozeß (-sse)	*process*
	(pp) geordert			*(vb)*	prüfen	*to test, check*
die	Ordnung (-en)	*order*			*(pp)* geprüft	
die	Organisation (-en)	*organisation*		die	Pumpe (-n)	*pump*
der	Ort (-e)	*place*		der	Punkt (-e)	*point*
das	Ostern	*Easter*		*(adj)*	pünktlich	*on time*
die	Ostsee	*Baltic*				
				das	Quadratmeter (-)	*square metre*
das	Paket (-e)	*package*		*(adj)*	qualifiziert	*qualified*
die	Palette (-n)	*palette*		die	Qualität (-en)	*quality*
das	Papier (-e)	*paper*				
(adv)	parallel	*in parallel*		das	Radio (-s)	*radio*
der	Partner (-)	*partner*		der	Rahmen (-)	*framework*
(vb)	passieren	*to pass*		die	Rahmenkondition (-e)	*general conditions*
	(pp) passiert			der	Rand ("er)	*edge*
die	Pastelfarbe (-n)	*pastel colour*		die	Range	*range*
das	Patent (-e)	*patent*		der	Raum ("e)	*area, space*
(adj)	perfekt	*perfect*		die	Raumersparnis (-sse)	*space saving*
die	Pflanze (-n)	*plant*		*(vb)*	reagieren	*to react*
das	Pfund (-e)	*pound*			*(pp)* reagiert	
(adj)	pharmazeutisch	*pharmaceutical*		die	Reaktion (-en)	*reaction*
der	Platz ("e)	*seat, space*		*(vb)*	rechnen	*to reckon*
(adv)	pneumatisch	*pneumatically*			*(pp)* gerechnet	
die	Polizeikontrolle (n)	*police check*		der	Rechner (-)	*computer*
die	Portion (-en)	*portion*		das	Rechnungswesen	*accounting*
(adj)	positiv	*positive*		*(adv)*	recht	*quite*
die	Post	*post*		der	Rechtsanwalt ("e)	*lawyer*
die	Präsentation (-en)	*presentation*		der	Rechtsvertreter	*legal representative*
(vb)	präsentieren	*to present*		*(vb)*	reden	*to talk*
	(pp) präsentiert				*(pp)* geredet	
(adv)	praktisch	*practically*		das	Regal (-e)	*shelf*
(adj)	praxisnah	*practice-based*		*(vb)*	regeln	*to regulate*
der	Preis (-e)	*price*			*(pp)* geregelt	
die	Preislage (-n)	*price bracket*		die	Reihe (-n)	*series*
die	Preisliste (-n)	*price list*		*(vb)*	rein'nehmen	*→ ein'nehmen*
das	Preisniveau (-s)	*price level*		die	Reise (-n)	*journey*
die	Preissituation (-en)	*pricing situation*		*(adv)*	relativ	*relatively*
die	Preisstruktur (-en)	*price structure*		*(vb)*	renovieren	*to renovate*
der	Preisunterschied (-)	*price difference*			*(pp)* renoviert	
(adj)	preiswert	*value for money*		die	Reparatur (-en)	*repair*
die	Presse	*press*		*(vb)*	reparieren	*to repair*
(adj)	prima	*first class!*			*(pp)* repariert	
die	Probezeit (-en)	*trial period*		die	Repräsentation (-e)	*representation*
(vb)	probieren	*to try*		*(vb)*	repräsentieren	*to represent*
	(pp) probiert				*(pp)* repräsentiert	
das	Problem (-e)	*problem*		*(adj)*	respektabel	*respectable*
das	Produkt (-e)	*product*		*(adj)*	restlich	*remaining*
die	Produktion	*production*		*(adj)*	richtig	*correct*
das	Produktionswerk (-e)	*production plant*		*(adv)*	richtig	*correctly*
die	Produktpalette (-n)	*product range*		die	Richtung (-en)	*direction*
(vb)	produzieren	*to produce*		die	Rinne (-n)	*gutter*
	(pp) produziert			der	Roboter (-)	*robot*
das	Profil (-e)	*profile*		das	Rohr (-en)	*pipe*
der	Profit (-e)	*profit*		der	Rohstoff (-e)	*raw material*
das	Programm (-e)	*programme, range*		die	Rolle (-n)	*role*
der	Projektleiter (-)	*project manager*		die	Rubrik (-en)	*heading*
der	Prokurist (-en, -en)	*authorised signatory*		*(adj)*	rückliegend	*previous*
der	Prospekt (-e)	*prospectus*		der	Rundgang ("e)	*walkabout*
das	Prozent (-e)	*per cent*		*(vb)*	runter'gehen	*→ unter'gehen*
der	Prozentsatz ("e)	*percentage*				

der	Sachbearbeiter (-)	*manager responsible*		(prep)	seit	*since*
die	Sache (-n)	*affair, thing, item*		(conj)	seitdem	*since*
(vb)	säen	*to sow*		die	Seite (-n)	*side*
	(pp) gesät			(adv)	seither	*since then*
(adj)	sämtlich	*entire*		die	Sekunde (-n)	*second*
(vb)	sagen	*to say*		(pron)	selber	*myself, ourselves etc*
	(pp) gesagt			(pron)	selbst	*by oneself*
das	Salz	*salt*		(adj)	selbstgesteuert	*self-access*
der	Same (-n, -n)	*seed*		(adv)	selbstverständlich	*of course*
(vb)	sammeln	*to collect*		die	Selbstverständlichkeit	*matter of course*
	(pp) gesammelt			(adv)	selten	*seldom*
der	Sand (-e)	*sand*		der	Sender (-)	*radio station*
(vb)	schaffen	*to create*		der	Sendersuchlauf	*reception search*
	(pp) geschaffen			die	Sendestation (-en)	*station*
(vb)	schalten	*to switch*		die	Serie (-n)	*series*
	(pp) geschaltet			(adj)	serienmäßig	*part of the series*
der	Schalter (-)	*switch*		die	Serviette (-n)	*serviette*
die	Schar (-en)	*plough share*		(vbs)	sich ab'zeichnen	*to stand out clearly*
(adj)	scharf	*sharp*			(pp) sich abgezeichnet	
der	Scheck (-e/-s)	*cheque*		(vbs)	sich an'siedeln	*to settle*
(vb)	schicken	*to send*			(pp) sich angesiedelt	
	(pp) geschickt			(vb)	sich bedanken	*to thank*
(adj)	schlecht	*bad*			(pp) sich bedankt	
(adv)	schlechthin	*purely and simply*		(vb)	sich befinden	*to be found*
(adj)	schleierhaft	*inexplicable*			(pp) sich befunden	
(vbi)	schließen	*to close*		(vb)	sich bemühen	*to take trouble*
	(pp) geschlossen				(pp) sich bemüht	
(adv)	schließlich	*finally*		(vb)	sich beschweren	*to complain*
der	Schluß ("sse)	*conclusion*			(pp) sich beschwert	
(vb)	schmecken	*to taste*		(vb)	sich eignen	*to be suitable*
	(pp) geschmeckt				(pp) sich geignet	
(vb)	schneiden	*to cut*		(vbs)	sich ein'bürgern	*become established*
	(pp) geschnitten				(pp) sich eingebürgert	
(adv)	schnell	*fast*		(vbs)	sich ein'stellen	*to adapt, prepare*
(vb)	schnuppern	*to sniff*			(pp) sich eingestellt	
	(pp) geschnuppert			(vb)	sich entscheiden	*to decide*
die	Schnur ("e)	*flex*			(pp) sich entschieden	
(adv)	schön	*nicely*		(vb)	sich entwickeln	*to develop*
(adv)	schon	*already*			(pp) sich entwickelt	
(adj)	schriftlich	*in writing*		(vb)	sich ergeben	*to be the result*
der	Schuh (-e)	*shoe*			(pp) sich ergeben	
(vb)	schulen	*to train*		(vb)	sich erstrecken	*to extend*
	(pp) geschult				(pp) sich erstreckt	
das	Schulkind (-er)	*school child*		(vb)	sich erweisen	*to turn out to be*
die	Schulung (-en)	*training*			(pp) sich erwiesen	
(adj)	schwach	*weak*		(vbs)	sich fest'legen	*to commit oneself*
(adj)	schwarz	*black*			(pp) sich festgelegt	
(adj)	schwer	*difficult, heavy*		(vb)	sich fragen	*to wonder*
die	Schwerindustrie (-n)	*heavy industry*			(pp) sich gefragt	
(adj)	schwierig	*difficult*		(vb)	sich freuen auf	*to look forward to*
die	Schwierigkeit (-en)	*difficulty*			(pp) sich gefreut auf	
die	Seeluft ("e)	*sea air*		(vb)	sich freuen über	*to be pleased with*
(vb)	segeln	*to sail*			(pp) sich gefreut über	
	(pp) gesegelt			(vb)	sich gewöhnen	*to get used to*
der	Segler (-)	*sailor*			(pp) sich gewöhnt	
(vb)	sehen	*to see*		(vb)	sich handeln um	*to be a question of*
	(pp) gesehen				(pp) sich gehandelt um	
(adv)	sehr	*very*		(vbs)	sich heraus'stellen	*to turn out to be*
(vb)	sein	*to be*			(pp) sich herausgestellt	
	(pp) gewesen					

(vb)	sich konzentrieren	to concentrate		(pron)	sowas	something like this
	(pp) sich konzentriert			(adv)	sowieso	in any case
(vb)	sich melden	to get in touch		(conj)	sowohl . . . .als auch	both . . . .and
	(pp) sich gemeldet			(adv)	sozusagen	so to speak
(vb)	sich nennen	to be called		(adv)	spät	late
	(pp) sich gemeldet			(adj)	später	later
(vb)	sich senken	to drop down	die		Späzle (plural)	dumpling
	(pp) sich gesenkt			(der)	Spaß (-e)	joke
(vb)	sich spezialisieren	to specialise	die		Speisekarte (-n)	menu
	(pp) sich spezialisiert		der		Spezialist (-en, -en)	specialist
(vb)	sich stellen	to arise (a question)		(adj)	speziell	specially
	(pp) sich gestellt			(adv)	spezifisch	specifically
(vb)	sich überlegen	to think about		(vb)	spielen	to play
	(pp) sich überlegt				(pp) gespielt	
(vb)	sich überzeugen	to satisfy oneself	die		Sprache (-n)	language
	(pp) sich überzeugt			(vb)	sprechen	to speak
(vbs)	sich um'hören	to make enquiries			(pp) gesprochen	
	(pp) sich umgehört		die		Spritzerei	injection
(vbs)	sich um'kehren	to turn round	die		Stadt ("e)	town
	(pp) sich um'gekehrt		die		Stadtmitte (-n)	town centre
(vb)	sich unterhalten	to talk		(adv)	ständig	continuously
	(pp) sich unterhalten		der		Stahl	steel
(vb)	sich verabschieden	to take one's leave	der		Stand	standing
	(pp) sich verabschiedet			(adj)	standardmäßig	as standard
(vb)	sich verlagern	to transfer		(vb)	stapeln	to stack
	(pp) sich verlagert				(pp) gestapelt	
(vb)	sich verschärfen	to intensify	das		Stapeln	stacking
	(pp) sich verschärft			(adj)	stark	strong
(vbs)	sich vor'stellen	to imagine		(vb)	starten	to start
	(pp) sich vorgestellt				(pp) gestartet	
(vbs)	sich zusammen'setzen	to sit down together	der		Status	status
	(pp) sich zusammengesetzt		der		Stecker (-)	plug
(adj)	sicher	sure		(vb)	stehen	to stand
die	Sicherheit (en)	certainty, safety, security			(pp) gestanden	
der	Sicherheitsbereich	security area		(vb)	steigen	to climb
(adv)	sicherlich	certainly			(pp) gestiegen	
(vbs)	sicher'stellen	to ensure		(adj)	steigend	rising
	(pp) sichergestellt			(vb)	steigern	to increase
die	Sicht (-en)	point of view			(pp) gesteigert	
(vb)	simulieren	to simulate		(vb)	stellen	to place
	(pp) simuliert				(pp) gestellt	
der	Sinn (-e)	sense		(vb)	stellen	to present itself
die	Situation (-en)	situation	die		Stellung (-en)	position
(vb)	sitzen	to sit		(adv)	stetig	constantly
	(pp) gesessen		der		Steuerberater (-)	tax consultant
(adj)	skeptisch	sceptical	der		Stil (-e)	style
(conj)	sobald	as soon as		(adv)	stolz	proudly
(adv)	sofort	immediately		(adj)	streng	strict
die	Software	software	der		Strom ("e)	current
(adv)	sogar	even		(vb)	studieren	to study
(adj)	sogenannt	so-called			(pp) studiert	
(adv)	solange	for such a long time	das		Studium	studies
(adj)	solch	such	das		Stück (-e)	item, piece, unit
(vb)	sollen	to be supposed to	die		Stückzahl (-en)	number of items, quantity
(adj)	solvent	solvent		(adj)	stumpf	blunt
der	Sonderfahrer(-)	special driver	die		Stunde (-n)	hour
(conj)	sondern	but		(vb)	stünden	would stand
(adv)	sonst	otherwise	die		Suche (-n)	search
(adj)	sonstig	remaining	der		Süden	south
das	Sortiment (-)	range		(adj)	super	super

(adj)	symmetrisch	symmetrical
das	System (-e)	system
(adj)	systematisch	systematic
der	Tag (-e)	day
der	Tagespunkt (-e)	item on the agenda
die	Tageszeitung (-en)	daily newspaper
(adv)	täglich	daily
(adj)	tätig	active
(adv)	tatsächlich	in fact
die	Technik (-en)	technology
(adj)	technisch	technical
die	Technologie (-n)	technology
der	Tee	tea
der	Teich (-e)	pond
die	Teigware (-n)	dough, product
der	Teil (-e)	part, share
der	Teilnehmer (-)	participant
das	Telefon (-e)	telephone
(vb)	telefonieren	to telephone
(pp) telefoniert		
der	Termin (-e)	appointment
der	Test (-s)	test
(vb)	testen	to test
(pp) getestet		
der	Testverkauf (″e)	sales test
(adj)	teuer	expensive
der	Text (-e)	text
das	Thema (-en)	theme
(adj)	theoretisch	theoretical
die	Tiefeneinstellung	depth adjustment
der	Tisch (-e)	table
die	Tochtergesellschaft	subsidiary
(adj)	toll	fantastic!
der	Tourist (-en, -en)	tourist
(adj)	traditionell	traditional
der	Transport	transport
(vb)	treffen	to make
(pp) getroffen		
der	Trinkbecher (-)	drinking beaker
(vb)	trinken	to drink
(pp) getrunken		
der	Trockenschutzschalter	boil-dry safety mechanism
(vb)	tun	to do
(pp) getan		
der	Typ (-en)	type
(adv)	überaus	extremely
der	Überblick (-e)	overview
(adv)	übereinander	one upon the other
(vbs)	über'gehen zu	to go over to
(pp) übergegangen zu		
(adv)	überhaupt	at all
(vb)	überlegen	to think about/over
(pp) überlegt		
(vb)	übernehmen	to take on
(pp) übernommen		
(vbs)	überschreiben	to entitle
(pp) übergeschrieben		
(vb)	übersetzen	to translate
(pp) übersetzt		
die	Überzeugung (-en)	conviction
die	Uhr (en)	o'clock
(prep)	um	around, round
(vbs)	um'ändern	to change round
(pp) umgeändert		
(vbs)	um'bauen	to re-build
(pp) um'gebaut		
(adj)	umkämpft	fought-over
der	Umsatz (″e)	turnover
die	Umsatzzahl (-en)	turnover figure
die	Umstellung (-en)	changeover
(adj)	unabhängig	independent
(adv)	unbedingt	necessarily
(adj)	unbekannt	unknown
(adj)	unbewußt	unconscious
(adv)	ungefähr	approximately
(adj)	ungewöhnlich	unusual
die	Ungunsten (plural)	disadvantage
(adj)	unproblematisch	unproblematical
(vb)	unterbrechen	to interrupt
(pp) unterbrochen		
(vb)	unterbreiten	to put forward, submit
(pp) unterbreitet		
(vbs)	unter'gehen	to go down
(pp) untergegangen		
die	Unterlage (-n)	documentation
das	Unternehmen (-)	company
der	Unterschied (-e)	difference
(vb)	unterschreiben	to sign
(pp) unterschrieben		
(vb)	unterstützen	to support
(pp) unterstützt		
die	Untersuchung (-en)	investigation
(adj)	unverkäuflich	unsaleable
der	Urlaub (-e)	vacation
(adv)	ursprünglich	originally
(phras)	im Verkauf	retail
der	VDE	Verband Deutscher Elektrotechniker
die	Veralgung (-en)	build-up of algae
(vb)	verankern	to anchor
(pp) verankert		
(adj)	verantwortlich	responsible
die	Verantwortung (-en)	responsibility
(vb)	verbessern	to improve
(pp) verbessert		
der	Verbraucher (-)	user
(vb)	verdienen	to earn
(pp) verdient		
der	Verdienst (-e)	gain, profit
(vb)	vereinen	to unite
(pp) vereint		
das	Verfahren (-)	process
(vb)	verfügen über	to be equipped with
die	Verfügung	disposal
die	Vergangenheit	past

(vb)	vergessen	to forget	(phras)	von vornherein	from the start
(pp)	vergessen		der	Vorabinteressent (-en, -en)	prospect
der	Vergleich (-e)	comparison	(vbs)	vor'bereiten	to prepare
(adj)	vergleichbar	comparable	(pp)	vorbereitet	
(vb)	vergrößern	to enlarge, increase	die	Vorbereitung (-en)	preparation
(pp)	vergrößert		(vbs)	vor'führen	demonstrate, present
das	Verhältnis (-se)	relation	(pp)	vorgeführt	
der	Verkauf (″e)	sales	(adj)	vorgefertigt	prepared
(vb)	verkaufen	to sell	(vbs)	vor'gehen	to go ahead
(pp)	verkauft		(pp)	vorgegangen	
die	Verkaufsbedingung (-en)	conditions of sale	(vbs)	vor'haben	to intend, plan
das	Verkaufsbüro(-s)	sales office	(pp)	vorgehabt	
der	Verkaufspreis (-e)	selling price	(adv)	vorher	beforehand
die	Verkaufszahl (-en)	sales figure	(adv)	vorhin	previously
die	Verkaufsziffer (-n)	sales figure	(vbs)	vor'liegen	to lie in front of
der	Verkehrsfunk	traffic broadcasts	(pp)	vorgelegen	
(vb)	verlängern	to extend	(vbs)	vor'nehmen	to undertake
(pp)	verlängert		(pp)	vorgenommen	
(vb)	verlassen	to leave	die	Vorrichtung (-en)	equipment
(pp)	verlassen		der	Vorschlag (″e)	suggestion
der	Verlauf	course	(vbs)	vor'schlagen	to suggest
die	Verluste (plural)	losses	(pp)	vorgeschlagen	
(adj)	vernünftig	reasonable	(vbs)	vor'sehen	to provide for
(vb)	verpacken	to pack	(pp)	vorgesehen	
(pp)	verpackt		die	Vorspeise (-n)	hors-d'oeuvre
die	Verpackungseinheit	packing unit	(vbs)	vor'stellen	to present
(adj)	verpflichtet	duty-bound	(pp)	vorgestellt	
der	Versand	forwarding	die	Vorstellung (-en)	presentation
(adj)	verschieden	various, different	der	Vorteil (e)	advantage
(vb)	verschrotten	to scrap	(vbs)	vor'ziehen	to prefer
(pp)	verschrottet		(pp)	vorgezogen	
(vb)	versehen	to equip			
(pp)	versehen		der	Wagen (-)	car
(vb)	verwenden	to use	die	Wahl (-en)	selection
(pp)	verwendet		(vb)	wählen	to choose
(vb)	versichern	to assure	(pp)	gewählt	
(pp)	versichert		(conj)	während	whereas
die	Verstärkung (-en)	reinforcement	(prep)	während	while
(vb)	verstehen	to understand	(vb)	wäre	would be (singular)
(pp)	verstanden		(adv)	wahrscheinlich	probably
die	Verstellbarkeit	adjustability	die	Ware (-n)	goods
(vb)	versuchen	to try	(vb)	warten	to wait
(pp)	versucht		(pp)	gewartet	
der	Vertrag (″e)	contract	das	Wasser	water
das	Vertrauen	trust	der	Wasserkocher (-)	water-boiler
(vb)	vertreten	to represent	der	Wechselkurs (-e)	rate of exchange
(pp)	vertreten		(vb)	wechseln	to change
der	Vertreter (-)	agent	(pp)	gewechselt	
(vb)	vertritt	→ vertreten	(conj)	weder . . . noch	neither . . . nor
(vb)	verwechseln	to confuse	der	Weg (-e)	way
(pp)	verwechselt		(prep)	wegen	on account of
die	Verwirklichung	realisation	(vbs)	weg'laufen	to run away
das	Verzeichnis (-se)	list	(pp)	weggelaufen	
die	Vertretung (-en)	agency	(conj)	weil	because
(adj)	viele	many	(vb)	weiß	→ wissen
(adv)	vielleicht	perhaps	die	Weite (-n)	width
das	Vierteljahr (-e)	quarter	(adj)	weiter	further
(adv)	völlig	completely	(vbs)	weiter'entwickeln	to develop
der	Vollprofit	full profit	(pp)	weiterentwickelt	
das	Volt (-)	volt	(pron)	welch	which

die	Welle (-n)	*axle, spindle*	*(adj)*	zeitlich	*chronological*
die	Welt	*world*	derne	Zeitpunkt (-e)	*point in time*
der	Weltmarktanteil (-e)	*world market share*	die	Zeitschrift (-n)	*magazine*
(adv)	weltweit	*world-wide*	*(adj)*	zentral	*central*
(adv)	weniger	*less*	das	Zentrum (Zentren)	*centre*
(adv)	wenigstens	*at least*	das	Zertifikat (-e)	*certificate*
die	Werbeagentur (-en)	*advertising agency*	die	Zielgruppe (-n)	*target group*
das	Werbematerial (-ien)	*publicity material*	*(adv)*	ziemlich	*fairly*
die	Werbung	*advertising*	*(adv)*	zirka	*approximately*
(vb)	werden	*shall/will, to become*	der	Zoll (″e)	*customs duty*
	(pp) geworden		*(adv)*	zuerst	*first of all*
(vb)	werden	*to be (passive)*	*(adj)*	zufrieden	*satisfied*
	(pp) geworden		*(adj)*	zugelassen	*authorised*
das	Werk (-e)	*factory, plant*	*(adj)*	zugeschnitten	*tailored*
das	Werkstück (-e)	*piece*	die	Zukunft	*future*
die	Werkstatt (″e)	*workshop*	*(adj)*	zukünftig	*future*
das	Werkzeug (-e)	*tool*	die	Zukunftsmusik	*music of the future*
der	Werkzeugbau	*machine tooling*	die	Zulassung (-en)	*authorisation*
der	Wert (-e)	*value*	die	Zulieferfirma (-en)	*supplier*
(adv)	wesentlich	*considerably*	die	Zulieferung (-en)	*supply*
der	Wettbewerb (-e)	*competition*	*(vbs)*	zu'machen	*to close*
das	Wetter	*weather*		*(pp)* zugemacht	
(adj)	wichtig	*important*	*(adv)*	zumindest	*at the very least*
das	Wichtigste	*the most important*	*(conj)*	zunächst	*to start with*
(adv)	wieder	*again*	*(vbs)*	zurück'nehmen	*to take back*
(adv)	wiederum	*in turn*		*(pp)* zurückgenommen	
der	Wille (-n, -n)	*will, intention*	*(adj)*	zusätzlich	*in addition*
(adv)	wirklich	*really*	*(vbs)*	zu'sagen	*to agree*
das	Wissen	*knowledge*		*(pp)* zugesagt	
(vb)	wissen	*to know*	*(adv)*	zusammen	*together*
	(pp) gewußt		die	Zusammenarbeit	*co-operation*
die	Woche (-n)	*week*	*(vbs)*	zusammen'fallen	*to fall apart*
(adv)	wohl	*to be sure*		*(pp)* zusammengefallen	
(vb)	wollen	*to want*	*(vbs)*	zusammen'hängen	*to be connected*
(vb)	worden	→ *werden (passive)*		*(pp)* zusammengehangen	
das	Wort (-e)	*word*	*(vbs)*	zu'sprechen	*to appeal to*
(vb)	wünschen	*to wish*		*(pp)* zugesprochen	
	(pp) gewünscht		*(vbs)*	zu'stimmen	*to agree*
(vb)	würde	*would*		*(pp)* zugestimmt	
(adj)	wunderbar	*wonderful*	*(prep)*	zuzüglich	*with the addition of*
			(adv)	zwangsläufig	*of necessity*
der	Zeichner (-)	*draftsman*	*(adv)*	zwar	*to be sure*
die	Zeichnung (-en)	*drawing*	*(adv)*	zweitens	*secondly*
(vb)	zeigen	*to show*	die	Zweitplatzierung (en)	*second positioning*
	(pp) gezeigt		die	Zwiebelsuppe (-n)	*onion soup*
die	Zeit (-en)	*time*	*(vbs)*	zwischen'schalten	*to interrupt*
die	Zeitdauer	*length of time*		*(pp)* zwischengeschaltet	

Sources of information and advice

Note The addresses and telephone numbers listed below are accurate at time of going to press.

Ministry of Agriculture Fisheries and Food
Government Buildings
Hook Rise South
Tolworth
Surbiton
Surrey KT6 7NF
Tel: 01–337 6611
For advice about exporting animals, animal products and fish.

BBC External Service
Export Liaison Unit
PO Box 76
Bush House
London WC23 4PH
Contact: H. Schroeder
Tel: 01–240 3456
Ext: 2200
For publicity via the BBC Overseas News Service

British Health-Care Export Council
5th Floor
2 Harewood Place
London W1R 9HN
Tel: 01–493 6699
For advice on exporting medical products and hospital equipment

British Industrial Biological Research Association (BIBRA)
Woodmansterne Road
Carshalton
Surrey SM5 4DS
Tel: 01–643 4411
For advice on food regulations

British Knitting and Clothing Export Council
British Apparel Centre
7 Swallow Place
Oxford Circus
London W1R 7AA
Tel: 01–493 6622
For advice on textile marketing overseas.

British Standards Institute Technical Help to Exporters (THE)
Linford Wood
Milton Keynes
MK14 6LE
Tel: 0908 220022
For all aspects of overseas safety laws and technical specifications.

Central Office of Information (COI)
Overseas Press Office
Hercules Road

London SE1 7EU
Tel: 01–928 2345
For trade fairs and publicity.

Department of Trade and Industry
contact Regional Offices (addresses below) for the following services:

Marketing Initiative
For independent professional advice on a company's marketing potential.
Export Market Research
For help and advice on researching your overseas markets.
Export Representative Service
For identifying potential representatives abroad and checking credentials.
Overseas Status Report Service
For providing impartial information to help assess a potential business partner overseas.
Export Intelligence Service
For identifying and dispatching to you information from overseas markets, relevant to your product area.

Trade Missions
  For the opportunity to join a
  mission and explore a target
  market at first hand.
Trade Fairs and In Store Promotions
  For help and financial support for
  companies wishing to exhibit
  abroad.

DTI publications
The Export Initiative – a guide to
  DTI export services
Hints to Exporters – country specific
  guides
Export guides for smaller firms – three
  short guides which introduce
  smaller firms to the key principles
  of exporting
Overseas Trade – a magazine
  providing regular news of export
  opportunities and practice, from:
  Room 235
  1 Victoria Street
  London
  SW1H 0ET
  Tel: 01–215 5492
Trade Promotions Guide – a quarterly
  supplement of *British Business
  Magazine*, giving details of
  forthcoming supported events,
  from:
  British Business
  Oakfield House
  Perrymount Road
  Haywards Heath
  West Sussex
  RH16 3DH
  Tel: 0444 440421

DTI regional offices
For information and guidance on
  general export matters and DTI
  services for exporters. (First
  contact with consular services
  should be through local DTI
  offices.)

East Midlands Regional Office
Severns House
20 Middle Pavement
Nottingham MG1 7DW
Tel: 0602–506181
Telex: 37143 DTI NOT G

North East Regional Office
Stanegate House
2 Groat Market
Newcastle-upon-Tyne NE1 1YN
Tel: 091–232 4722
Telex: 53178 DOT TYN G

North West Regional Office
Sunley Building
Piccadilly Plaza
Manchester M1 4BA
Tel: 061–236 2171
Telex: 667104 DTI MCHR

South East Regional Office
Ebury Bridge House
2–18 Ebury Bridge Road
London SW1 8QD
Tel: 01–730 9678
Telex: 297124/5/6 a/b SEREX G

South West Regional Office
The Pithay
Bristol BS1 2PB
Tel: 0272–272666
Telex: 44214 DTI BTL G

West Midlands Regional Office
Ladywood House
Stephenson Street
Birmingham B2 4DT
Tel: 021–632 4111
Telex: 337919 DTI BHM

Yorkshire and Humberside
  Regional Office
Priestley House
Park Row
Leeds LS1 5LF
Tel: 0532–443171
Telex: 557925 DTI LDS G

Industrial Development Board for
  Northern Ireland
IDB House
64 Chichester Street
Belfast BT1 4JX
Tel: 0232–233233
Telex: 747223

Scottish Office
Industry Department for Scotland
Alhambra House
45 Waterloo Street
Glasgow G2 6AT

Tel: 041–248 2853
Telex: 777883 SEPD G

Welsh Office
New Crown Building
Cathays Park
Cardiff CF1 3NQ
Tel: 0222–825097
Telex: 498228

Department of Transport
International Road Freight Office
Westgate House
Westgate Road
Newcastle-upon-Tyne NE1 1TW
Tel: 091–3610031
For advice about international
  aspects of vehicle safety,
  construction and use overseas.

Directory of British Associations
Benn Business Information Services
  Ltd.
PO Box 20
Sovereign Way
Tonbridge
Kent
TN9 1RQ

Exhibition Bulletin
The London Bureau
266/272 Kirkdale
Sydenham
London SE26 4RZ
Tel: 01–778 2288
For worldwide list of trade fairs and
  exhibitions classified by countries
  and product groups. Published
  monthly.

Food and Drink Federation
6 Catherine Street
London WC2B 5JJ
Tel: 01–836 2460

German Chamber of Industry &
  Commerce in the UK
12/13 Suffolk Street
St. James's
London SW1Y 4HG
Tel: 01–930 7251

German Embassy
Embassy of the Federal Republic of
  Germany

23 Belgrave Square
London SW1
Tel: 01–235 5033

**Pharmaceutical Society of Great
Britain**
1 Lambeth High Street
London SE1 7JN
Tel: 01–735 9141
For advice about drugs regulations.

**SITPRO – Simplification of
International Trade Procedures
Board**
Almack House
26 King Street
London SW1W 6QW
Tel: 01–930 0532
Telex: 919130 SITPRO G
For advice on documentation.

Small Firms and Tourism Division
Department of Employment
Steel House
Tothill Street
London SW1H 9NF
For advice on exporting for small
firms.

The Institute of Linguists
24a Highbury Grove
London N5 2EA
Tel: 01–359 7445/6386
For advice about translation services

Addresses in Germany

AUMA
The German Council of Trade Fairs
& Exhibitions
Lindenstrasse 8
D 5000 Köln 1
Tel: 0221 21 90 91
For advice on type and location of
trade fairs.

**British Chamber of Commerce in
Germany**
Heumarkt 14
D 5000 Köln 1
West Germany
Tel: 0221 234284
Telex: 08 0883 400
Cables: Grittrude Köln

**Federation of German Trade
Agents and Brokers Association**
Geleniusstrasse 1
D 5000 Köln 41
For copies of German agency law

British Embassy
Friedrich Ebert Allee 77
D 5300 Bonn 1
Tel: 0228 23 40 61
For general information.

The British commercial
representatives in Germany are as
follows:
Bonn
Counsellor (Commercial)
Commercial Department British
Embassy
Friedrich Ebert Allee 77
D 5300 Bonn 1
Tel: 0228 23 40 61
Telex: 886887 a/b BRINF D

Berlin
Consul General
British Consulate-General
Uhlandstrasse 7–8
D 1000 Berlin 12
Tel: 030 309 5295/7
Telex: 1894268 a/b UKBLIN D

Frankfurt
Consul General
British Consulate-General
Bockenheimer Landstrasse 51–53
D 6000 Frankfurt am Main
Tel: 069 720406/9
Telex: 414932

Düsseldorf
Consul General
British Consulate-General
Nordsternhaus
Georg-Glock-Strasse 14
D 4000 Düsseldorf 30
Tel: 0211 43740
Telex: 8–584855 a/b BRIN D

Hamburg
Consul General
British Consulate-General
Harvestehuderweg 8a
D 2000 Hamburg 13
Tel: 04044 60 71
Telex: 231562 a/b BRHBG

Munich
Consul General
British Consulate-General
Amalienstrasse 62
D 8000 Munich 40
Telex: 08939 40 15/9
Telex: 529959 a/b UKMUN D

Stuttgart
British Marketing Office (Advanced
Technology)
Kronprinzstrasse 14
D 7000 Stuttgart 1
Tel: 0711 293216
Telex: 722397 a/b UKST D